TIME

ANNUAL

1993: The Year In Review

TIME

ANNUAL

1993

The Year In Review

By the Editors of TIME

TIME Annual 1993

The Year In Review

EDITOR-IN-CHIEF: Jason McManus
EDITORIAL DIRECTOR: Henry Muller
EDITOR OF NEW MEDIA: Walter Isaacson

TIME INC.
CHAIRMAN, CEO: Reginald K. Brack Jr.
PRESIDENT: Don Logan

TIME

Founders: Briton Hadden 1898-1929   Henry R. Luce 1898-1967

MANAGING EDITOR: James R. Gaines
DEPUTY MANAGING EDITOR: John F. Stacks
EXECUTIVE EDITOR: Richard Duncan
ASSISTANT MANAGING EDITORS: Joelle Attinger, James Kelly, Oliver Knowlton (Operations), Christopher Porterfield
SENIOR EDITORS: Charles P. Alexander, Howard Chua-Eoan, James Collins, Nancy R. Gibbs, S.C. Gwynne, Bruce Handy, Stephen Koepp, Johanna McGeary, Priscilla Painton, Barrett Seaman (Special Projects), Claudia Wallis
ART DIRECTOR: Arthur Hochstein
GRAPHICS DIRECTOR: Nigel Holmes
CHIEF OF RESEARCH: Betty Satterwhite Sutter
PICTURE EDITOR: Michele Stephenson
COPY CHIEF: Susan L. Blair   **PRODUCTION MANAGER:** Gail Music
SENIOR WRITERS: George J. Church, Richard Corliss, Martha Duffy, Paul Gray, John Greenwald, William A. Henry III, Robert Hughes, Richard Lacayo, Eugene Linden, Lance Morrow, Bruce W. Nelan, Richard Zoglin
ASSOCIATE EDITORS: Richard Behar, Janice Castro, Philip Elmer-DeWitt, Christine Gorman, Sophfronia Scott Gregory, Michael D. Lemonick, Thomas McCarroll, Marguerite Michaels, Richard N. Ostling, Jill Smolowe, Anastasia Toufexis, David Van Biema
STAFF WRITERS: Gina Bellafante, Christopher John Farley, Kevin Fedarko
CONTRIBUTORS: Bonnie Angelo, Laurence I. Barrett, Jesse Birnbaum, Stanley W. Cloud, Jay Cocks, Barbara Ehrenreich, John Elson, Pico Iyer, Edward L. Jamieson (Consulting Editor), Leon Jaroff, Michael Kinsley, Charles Krauthammer, Richard Schickel, Walter Shapiro, R.Z. Sheppard, John Skow, Martha Smilgis, Richard Stengel, George M. Taber, Andrew Tobias
ASSISTANT EDITORS: Ursula Nadasdy de Gallo, Andrea Dorfman, Brigid O'Hara-Forster, William Tynan, Sidney Urquhart, Jane Van Tassel (Department Heads); Bernard Baumohl, David Bjerklie, Val Castronovo, Mary McC. Fernandez, Georgia Harbison, Ratu Kamlani, Sue Raffety, Susan M. Reed, Elizabeth Rudulph, Susanne Washburn, Linda Young
REPORTERS: Elizabeth L. Bland, Hannah Bloch, Barbara Burke, Tresa Chambers, Wendy Cole, Tom Curry, Kathryn Jackson Fallon, Janice M. Horowitz, Jeanette Isaac, Daniel S. Levy, Michael Quinn, Jeffery C. Rubin, Andrea Sachs, Alain L. Sanders, David Seideman, David E. Thigpen
COPY DESK: Judith Anne Paul, Shirley Barden Zimmerman (Deputies); Barbara Dudley Davis, Evelyn Hannon, Jill Ward (Copy Coordinators); Minda Bikman, Doug Bradley, Robert Braine, Bruce Christopher Carr, Barbara Collier, Julia Van Buren Dickey, Dora Fairchild, Judith Kales, Sharon Kapnick, Claire Knopf, Jeannine Laverty, Peter J. McGullam, M.M. Merwin, Maria A. Paul, Jane Rigney, Elyse Segelken, Terry Stoller, Amelia Weiss (Copy Editors)
CORRESPONDENTS: Joelle Attinger (Chief), Paul A. Witteman (Deputy), Suzanne Davis (Deputy, Administration); **Chief Political Correspondent:** Michael Kramer **Washington Contributing Editor:** Hugh Sidey **Senior Correspondents:** David Aikman, Jonathan Beaty, Sandra Burton, Richard Hornik, J. Madeleine Nash, Bruce van Voorst, Jack E. White
Washington: Dan Goodgame, Ann Blackman, Margaret Carlson, James Carney, Michael Duffy, Julie Johnson, J.F.O. McAllister, Jay Peterzell, Suneel Ratan, Elaine Shannon, Dick Thompson, Adam Zagorin, Melissa August **New York:** Janice C. Simpson, Edward Barnes, John F. Dickerson **Boston:** Sam Allis **Chicago:** Jon D. Hull, Elizabeth Taylor **Detroit:** William McWhirter **Atlanta:** Michael Riley **Houston:** Richard Woodbury **Miami:** Cathy Booth **Los Angeles:** Jordan Bonfante, Jeanne McDowell, Sylvester Monroe, Jeffrey Ressner, James Willwerth, Patrick E. Cole **San Francisco:** David S. Jackson
London: Barry Hillenbrand **Paris:** Thomas A. Sancton, Margot Hornblower **Brussels:** Jay Branegan **Bonn:** James O. Jackson **Central Europe:** James L. Graff **Moscow:** John Kohan, Sally B. Donnelly, Ann M. Simmons **Rome:** John Moody **Istanbul:** James Wilde **Jerusalem:** Lisa Beyer **Cairo:** Dean Fischer **Beirut:** Lara Marlowe **Nairobi:** Andrew Purvis **Johannesburg:** Scott MacLeod **New Delhi:** Jefferson Penberthy **Beijing:** Jaime A. FlorCruz **Southeast Asia:** William Dowell **Tokyo:** Edward W. Desmond, Kumiko Makihara **Ottawa:** Gavin Scott **Latin America:** Laura López
Administration: Susan Lynd, Denise A. Carres, Sheila Charney, Breena Clarke, Donald N. Collins, Joan A. Connelly, Corliss M. Duncan, Ann V. King, Lina Lofaro, Anne D. Moffett, Judith R. Stoler **News Desks:** Brian Doyle, Waits L. May III, Susanna Schrobsdorff, Pamela H. Thompson, Diana Tollerson, Ann Drury Wellford, Mary Wormley
ART: Linda Louise Freeman (Covers); Steve Conley, Paul Lussier, Thomas M. Miller, Billy Powers (Associate Art Directors); Joseph Aslaender, Kenneth B. Smith (Assistant Art Directors); David Drapkin, Leah M. Purcell (Designers); John P. Dowd (Traffic) **Maps and Charts:** Joe Lertola (Associate Graphics Director); Paul J. Pugliese (Chief of Cartography); Leslie Dickstein, Steven D. Hart, Deborah L. Wells **Administration:** Marilyn Rudnick-Salinger
PHOTOGRAPHY: Richard L. Booth, MaryAnne Golon (Deputy Picture Editors); Robert B. Stevens (Associate Picture Editor); Kevin J. McVea (Operations); Renee Mancini (Syndication); Dorothy Affa Ames, Sarah Buffum, Gary Roberts, Nancy Smith-Alam, Mary Worrell-Bousquette (Assistant Editors); Cristina T. Scalet, Marie Tobias (Researchers) **Bureaus:** Martha Bardach, Sahm Doherty, Leny Heinen, Stanley Kayne, Glenn Mack, Barbara Nagelsmith, Anni Rubinger, Mary Thompson, Simonetta Toraldo **Photographers:** Forrest Anderson, Terry Ashe, P.F. Bentley, William Campbell, Greg Davis, Dirck Halstead, Barry Iverson, Kenneth Jarecke, Cynthia Johnson, Shelly Katz, Steve Liss, Peter Magubane, Christopher Morris, Robin Moyer, Carl Mydans, James Nachtwey, Robert Nickelsberg, Chris Niedenthal, David Rubinger, Anthony Suau, Ted Thai, Diana Walker
MAKEUP: Robyn M. Mathews (Chief)
TECHNOLOGY: Ken Baierlein, Hope Almash, David Richardson (Managers); Nora Jupiter, Kevin Kelly, George Mendel, Peter K. Niceberg, Michael M. Sheehan, Lamarr Tsufura **IMAGING:** Mark Stelzner (Manager); Gerard Abrahamsen, Raphael Joa, Lois Rubenstein (Supervisors); Steven Cadicamo, Charlotte Coco, John Dragonetti, Paul Gettinger, John Goodman, Kin Wah Lam, Carl Leidig, Linda Parker, Mark P. Polomski, Richard Shaffer, David Spatz, Lorri Stenton
PRODUCTION: Trang Ba Chuong, Theresa Kelliher, L. Rufino-Armstrong (Supervisors); Silvia Castañeda Contreras, Michael Dohne, Garry Hearne, Sandra Maupin, Michael Skinner
ADMINISTRATION: Alan J. Abrams, Catherine M. Barnes, Denise Brown, Anne M. Considine, Tosca LaBoy, Marilyn V.S. McClenahan, Ann Morrell, Teresa D. Sedlak, Deborah R. Slater, Marianne Sussman, Raymond Violini
EDITORIAL FINANCE: Genevieve Christy (Manager); Esther Cedeño, Carl Harmon, Morgan Krug, Katherine Young (Domestic); Camille Sanabria, Aston Wright (News Service); Linda D. Vartoogian, Wayne Chun, Edward Nana Osei-Bonsu (Pictures)
LETTERS: Amy Musher (Chief); Gloria J. Hammond (Deputy); Marian Powers (Administration)

TIME INC. EDITORIAL OPERATIONS
Director: Sheldon Czapnik **Editorial Services:** Christiana Walford (Director); Hanns Kohl (Photo Lab); Lany Walden McDonald (Library), Beth Bencini Zarcone (Picture Collection)

TIME INTERNATIONAL
Managing Editor: Karsten Prager
Assistant Managing Editor: José M. Ferrer III
Senior Editors: Christopher Redman, George Russell, John Saar
Senior Writers: Michael S. Serrill, James Walsh
Associate Editors: William R. Doerner, Barbara Rudolph
Staff Writer: Emily Mitchell
Contributors: Robert Ball, Marguerite Johnson, Dominique Moisi, Christopher Ogden, Frederick Painton, Michael Walsh
Assistant Editors: Tam Martinides Gray (Research Chief), Ariadna Victoria Rainert (Administration), Oscar Chiang, Lois Gilman, Valerie Johanna Marchant, Adrianne Jucius Navon
Reporters: Sinting Lai, Lawrence Mondi, Megan Rutherford, Sribala Subramanian
Art: Jane Frey (Senior Associate Director); James Elsis (Associate Director); Nomi Silverman (Assistant Art Director); Victoria Nightingale (Designer)
Photography: Julia Richer (Associate Editor); Eleanor Taylor, Karen Zakrison (Assistant Editors)
Makeup: Alison E. Ruffley (Chief)
Administration: Helga Halaki, Barbara Milberg

PRESIDENT: Elizabeth Valk Long
PUBLISHER: John E. Haire
FINANCIAL DIRECTOR: Daniel M. Rubin
CONSUMER MARKETING DIRECTOR: Kenneth Godshall
PRODUCTION DIRECTOR: Brian F. O'Leary
BUSINESS MANAGER: A.P. Duffy
MARKETING DIRECTOR: Linda McCutcheon Conneally
PUBLIC AFFAIRS DIRECTOR: Robert Pondiscio

TIME ANNUAL 1993: THE YEAR IN REVIEW

Editor
Edward Jamieson

Managing Editor
Kelly Knauer

Art Director
Janet Waegel

Picture Editor
Jay Colton

Research Director
Leah Gordon

Editorial Production Director
Michael Skinner

Essays
Michael Duffy, Lance Morrow

Information Design
Joe Lertola, Paul Pugliese

Design Associate
Gigi Fava

Research Associates
Anne Hopkins, Sue Raffety

Copy Desk
Doug Bradley, Bob Braine, Bruce Carr,
Barbara Dudley Davis, Peter McGullam

Thanks to:
Susan Blair, Kate Boal, John Dragonetti, Richard Duncan,
Linda Louise Freeman, Arthur Hochstein, Rudy Hoglund,
Nora Jupiter, Kevin Kelly, Oliver Knowlton,
Bob Marshall, George Mendel, Gail Music, Lois Rubenstein,
Betty Satterwhite Sutter, Michael Shea, Mark Stelzner,
Michele Stephenson, Lamarr Tsufura, Robert F. Warren Jr.,
the Time Inc. Consumer Marketing Staff

NEW BUSINESS DEVELOPMENT

Director
David Gitow

Assistant Director
Mary Warner McGrade

Production Director
John Calvano

Operations Director
David Rivchin

The work of the following TIME writers and editors is represented in this volume:
Kurt Andersen, Margaret Carlson, George J. Church, Howard Chua-Eoan, Richard Corliss, Philip Elmer-DeWitt, Martha Duffy, Michael Duffy, Christopher John Farley, Nancy R. Gibbs, Paul Gray, John Greenwald, William A. Henry III, Robert Hughes, Michael Kramer, Richard Lacayo, Michael D. Lemonick, J.F.O. McAllister, William McWhirter, Bruce W. Nelan, Richard N. Ostling, Dennis Overbye, Richard Schickel, Hugh Sidey, John Skow, Jill Smolowe, Paul A. Witteman, Richard Zoglin

The Year It Rained News

By LANCE MORROW

IMAGINE THAT A YEAR HAS ONE event containing a hidden explanation for everything else that happened: a metaphorical code, something like the year's DNA. Find that, and all else follows.

If such a metaphor were to lie buried in the jumble of 1993, it might be the one that fell from the sky in the exact middle of the year, upon the middle of America—a perfectly centered symbol, but a terrible mess.

It fell and fell, week after week, a drenching, interminable rain that lifted the Mississippi out of its course and set it loose upon the landscape. As the wet sky all but fused with a liquefying earth and the air became a lighter

layer of water, the weather and the river explored new possibilities of relentlessness and disorder. Whole landscapes, expanses of entire states went under. The Mississippi, T. S. Eliot's "strong brown god," dissolved into a sort of hydro-chaos that flowed undifferentiated over farms and highways and lowland cities.

On moral and political and scientific floodplains around the world, boundaries and familiar landmarks were similarly vanishing, eroded and washed away by border-crumbling economic tides, surging political swells and new streams of powerful electronic information. Through it all, except for a transforming vision here and

1

there, occurred terrible seepages from the ugliest regions of human nature: the most vicious ethnic savagery, the growth of sexual assaults and a rush of violent and unfathomable crime—the new frontiers of swampland and id.

THE SPECTACLE OF THE MIDWESTERN FLOODS, the worst in U.S. history, produced, at the time, one of those uneasy, subliminal, anything-can-happen moments. It prompted a kind of mild amazement that fitted perfectly with a sense that the world was up to surprising things, that old records and old values and familiar patterns might not stand: that the globe itself was rapidly and sometimes dangerously changing. A boundary, after all, may be a limitation upon freedom (therefore bad) or a necessary defense and insulation (therefore good). Or both. So the destruction of old borders may be a blessing (as in Eastern Europe, outside Yugoslavia) or a catastrophe (Yugoslavia) or both (the former Soviet Union's republics, several of them now dissolved in civil war).

In truth, the year was probably no more disillusioning or shattering than most others. As Flaubert wrote to George Sand more than a century ago, as the two tried to account for some atrocious crime or other: "Our ignorance of history makes us slander our own time. People have always been like this."

That truth—the more or less constant flaw—could be seen in the arrest of fundamentalist Muslims suspected of attempting to blow up the World Trade Center, in David Koresh's determination to lead his cult into immolation in Waco, and in the racially motivated shooting of 23 people on the Long Island Rail Road during the holiday season. But especially in its closing weeks, 1993 also produced signs of hopeful change: some signals of an improving American economy, approval of the NAFTA treaty (which again called forth images of crumbled borders and economic seepages), the possibility of peace in the Middle East and South Africa.

But the dilemma remains: a frequently low human nature working with high technology. People before and after Hiroshima may be the same, but who would deny that something is forever different? If the free-floating year of 1993 induced a queasiness, that was caused in good part by the barely assimilable sense of accelerated technological change, by the speed of communication and the velocity of global culture. Some of that sense of unease arose from the borderless quality of television—its strange simultaneous world-scope and intimacy. Television changes the perspectives of normality. It seeks the abnormal, because it has an appetite for drama, even as it obliterates distance and boundaries and brings the most disturbing events inside the brain, rendering them as intimate as thought —or fear.

Instant global communication (TV, faxes, telephones, computers, the incipient information highway) has already given the world a fourth dimension. Now it is pointing to a kind of fifth dimension that may lie somewhere down the road, a mental universalization in which the entire world will be absorbed into an interlinked network. For the moment, however, a society whose institutions of authority tend to be washing away is left with television to dramatize the spectacle of floodwaters driving the snakes (murderers, rapists, "ethnic cleansers," and all of the merely vicious oddities) up into the open air, into the trees and onto the daytime news and talk shows.

The motif of a dangerous borderlessness was evident in the spread of AIDS and the comeback of malaria and TB. The planet's safe havens seem fewer now, as the world grows smaller year by year. At the same time, AIDS induces a regressive terror of plague, a kind of collective memory of the black death, that coexists with the astonishing news of the first cloning of human beings. A sort of brutal metaphysical win-some-lose-some spirit fills the air. Those watching the border between life and death have seen strange traffic in both directions. Mass abortion and Kevorkian's easeful-death desires move in one direction, matched by life desires going the other way: ingenious inseminations, for example, surrogate parenthoods, biotechnical feats. What once were accepted as the gift of life and the fate of death must soldier now as issues of political rights.

FOR AMERICANS, SOME OF THE YEAR'S UN-ease involved growing pains and immaturity: the sulking and self-pity, the tantrum-prone adolescence, of an almost entirely new national identity. America today is a rapidly feminizing multicultural nation engaged in redrawing its social contract, redefining its place in the world and trying, in the process, to keep from committing suicide by gun glut, drugs, illiteracy, stupidity and bad manners.

The central article of the American credo, the dynamo of its optimism, has always been Progress: a conviction that American history is not only ascendant but indeed divinely endorsed. That belief persists, but it has become provisional in ways it never was before. Part of the national mood is a chilly intimation that history may be on a downslide, that the Golden Age was long ago and the future can only be a steady darkening. In the days when two great oceans protected the American exceptionalism, and a few thousand miles meant something, Americans thought they operated the nation on a contract with God. Today, in a new world, in a post-American century, they are busy drawing up, for the first time, a thousand contracts between themselves and everyone else on the planet.

Simultaneously, Americans are struggling to discover the terms of a fresh internal social contract that will cope with the tremendous floodwaters of their grievances: their drugs and crime, their gender and cultural complaints, their pervasive, litigious sense of injustice. The goal is that, through their struggle, they will come upon a new way to live with themselves—something that, by all appearances, they find increasingly difficult to do. ∎

IMAGES '93

MALIBU In California a woman escapes the November fires that caused about $1 billion in damage.

"There's not really all that much you can do . . . The fires stop when the wind does and when they're out."

—JAMES PETRONI, CALIFORNIA OFFICE OF EMERGENCY SERVICES

4

MOGADISHU The body of a U.S. soldier is dragged past jeering Somalis. Army Rangers hunting General Aidid were killed when trapped under fire for ten hours.

❝War is really very sad and kills everyone in some way.❞ —ARMY PRIVATE FIRST CLASS RICHARD KOWALEWSKI, 20, KILLED IN OCTOBER, IN A LETTER HOME

WASHINGTON With a nudge from Bill Clinton, Israeli Prime Minister Yitzhak Rabin and P.L.O. chief Yasser Arafat make a tentative peace.

❝You know, we are going to have to work very hard to make this work.❞ —RABIN

❝I know. I am prepared to do my part.❞ —ARAFAT

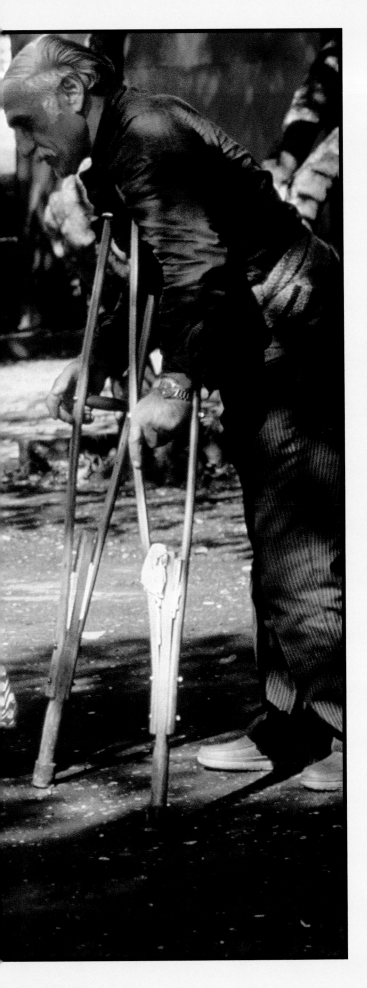

GEORGIA A Georgian soldier and boy run for cover as rebels besiege Sukhumi, capital of the breakaway republic of Abkhazia. Photographer Andrey Salaviov was killed shortly after taking this picture.

❝The city is being shelled. There is no water, no bread, no light, and hope is dwindling. Regardless of what happens, I will not leave this town.❞

—EDUARD SHEVARDNADZE, DAYS BEFORE FLEEING SUKHUMI

A child passes a hand grenade to a soldier in Ochamchire, as Georgian families prepare to flee advancing rebels.

❝May I be forgiven by my contemporaries and posterity.❞

—SHEVARDNADZE, ON THE DAY OF HIS FLIGHT

SARAJEVO A man digs graves, as snow blankets the city that once played host to the Winter Olympics. The Bosnian capital regularly suffered Serb shelling.

"This war is needed by no one, but we are not clever enough to stop it."
—NENAD GUSTIMIROVIC, SERB FIGHTER

JAPAN The wedding of Crown Prince Naruhito to
Harvard grad (and former diplomat) Masako
Owada promised to loosen up the ancient dynasty.

❝It's a pity for Masako Owada's career.❞
— KEIKO HIGUCHI, PROFESSOR OF
WOMEN'S STUDIES AT TOKYO KASEI UNIVERSITY

SPACE Perched on the shuttle *Endeavour's* remote manipulator arm 325 nautical miles above the west coast of Australia, NASA astronauts F. Story Musgrave and Jeffrey Hoffman repair the Hubble telescope.

"Piece of cake."
—ASTRONAUT KATHRYN THORNTON,
AS SHE WORKED ON THE HUBBLE

HAMBURG In April, a knife attack at courtside by an unemployed lathe operator and fan of Steffi Graf's sidelined No. 1–ranked tennis star Monica Seles.

❝ I've got to start all over. I love this sport too much, and I'm not going to let anyone take it away from me. I'm going to go out on my own terms. ❞

—MONICA SELES

LAS VEGAS Piloting a paraglider, James Miller dropped in unexpectedly during the heavyweight title fight between Riddick Bowe and eventual winner Evander Holyfield.

❝ I remembered that tennis lady who got stabbed, and I didn't know what was going on. I thought about running out of the ring. ❞

—HOLYFIELD, WHEN HE SAW THE INTRUDER LANDING

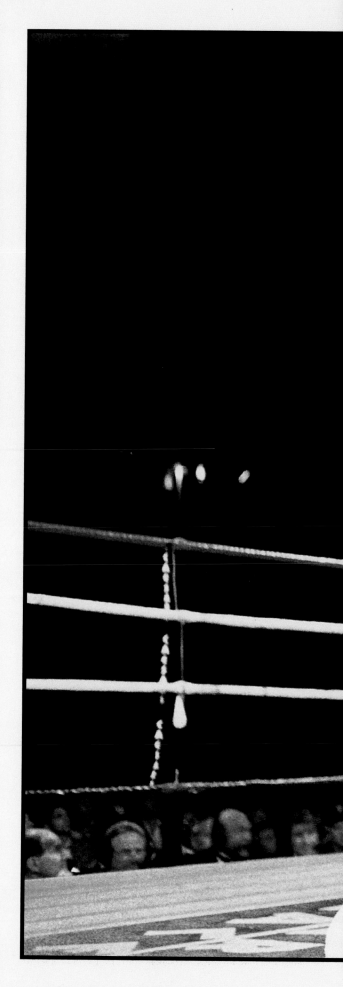

"LIAR, LIAR, PANTS ON FIRE!"

—John Sununu to George Stephanopolous, on CNN's *Crossfire*

"Sleep around all you want, but don't get married."

—Wisconsin lawyer Debra Koenig, giving advice to a class of 7th-grade girls on Take Our Daughters to Work day

"A GIANT SUCKING SOUND"

–Ross Perot, on U.S. jobs heading south if NAFTA passed

IF YOU Ding It, Bash It, Crunch It Or Smash It, WHO PAYS FOR IT?

In Most Cases, Truck Rental Is Not Covered By Your Auto, Home, Credit Card Or AAA Insurance.

RYDER

"He said he was sorry for the language, that he couldn't say every word right . . . but he could say 'refund.'"

—Ryder agent Patrick Galasso, on World Trade Center bombing suspect Mohammed Salameh's attempt to get his deposit back

"I wasn't aware that the world

"I'm going to make her cry. I'm going to sing *Dixie* until she cries."

"Senator, your singing would make me cry if you sang *Rock of Ages.*"

—Exchange between Senator Jesse Helms and black Senator Carol Moseley-Braun, on an elevator with Senator Orrin Hatch

"This sucks . . . heh, heh, heh."

—Beavis and Butt-head, on just about everything

"People will be hunting Democrats with dogs by the end of the century."

—Senator Phil Gramm, on Clinton's health plan

"I'm an average Joe. I just have a unique ability to accessorize."

—RuPaul, drag queen and pop star

"IT'S JUST LIKE PEPSI-COLA!"

—Georgian leader Eduard Shevardnadze, after sampling Coca-Cola

"HE ATE EVERYTHING BUT THE DRAPES."

—Tom Brokaw, NBC anchor, on Clinton's eating habits

"Let it burn down, because I don't live there anymore."

—Dodgers outfielder Darryl Strawberry, on the L.A. fires

❝I rat the tar out of it, spray the hell out of it. I get it up there and defy gravity.❞
—Texas Governor Ann Richards' hairdresser, Gail Huitt

❝I think that Amy Fisher shot the wrong Buttafuoco, and she aimed too high.❞
—Audience member to Joey Buttafuoco, on the Phil Donahue show

"I FEEL STRONGLY THAT SOCIETY NEEDS TO CONDEMN A LITTLE MORE AND UNDERSTAND A LITTLE LESS."
—Prime Minister John Major, on the slaying of a two-year-old by two 10-year-olds

"I AM NOT A WARLORD."
—Mohammed Farah Aidid, after emerging from hiding

thought I was so weird and bizarre.❞
—Michael Jackson, accepting a special career Grammy award

❝IF HE WANTS ME TO BE A CHARACTER WITNESS, I'LL BE THERE.❞
—Senator Bob Packwood, on the inquiries into Rep. Dan Rostenkowski

"IT HURT A LOT."
—John Wayne Bobbitt, on the penisectomy administered by his wife

❝We've made a lot of progress on, you know, pasta and things like that—but tofu has been hard for us.❞
–Hillary Rodham Clinton, on the effort to improve the President's eating habits

❝When we were together she was so sweet and understanding. If I said to her, 'Go shoot that guy!' she'd shoot him without even thinking if it was right or wrong. We were that tight.❞
—Ike Turner, reminiscing about his marriage to Tina

"An excellent experience–for a disaster."
—A California school superintendent, on a successful evacuation drill during the wildfires

❝You know you're out of power when your limousine is yellow and your driver speaks Farsi.❞
—James Baker

Looking History in the Eye

Each year offers its own cast of characters: some are familiar, others blink for a moment in the bright lights of attention, then vanish forever. In this portrait gallery, a wide variety of artists contribute their impressions, in a wide variety of styles, of some of the most interesting newsmakers of 1993. Using a combination of artistic reportage and symbolism, they bring to their subjects a view that is at once both incisive and complex. Their art, in the best tradition of political cartooning, finds a deeper truth in exaggeration.

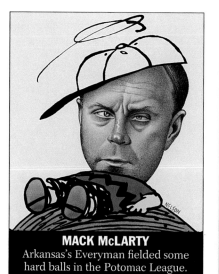

MACK McLARTY
Arkansas's Everyman fielded some
hard balls in the Potomac League.

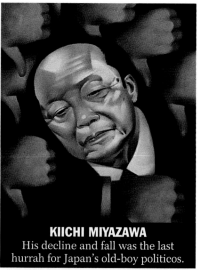

KIICHI MIYAZAWA
His decline and fall was the last
hurrah for Japan's old-boy politicos.

KATHERINE ANN POWER
A flashback from the '60s, she
surfaced after 23 years on the lam.

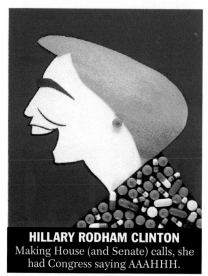

HILLARY RODHAM CLINTON
Making House (and Senate) calls, she
had Congress saying AAAHHH.

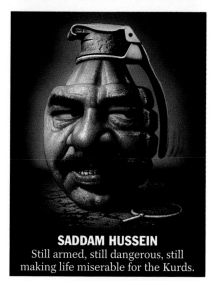

SADDAM HUSSEIN
Still armed, still dangerous, still
making life miserable for the Kurds.

CLINTON-SAN
He threw his weight around
in Tokyo at his first G-7 summit.

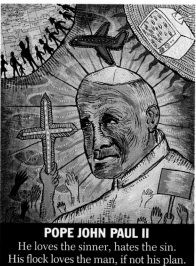

POPE JOHN PAUL II
He loves the sinner, hates the sin.
His flock loves the man, if not his plan.

MOYNIHAN AND ROSTENKOWSKI
What politics makes.
They cozied up on Bill's budget bill.

SHEIK OMAR ABDEL RAHMAN
Like justice, he was blind.
And there the similarity ended.

INDIANA CLINTON
Domestic problems? Tell it
to Somalia, Haiti and Bosnia.

CHINESE WOMEN RUNNERS
The magic to making world records
vanish? Eat more worms.

ARAFAT AND RABIN
The artful dodger and the soldier-
statesman gave peace a chance.

SENATOR ROBERT PACKWOOD
He dragged the Senate into the mire,
and Senator Byrd was not amused.

JEAN-BERTRAND ARISTIDE
Awaiting his homecoming, he was
all dressed up—with no place to go.

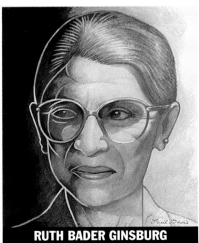

RUTH BADER GINSBURG
Bill Clinton's supreme appointment.
Even Republicans applauded.

PABLO ESCOBAR
The king of cocaine was killed
16 months after taking a powder.

MAJ. GEN. HAROLD CAMPBELL
For shame! He called the President
names at an Air Force banquet.

A New Kind of Summit

Freshman President Bill Clinton met Russian President Boris Yeltsin for the first time in Vancouver, British Columbia, in early April, shortly after one of Yeltsin's run-ins with the balky Soviet-era Congress of People's Deputies. It was a new kind of summit meeting. Instead of bickering over missile throw weights and Third World hot spots, Clinton and Yeltsin spent most of their several hours together poring over loan schedules, monetary policy and investment strategies as they mapped out a program of aid for Russia from the West. Clinton reaffirmed his support for Yeltsin's reforms but said he could not fund them; he offered the embattled Russian leader only $1.6 billion, no more than a down payment on the total amount Yeltsin would need to transform Russia's economy.

Clinton and Yeltsin: money talks in Vancouver.

Striking Back at Saddam

Air-raid sirens woke the residents of Baghdad early Sunday morning, June 27, as a flight of 23 Tomahawk cruise missiles launched from two U.S. warships converged in an attack on the headquarters of the Iraqi Intelligence Service. President Clinton ordered the raid in response to an attempt in April to assassinate former President George Bush during his visit to Kuwait. Clinton said he approved the retaliation after receiving "compelling evidence" that Iraq had been responsible for planning the foiled assassination attempt. "From the first days of our Revolution," said Clinton, "American security has depended on the clarity of this message: Don't tread on us."

Home Run at the High Court

Bill Clinton stumbled early in his presidency with appointment problems, but when he got his chance to name a Supreme Court Justice, he hit a

Rob Brennan hosed down his roof in Laguna Beach.

homer of Ruthian proportions. After some characteristic dillydallying, the President in June chose Ruth Bader Ginsburg, 60, of the U.S. Court of Appeals to replace the seat vacated by Justice Byron White. Ginsburg had been in the vanguard of litigating sex-discrimination cases to secure equal rights for women. She was a jurist with liberal credentials and centrist views whose conservative friends included Supreme Court Justice Antonin Scalia. Standing next to the President on the day he announced her nomination, Ginsburg recalled graduating first in her class at Columbia Law School, after which, she said, "Not a single law firm in the entire city of New York bid for my employment." Her nomination was universally hailed, and she sailed through the approval process in the Senate.

LINCOLN IS SAFE

"We do not assassinate dead people."

—ABDUL JABBAR MUHSIN, SADDAM HUSSEIN'S PRESS SECRETARY, DENYING THE PLOT TO KILL GEORGE BUSH

Packwood: Time to Pack?

In the capital's longest-running sex scandal, Oregon Senator Robert Packwood resisted ongoing cries to step down. The demands came not only from his constituents, who relentlessly demonstrated against him when he showed his face in his home state, but even from such fellow Republicans as Senator Nancy Kassebaum of Kansas, who said, "It's time to go." Packwood, accused of sexual harassment over the years by a total of 26 women, steadfastly battled to remain in office. When the Senate ethics committee investigating the charges subpoenaed his private diaries in October, Packwood took to the Senate floor to plead for his privacy, then fought the subpoena in court. Later, his secretary of 24 years testified that Packwood had altered portions of the diaries. Because of earlier revelations from the diaries, the charges against

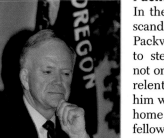

Packwood: embattled, but not embarking.

Packwood had grown to include influence peddling as well as sexual misconduct. The Senator's lawyer, Jacob Stein, acknowledged that the inquiry kept expanding "like a balloon."

Clinton to Iraq: "Don't tread on us."

The Wildfires of California

If Southern California were a building, it would fail fire inspection. Every year for five months virtually no rain falls. And every year from mid-September to November the Santa Ana winds, superheated in the Mojave Desert, blow through the hundreds of canyons leading coastward from the mountains, turning them into gigantic firetraps. 1993 seemed a lucky year, with few major conflagrations, until October 26, when fires began to spring up in Ventura County. Two days later, 100 fires were raging through the state, 13 of them major. Flames shot 70 feet in the air, palm trees exploded and million-dollar homes seemed to combust spontaneously. Some 6,000 firefighters scurried around the state, but they could not stop the flames. Before the fires were quenched, 200,000 acres were burned and thousands were homeless. President Clinton declared six counties federal disaster areas. Saddest of all, arson was suspected as a cause in 20 of the 26 major blazes.

Sons and Murderers

In a case that transfixed the nation, the Menendez brothers, Lyle, 24, and Erik, 21, went on trial in California for the murder of their parents on the night of August 20, 1989, in their Beverly Hills mansion. No one denied that the two had killed Jose and Kitty Menendez with 15 shotgun blasts. Instead the trial revolved around the brothers' so-called battered-child defense. The brothers contended that they had acted in fear for their lives after years of sexual and emotional torture, even though the state presented evidence of a $700,000 spending spree with the insurance money after the deaths. As millions watched the proceedings live on Court TV, ratings for the all-trial cable channel escalated sharply.

The Brothers Menendez: Did abuse lead to homicide?

Florida's Endangered Tourists

German tourist Uwe-Wilhelm Rakebrand and his wife Kathrin were perfectly willing to start their belated honeymoon by behaving like urban guerrillas. Before departing in their rental car from the Miami airport, they mapped out their route, then they stashed their valuables and, keeping to the main road, drove at a brisk pace while Kathrin read from a safety brochure distributed in seven languages by the car rental company. It was to no avail: a truck rammed them twice from behind, and when Rakebrand refused to fall for the "bump-and-rob" ploy, a frustrated 20-year-old blasted a .30-cal. slug through the window and into the back of the 33-year-old agricultural engineer, who died instantly. His wife, four months pregnant, somehow survived the ensuing crash.

Rakebrand was the eighth of nine foreign tourists to be killed in the state in 1993. Fearful for its valuable tourist business, Miami and the state of Florida took strong measures to improve security, but the area's image as a fun-in-the-sun playground suffered serious damage from the brutal series of homicides, and tourism revenues decreased.

Shall

We Dance?

The Clintons waltzed, Hollywood swooned, and the Democrats cheered as they recaptured the White House. But the First Family's honeymoon faded fast

COMPUTER WIZARDS PLAY THE game of virtual reality. In 1992 Bill Clinton, like Ronald Reagan before him, mastered a more dangerous skill—virtual fantasy—and the nation played along. During the long presidential campaign, TV screens showed Clinton gradually transformed, morphed, from a wannabe to a has-been to a third-place candidate to a front runner. And from a politician to a youthful superstar. He was fresh, and everyone else was tired.

That was never truer than at the swearing-in ceremony on Inauguration Day. The new President radiated the confidence of a young star athlete who couldn't wait for the coach to send him into the big game. Twice while taking the oath of office, he nearly stepped on Chief Justice William Rehnquist's lines. Meanwhile, George Bush, who was married before Clinton was born, wore an understandably defeated look. He stared at Clinton with the naked anguish of a father whose teenage boy had just beaten him at arm wrestling for the first time.

You didn't have to be from the G.O.P. to feel like a wallflower at this '90s party; you only had to be from the '80s. At the swearing-in ceremony, Geraldine Ferraro was looking lost and alone in her mediocre seat. At one of the fancy private dinners, Walter Mondale and Michael Dukakis were planted in a dark corner and remained unintroduced throughout the evening.

But there was no lack of candlepower in Bill Clinton's Washington. In celebration of his Inauguration, movie and music stars descended on Washington in numbers not seen since the bond drives of World War II. The whole wide world of American tinsel and twang—Oprah Winfrey, Little Richard, Kenny Rogers, Bill Cosby, Kathleen Battle, Macaulay Culkin, Harry Belafonte—showed up, swelling the Rat Pack of John F. Kennedy's day to Hamelin proportions, offering its best wishes to a new Administration. Jack Nicholson read the words of Abraham Lincoln. Aretha Franklin, a natural woman in a natural fur, sang a hymn to single motherhood from *Les Misérables.* Kermit the Frog sent Gonzo searching for the White House. Barbra Streisand performed a knockout set and gave her benediction to the party's Arkansas hosts. En Vogue and Boys II Men showed that a cappella renditions of *The Star-Spangled Banner* could have art and soul. Michael Jackson led a chorus of

POWER DANCE: **100,000 visitors, constellations of Hollywood stars, 13 Inaugural balls—and one couple in the center of it all.**

glamourati in *We Are the World.* Rapper L.L. Cool J had the word from a new generation: "Ninety-three! You and me! U-ni-tee!/ Time to par-tee with Big Bill and Hillaree."

At this multimillion-dollar partee, Big Bill Clinton— excuse us, William Jefferson Clinton—often played the role of First Audience. Celebrity has its muscle in America, but politics has the power. So the artists, most of them liberal Democrats, came to celebrate the politics of inclusion: after 12 years, or maybe 30, they were back on a party line to Washington clout.

The stars came out in constellations because they recognized in Clinton one of their own. Not just that he played the saxophone. Or that Hillary was a smart, tough lawyer, like most Hollywood moguls. Or that Tipper Gore was a photojournalist with a motherly interest in pop music. Or that Chelsea was working her camcorder at the Inaugural. What mattered was that Clinton was a prime communicator, a beacon of middle-class charisma, a believer in the importance—perhaps the primacy—of image, metaphor, style. And an ace manipulator of media, selling his symbols directly to the people, on TV, without the interference of pesky journalists. It all made for a wondrous '90s blend of show biz and politics, of Hollywood and heartland.

When Clinton himself took center stage at the West Front of the Capitol for the Inaugural ceremony, he captured the spirit of the occasion in an address whose recurring mantra was the necessity of change. "Thomas Jefferson believed that to preserve the very foundations of our Nation, we would need dramatic change from time to time," declaimed Jefferson's 39th successor. "The urgent question of the time is whether we can make change our friend and not our enemy."

In a speech of marked brevity and discipline, the new President spoke of the need to "face hard truths and take strong steps." He challenged young Americans especially to help end what he termed America's "drifting," and to create a new season of American renewal. "There is nothing wrong with America that cannot be cured by what is right with America," claimed the youngest Pres-

ident to assume office since Kennedy. "This is our time. Let us embrace it."

At times it seemed Clinton had an embrace for every one of the more than 100,000 visitors who crowded the capital for the occasion, from the Hollywood set to the civilians who lined up for the big parade, where the Lesbian & Gay Bands of America played and Girl Scouts passed out American flags and AIDS ribbons. A Clinton spotting could cue an impromptu chant of "Chel-*sea!* Chel-*sea!*" at the hot-ticket MTV Ball. Though the rockers booed Tipper Gore for her lyric-sanitation campaign, they gave a hand to Clinton's rowdy half brother Roger. And so did the music industry. Atlantic Records snagged him to preserve forever his rendition of Sam Cooke's *A Change Is Gonna Come.* Let's sing along: "Then I go to my brother,/ And I say, brother, help me please." Well, Bill did help Roger get famous. Fifteen minutes and counting, bro.

Bill Clinton has also been known to party hearty, but in his soul he may be a wonk. He is no more afraid to be square in his musical taste (his favorite sax player— Kenny G?) than Maya Angelou was to be passionate, politically correct and perfectly understood in her Inaugural Day poem. At 13 balls that night, Clinton was like the college grind who drops in on frat bashes the night before the exam to show he's one of the guys, then sneaks back to his dorm to cram. At Woodstock on the Mall, actor Edward James Olmos quoted Lincoln: "We must disenthrall ourselves, and then we shall save our country." Clinton, a good student with a good memory, mouthed the words as Olmos spoke them. Clinton must have realized that, in a different sense and a different era, America faces the task of disenthralling itself, of shaking off the Hollywood stardust and facing facts.

In 1992 Clinton vended optimism; as President he would have to become a pitchman for austerity. His eloquent appeal for change was stirring, but he must have known that if he could not deliver it, the man from Hope would become the man called Hype. All the big stars and better angels would leave him out in the spotlight, stranded, unmasked. ∎

From Nannygate To NAFTA

Winning ugly, Bill Clinton takes on the budget, trade—and himself

BILL CLINTON ENTERED THE OVAL OFFICE TOTing a heavy load of promises. In his successful campaign for the presidency he had declared he would tackle some of the toughest problems facing the American people, including the ever-expanding federal budget deficit and the ballooning costs and complications of American health care. But as he set out to slay these domestic dragons, the new President found himself tripping over an unexpected enemy: himself. Fighting a series of self-inflicted wounds, Clinton devoted the first third of his year simply to getting his White House in order. In the late spring and summer he was consumed by his battle for a new U.S. budget. In the fall his campaign to reform America's health-care system was sidetracked by an issue the President decided was more pressing: passage of the North American Free Trade Agreement.

ROCKY START. It may have been the shortest presidential honeymoon on record. In his inaugural speech, Clinton promised "to reform our politics so that power and privilege no longer shout down the voice of the people." Two days later, his nominee for Attorney General, Connecticut corporate lawyer Zoë Baird, withdrew her nomination after it was found she had employed illegal aliens and had failed to pay Social Security and other taxes on them. Baird's "Nannygate" problem touched a nerve with ordinary Americans, who detected power and privilege at work in her flouting of the laws and

> **"I was acting more as a mother than as someone . . . who would be Attorney General."**
> ZOE BAIRD, **TO THE SENATE JUDICIARY COMMITTEE**

Nannygate: Zoë Baird's tax evasions touched a nerve.

> **"Americans with one-fiftieth [your] income have to take care of their children, and they do not violate the law."**
> SEN. JOE BIDEN, **CHAIRMAN OF THE JUDICIARY COMMITTEE**

denounced her on radio talk shows and in letters and phone calls to Congress.

That problem was troublesome enough in itself, but two weeks later another respected woman with a high-profile career watched her reputation shredded in similar fashion. Clinton's second choice for Attorney General was New York Federal District Judge Kimba Wood, who, it turned out, had also employed an illegal alien as a baby sitter, though before the passage of a federal law that forbade the hiring of illegal aliens. Wood had paid the appropriate taxes and filed the required papers for her employee. Still, fearful that the public would not see the difference between Wood and Baird, the Administration pressured Judge Wood to withdraw from consideration. Nannygate had become an acute embarrassment to Clinton.

Yet even before the second nomination failed, a President scarcely two weeks in office found himself in a far stickier political quagmire: he was at war with the Joint Chiefs of Staff, as well as members of his own party in Congress, over the issue of the nearly 50-year-old ban on gays in the military. Clinton had first promised to lift the ban if elected in a speech in October 1991. During the transition a Clinton deputy found the Joint Chiefs willing to end the practice of asking recruits about their sexual preferences, but strongly opposed to lifting the ban on gays in uniform immediately. Despite their resistance, the President moved ahead with his plan to eliminate the ban by a single Executive Order within six months.

Clinton magnified his problem by failing to seek the advice and support of Senator Sam Nunn of Georgia, the powerful chairman of the Senate Armed Services Committee. Nunn expressed contempt for Clinton's approach, and he found support among Senate Republicans. Unable to win Nunn's approval, Clinton backed off and assigned the subject to a committee for review; eventually it was Nunn's policy of "Don't ask, don't tell," a vastly watered-down version of Clinton's original promise, that was adopted during the summer. The President was humbled; both his judgment and political savvy were questioned. In one stroke he had not only annoyed important forces on Capitol Hill and in the Pentagon, but had let down his gay supporters. And he had done so in championing a cause far away from the mainstream economic issues he had promised to focus on "like a laser beam" during the campaign.

> ## "Whatever war you were in, I know it was before the Clinton fags-in-the-foxhole [proposal]."
> **WARREN BARRY, VIRGINIA STATE SENATOR, AT A REPUBLICAN DINNER**

As Clinton concluded his first four months in office, his approval rating was at a record low for a President that far into his term. Even his own advisers were concerned: White House Budget Director Leon Panetta went so far as to tell reporters the President needed to "define his priorities" more clearly.

Clinton's year reached its nadir in May, when he was accused of delaying air traffic at Los Angeles International Airport while he received a $200 haircut aboard Air Force One from Beverly Hills hairdresser-to-the-stars Cristophe. Though the reported delays of other flights turned out to be false, the perception lingered that the candidate who had claimed to be a down-home Arkansas populist was really a star-struck élitist. In the same week, a mishandled, abrupt firing of seven employees in the White House Travel Office opened Clinton to new charges of cronyism and poor judgment.

> ## "You don't need to be 'straight' to fight and die for your country. You just need to shoot straight."
> **BARRY GOLDWATER, FORMER U.S. SENATOR FROM ARIZONA**

After desperately seeking advice on how best to right his troubled Administration, Clinton—now pictured as the "incredible shrinking President" on the cover of TIME—turned to an unexpected source for help: a Republican. He tapped David Gergen, a veteran of the Nixon and Reagan White Houses, to join his staff as communications director. Even this decision was made in the fashion that was emerging as typical for Clinton: without much warning, late at night, and with a last-minute O.K. from Hillary Rodham Clinton.

Only a week later Clinton dropped the nomination of the controversial Lani Guinier, a law professor at the University of Pennsylvania, to be Assistant Attorney General for Civil Rights. Guinier was the third woman to have her nomination withdrawn by the White House after a public period of indecision. Clinton's stumbles seemed to have taken on a certain farcical rhythm. Every time he appeared to bottom out, ready to dust himself off and get started again, he found a new hole in the floor to fall through.

Gergen's advent and Guinier's departure marked a turning point in Clinton's year. Headlines mocked Clinton as "Bumblin' Bill" and "President Jell-O." The President preferred another epithet: "The Comeback Kid." And come back he did, taking control of his presidency and managing the rest of the year with improved focus and a surer sense of control.

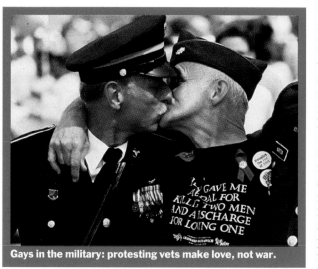
Gays in the military: protesting vets make love, not war.

BATTLE OF THE BUDGET. In February Clinton had launched his attack on the federal budget deficit with a speech to a joint session of Congress. He announced a plan that would raise taxes by $246 billion and cut spending by $247 billion, then apply $325 billion of the new funds to cutting the deficit and $169 billion to "investment spending." The plan included hikes in personal and corporate taxes and proposed a broad-based new tax on energy. Despite the huge new taxes it proposed, the speech was well received at first; even Ross Perot termed it "excellent." But its first portion, a $16 billion package designed to jump-start the nation's economy, succumbed to a Republican filibuster in the Senate; its death was one of Clinton's early setbacks.

When the full economic plan came before the Congress, the President once again found himself scrounging for two or three votes for a half-trillion-dollar economic package. With an eye to the 1994 elections, Republicans uniformly opposed the bill, while many moderate Democrats faulted it for raising taxes more than it cut spending. In May, a House version of the bill squeaked through, winning by a margin of only six votes. But during the Senate approval process, the President's broad-based energy tax was dropped in favor of a 4.3¢-per-gallon tax on gasoline. The compromise version of the bill finally passed both houses in early August, prevailing by two votes in the House and by one vote in the Senate, where Vice President Al Gore broke a 50-50 tie. However flawed, the final version of the bill did include most of the broad steps the President had originally called for, including $250 billion in spending cuts, $243 billion in revenue raises and the hope of reducing the deficit by about $490 billion—just shy of Clinton's cherished $500 billion figure—over five years. The bill's passage was doubly significant, since it represented the first real rejection of Reaganomics on Capitol Hill since the Republicans took the White House in 1980.

Clinton next turned to his plan to restructure the nation's health care, kicking it off in a speech to a joint session of Congress that won strong public approval. Almost immediately, though, Clinton plunged into a struggle that diverted him from the health plan, but emerged as one of his triumphs: the contretemps over the free trade agreement with Mexico and Canada.

THE GREAT NAFTA DEBATE.
The North American Free Trade Agreement, or NAFTA, had been negotiated during the Bush Administration. The pact, which would tear down most trade barriers between the U.S., Mexico and Canada, was unpopular with labor unions and many workers, who believed it would create an exodus of American manufacturing jobs to Mexico. Ross Perot agreed, claiming in a memorable sound bite that American jobs would drain south to Mexico "with a giant sucking sound." Environmentalists also opposed the treaty, believing it did not clamp down hard enough on Mexico's deficient safety and pollution regulations.

As a "new Democrat," Clinton had a long-standing commitment to eliminating trade barriers as a way to boost growth. In fact, it was one of the centrist positions that aligned younger Democrats with Republicans. Still, Clinton had refrained from endorsing the agreement until late in his presidential campaign and had not pushed it once in office. Now he decided to support it strongly, though it would place him in opposition to labor, a key constituent of his party.

Once the President picked up NAFTA's banner, the enormous importance he placed on the pact made its passage a defining test of his power. The lines were drawn. Perot traveled the country, denouncing the pact in rallies of his United We Stand America organization. Odd, makeshift alliances were forged. Ralph Nader,

> ## "Could we have an unnatural event and [you] try not to interrupt me?"
>
> ROSS PEROT **TO AL GORE, NAFTA DEBATE**

Jesse Jackson and Pat Buchanan lined up with Perot. Clinton signed up all five living ex-Presidents to endorse the agreement and also enlisted a host of bipartisan supporters, including longtime Chrysler boss Lee Iacocca and conservative talkshow host Rush Limbaugh. Mainstream economists, while siding with the President, believed the free trade pact would have only modest economic effects, and would most probably result in a small net gain of American jobs.

Then the President surprised everyone: he invited Ross Perot to debate Vice President Al Gore on NAFTA. Commentators, even his own advisers, felt Clinton had stumbled by offering Perot a platform. "There hasn't been enough oxygen for Perot, and now we've gone and given him a whole lot more," said one White House aide. But Clinton had his reasons. Polls showed Perot's support slipping badly. The White House felt that by reminding people that Perot was the voice of opposition to NAFTA, the Administration might garner support for it.

An oxygen-depleted Perot was delighted, and a deal was struck for a single, 90-minute Gore-Perot debate on Larry King's TV show. The Administration's gamble paid off. Gore debated like the newspaper reporter he once was, hammering Perot with facts, even stealing a page from the billionaire's book and presenting him with a framed picture of Hawley and Smoot, the congressional architects of the 1930s tariff that crippled the U.S. economy.

NAFTA debate: Perot and Gore exchange unpleasant charges.

Perot, who began the debate by arguing about the ground rules, was increasingly stymied, annoyed, and impolite. A TIME/CNN poll taken after the debate showed that only 18% of those surveyed thought Perot had won, vs. 47% for Gore. In one stroke, the White House had not only successfully defended its policy, but had deflated its most nagging critic.

> ## "He started out as the head of United We Stand, and I'm afraid he'll end up as the head of Divided We Fall."
>
> AL GORE **ON ROSS PEROT, NAFTA DEBATE**

The following week the House passed NAFTA by a vote of 234 to 200. A majority of Democrats voted against the treaty; a strong majority of Republicans voted with the President. Clinton had embraced a treaty fashioned by Republicans, defeated a majority in his own party, and taken on a key segment of his support, organized labor, in the name of a "new Democrat" cause. It was the biggest win of Clinton's presidency, and it promised that his year of living dangerously might pay off as he faced his next great domestic challenge: building a centrist coalition to pass a plan to restructure health care in America. ∎

All the Cares of The World

A trio of persistent headaches dominates Clinton's foreign policy

THE END OF THE COLD WAR, BILL CLINTON claimed on taking office, would allow him to concentrate on solving America's domestic problems. But he soon found he could not make the world go away. Under Clinton and his first foreign policy team—Secretary of State Warren Christopher, Secretary of Defense Les Aspin and National Security Adviser Anthony Lake—American policy zigged and zagged, talked tough only to back down, and seemed to be cut to fit the current week's crisis. In mid-December the President reorganized. He dropped Aspin and initially named long-time defense insider Bobby Ray Inman, a retired Admiral, to replace him, and also elevated Russian specialist Strobe Talbott to Deputy Secretary of State under Christopher.

> **"Failure in Bosnia will prolong the agony and threaten our national interest."**
> WARREN CHRISTOPHER, JANUARY 13

Clinton's challenge was to define a role for the U.S. as the world's only superpower. The paradox: Americans wanted immaculate interventions, commitments without consequences. They longed to stop the fighting in the Balkans, feed the hungry in Somalia, restore Haiti's rightful President to power. But they recoiled from seeing U.S. troops lost in the process. And without that resolve, the U.S. might become, as Richard Nixon had argued when the same issue arose in Vietnam, "a pitiful, helpless giant." Too often in 1993, that was just how Clinton's America appeared.

> **"Bosnia involves our humanitarian concerns, but not our vital interests."**
> WARREN CHRISTOPHER, JUNE 3

THE BALKANS. The ongoing warfare in the republics of the former Yugoslavia presented Clinton with his first and most intractable challenge. Here, Serbs and Croats continued their campaigns of "ethnic cleansing," overrunning Muslim Bosnia and Herzegovina and surrounding cities like Sarajevo, Mostar, Gorazde and Srebrenica, then slowly shelling and starving them to death. Clinton and the U.S. had no vital interest in the region, but the ongoing slaughter was an affront to humanity, and the continuing instability of the region threatened to lead to wider war. Clinton was presented with a quagmire with no good options, but growing public outrage over the genocide forced the struggle to the top of his agenda. Eager to take some action to lessen the suffering, in the late winter the President authorized relief drops from U.S. bombers stationed in Germany to the starving Muslims in the mountains of Bosnia.

During his campaign for the White House, Clinton said he would consider tougher action against Serb aggression. He criticized the peace plan put forth by former U.S. Secretary of State Cyrus Vance and Britain's Lord Owen for in effect rewarding the aggressors by partitioning Bosnia and Herzegovina and awarding large portions of them to the Serbs. But when the time came to settle on a better policy, Clinton found himself boxed in: by the West's past failures to act, by circumstances on the ground and by European allies and the U.N. Security Council, both of which opposed any use of force. Eating crow, the President eventually agreed to support the Vance-Owen plan as the best way to end the killing.

In May, eager to push the Bosnian Serbs to the peace

Bosnia: aid packages dropped by U.S. cargo planes in March.

table, Clinton proposed a series of limited air strikes by Western allies, coupled with a rearming of the Muslims. He dispatched Warren Christopher to sound out the European allies about joining the effort, but the U.S. initiative was side-tracked when the leader of the Bosnian Serbs, Radovan Karadzic, unexpectedly announced he would accept the Vance-Owen plan. As the allies scrambled to come to terms with the surprising offer, the self-designated Bosnian Serb parliament defied Karadzic, their own leader, as well as their backer in neighboring Serbia, President Slobodan Milosevic, by overwhelmingly turning down the plan.

> ## "[General Aidid?] He's no hero, he's basically a thug."
> JOE SNYDER, **STATE DEPARTMENT SPOKESMAN, JUNE 14**

Clinton and the U.S. were effectively stymied. In August, a new round of talks over Vance-Owen in Geneva seemed close to success, but collapsed when some ill-timed tough talk by Clinton about possible NATO air strikes against the Serbs persuaded the leader of the Muslims, Bosnia's President Alija Izetbegovic, to hold out for better terms rather than sign the partition plan.

Early in the year, Christopher had proclaimed: "Bold tyrants and fearful minorities are watching to see whether 'ethnic cleansing' is a policy the world will tolerate." By the fall, both tyrants and minorities had their answer. As their inability to break the stalemate and their willingness to tolerate it became clear,

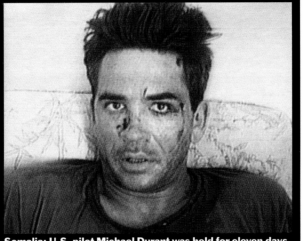

Somalia: U.S. pilot Michael Durant was held for eleven days.

Clinton and Christopher lowered the volume. Bosnia was placed on a back burner. Oddly enough, the President was aided in his attempt to turn the public's gaze away from the former Yugoslavia by two new crises that erupted in the fall, in Somalia and Haiti.

SOMALIA. In his last weeks in office, lame-duck President George Bush launched Operation Restore Hope, the U.S. mission under U.N. auspices to relieve starvation in Somalia. The American public, galvanized by pictures of starving Somali children, was solidly behind the operation, especially because Bush promised that the American troops would begin to withdraw before Inauguration Day, January 20. For a while after U.S. troops waded ashore in Mogadishu, the capital city, things went well. So well, in fact, that in March, with its forces being cut from 28,000 to 4,500, the U.S. agreed to help the U.N. set up regional councils to pave the way for nationwide elections leading to a stablized government. That worried Somali warlord General Mohammed Farrah Aidid, the strongman who had the most to lose if the U.N. plan took effect. In June his forces ambushed Pakistani troops serving under the U.N. who were inspecting unguarded weapons depots, killing 24. Eleven days later, the U.S. and U.N. plastered the bombed-out buildings of Mogadishu with posters offering a $25,000 reward for information leading to Aidid's capture.

At that moment the humanitarian mission became a mini-war against Aidid, who proved impossible to run down, even by specially trained forces. Then the manhunt turned into an American tragedy. On October 3, a group of Army Rangers swarmed down ropes from helicopters and stormed a building near the Olympic Hotel in Mogadishu in an attempt to snatch Aidid. They missed him, but captured 19 of his supporters. As they led the Somalis away, the Rangers were met with a hailstorm of fire, pinned down and surrounded in the nearby streets of the Bakhara marketplace by howling, armed Somali mobs. The Somalis shot down three hovering helicopters, then barricaded the area with burning tires. Rescue helicopters could not land in these narrow streets; the only way out was by ground. Two U.N. rescue columns fought to reach the American troops, but it was not until 10 hours after the Somali attack began that reinforcements arrived. By that time, 14 U.S. soldiers were dead, 77 wounded and one helicopter pilot, Chief Warrant Officer Michael Durant, taken prisoner. A few days later, a mortar attack by Aidid's men on Ranger forces at the Mogadishu airport killed another U.S. soldier and wounded 12 more.

Across America, TV screens suddenly seemed to carry only two images. In one, the white body of a U.S. soldier, naked except for green underwear, was being dragged through the street while Somalis kicked and stomped him. In the other, Durant, the terrified U.S. helicopter pilot, was being interrogated by his Somali captors. The response was overwhelming: thousands of horrified Americans wrote and phoned the offices of their representatives in Washington, posing angry questions that soon coalesced into a single demand: Get out! All the way. And never mind what kind of precedent was set by withdrawing.

> ## "[General Aidid] is a clan leader with a substantial constituency in Somalia."
> DEE DEE MEYERS, **WHITE HOUSE PRESS SECRETARY, OCTOBER 19**

The heat landed squarely on the White House, but Clinton and his advisers never even discussed immediate withdrawal. Clinton's policy in Somalia seemed in complete disarray, however, and he moved quickly to repair the damage. Meeting with congressional leaders, who argued that the U.S. had no vital interest in Somalia, he replied, in an odd echo of the kind of arguments he might surely have rejected as a Vietnam War protester, that the vital interest at stake was the credibility of U.S. power.

Shortly after the meeting, Clinton spoke to the nation from the Oval Office, proclaiming his revised policy. He would, he said, send 1,700 more crack troops to Somalia, and more tanks, personnel carriers and helicopters. Stationed offshore, and ready to go in if needed, would be 3,600 Marines. The hunt for Aidid would be downgraded. Robert Oakley, a retired U.S. ambassador, would be dispatched to find a political solution to the Aidid problem. Most important, Clinton set a firm deadline of March 31, 1994, for withdrawal of all American troops.

The revised early-departure policy succeeded in calming both Congress and the public. More important, it immediately defused the unproclaimed war with Aidid. Two days after Clinton's speech, Aidid accepted a nonexistent offer of a cease-fire from the Americans; shortly thereafter, Clinton's envoy Oakley met with five of Aidid's aides, and Aidid released Durant, the captured U.S. helicopter pilot. Meeting with reporters and looking dapper in a blue pinstripe shirt and red polka-dot tie and sporting a gold-tipped cane, Aidid congratulated the U.S. on having "decided to address its past mistakes"—meaning its attempts to take him prisoner. Before too long he was flying to peace conferences aboard a U.S.-supplied airplane.

HAITI. Just as the situation in Somalia was coming under control, a crisis erupted far closer to U.S. shores, in Haiti. Much as Aidid had thumbed his nose at U.S. power, local strongmen in this impoverished Caribbean nation succeeded in making the U.S. look impotent in the face of a rioting mob of no more than 200 protesters. The chief villains were Lieut. General Raoul Cédras, head of the Haitian army, and Joseph Michel François, the commander of Haiti's military police. Acting with other military leaders, they had deposed democratically elected President Jean-Bertrand Aristide in 1991. But a U.S.-led embargo had pushed them into agreeing to let Aristide return to power on October 30, 1993.

As the deadline neared, the troopship U.S.S. *Harlan County* arrived in Port-au-Prince on October 11, carrying 193 U.S. and 25 Canadian engineers and specialists who were to repair roads, hospitals and schools and train a new Haitian police force. Some carried only sidearms, some no guns at all. But as the ship anchored, thugs surged through the dock area brandishing pistols, screaming "Get out!" and kicking at or banging on cars, including one carrying U.S. chargé d'affaires Vicki Huddleston. It was "all show," according to one Haitian with close ties to the military regime: "As wild and scary as it appeared, [the supposed riot] was very carefully choreographed by the Haitian military." The U.S. President, deciding he could not risk sending lightly armed troops to face the mob, ordered the *Harlan County* to pull up anchor and steam away. The image of U.S. helplessness was heightened by the taunts of the rioters in Port-au-Prince; they shrieked threats to create "another Somalia."

On Haiti, Clinton had faltered early. In the opening days of his Administration, he decided to continue George Bush's policy of sending Haitian refugees back—a policy he had denounced during the campaign. But the Administration brokered the agreement under which Aristide was to be restored to power; it was signed on American soil in July. Now, with the Haitian strongmen defying him, Clinton acted to increase the pressure. At U.S. request, the U.N. Security Council voted to reimpose its embargo on oil and arms shipments to Haiti.

The regime answered with murder. Only hours after the President, in a Washington news conference, expressed concern for the safety of members of Aristide's putative government, gunmen riddled the car of Justice Minister Guy Malary with bullets as it drove along a quiet street in Port-au-Prince. The minister, his chauffeur and two bodyguards were killed. The U.S. then sought, and got, U.N. Security Council approval to impose what would amount to a blockade of Haiti, though it did not use that word. The President dispatched six warships to stop and search vessels headed for Haiti, and also sent a reinforced rifle company of 600 Marines to be placed on alert at the U.S. naval base at Guantanamo Bay in Cuba. The show of force stabilized the situation. Still, at year's end, Aristide remained an exile in Washington and Cédras and François were firmly in command in Haiti. ∎

> ## "Another Somalia! Another Somalia! Another Somalia!"
> **ANTI-U.S. CHANT OF HAITIAN RIOTERS IN PORT-AU-PRINCE, OCTOBER 11**

Haiti: a protester attacks U.S. diplomat Huddleston's car.

> ## "[The Haitian military] must not delude themselves that they have destroyed the democratic process."
> **PRESIDENT CLINTON, OCTOBER 29**

Radical Surgery

THE CLINTON PLAN TO REMAKE HEALTH CARE

NOT SINCE MOSES CAME DOWN FROM THE mountain bearing the Ten Commandments, Hillary Rodham Clinton joked in September, had a document been so anxiously awaited as her husband's proposal to reorganize the nation's ailing health-care system. That plan, bigger even than F.D.R.'s institution of Social Security half a century ago, would represent the boldest, most expensive social initiative since the New Deal. It would affect the health and livelihood of every American, and it would involve almost every employer in the United States, from the largest, most diverse industries to the tiniest shops.

Clinton had vowed during his campaign to take on the task of rebuilding America's health-care system; the issue was one of the biggest vote getters among his campaign promises. Polls showed the public was overwhelmingly in favor of the general idea of reform, an issue that touched their everyday lives more than anything else on the President's agenda. Clinton assured that the issue would be a touchstone of his presidency by vowing to deliver a complete proposal to overhaul the country's health-care system within 100 days of taking office.

The President missed his May deadline, but when he did appear before a joint session of Congress on September 22 to announce his new plan—following months of task forces, internal battles, trial balloons and leaks—he succeeded in communicating his personal passion for the issue in terms every Congressman and citizen could understand. "This health-care system of ours is badly broken," Clinton declared, "and it is time to fix it."

There were few who would argue with Dr. Clinton's diagnosis. Most Americans, including individuals and groups with a special interest in the system, had recognized for years that the nation's management of health care was grievously flawed. In fact, America's health-care system is not really a system at all, but a hydra-headed monster that has grown by accretion over decades without any direction. In the President's analysis, "Our health care is too uncertain and too expensive, too bureaucratic and too wasteful. It has too much fraud and too much greed."

Clinton's initial direction of the plan's development, burdened by his 100-day pledge, reflected the erratic progress of the beginning months of his presidency. He appointed his wife to head a task force that would draw up the plan. The First Lady, who believed passionately in the cause of health-care reform, gained the admiration of most Americans for her tenacious pursuit of a better system, a pursuit that took her around the nation to hold hearings and create momentum for reform. Less popular was the brilliant business consultant the Clintons chose as day-to-day manager of the task force, Ira Magaziner, a policy wonk's policy wonk who was seen as obsessed with process, overly secretive and given to spouting a mystifying bureaucratese. Elementary prudence—not to mention Clinton's usual habit of seeking to accommodate everybody—would seem to have dictated trying to bring the major interest groups aboard the process from the start, at least to the extent of listening to their views and thus giving them a stake in a plan they could feel they had helped shape. Instead, the White House turned the job over to a 511-member task force, whose very names were kept secret. When the Administration grudgingly issued a list, the task-force members turned out to be mostly congressional assistants, academics and think tankers little known even inside the Washington Beltway. While the Administration did finally begin to invite the opinions of about 50 well-known health-care experts, the sense of exclusion created by the task force alienated some of the groups essential to the plan's

DR. CLINTON'S PRESCRIPTION

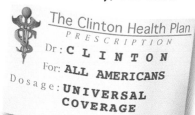

The Clinton Health Plan
PRESCRIPTION
Dr: **C L I N T O N**
For: **INSURERS**
Dosage: **MANAGED COMPETITION**

IN HIS SEPTEMBER 22 SPEECH ON HEALTH CARE, President Bill Clinton proposed a plan based on six principles: security, simplicity, savings, choice, quality and responsibility. As sketched by the President, the plan aimed to:

COVER EVERYONE By guaranteeing a generous minimum package of health insurance to all Americans. The basic array of benefits would be comparable to that offered by most major corporations and would include extra benefits for primary and preventive care.

NEVER LAPSE By safeguarding the security and "portability" of health insurance, even for workers who change jobs, are laid off or develop chronic illnesses.

LOWER PRICES By making health insurance more affordable through a system of "managed competition." Under this provision, health-insurance buyers would band together in large "alliances" to bargain with competing networks of doctors, hospitals and other health-care providers for the best service at the best price. The plan would also strictly enforce limits on health-care spending through a powerful new National Health Board that would regulate charges.

INVOLVE MORE EMPLOYERS By requiring all employers to contribute to the cost

The Clinton Health Plan
PRESCRIPTION
Dr: **C L I N T O N**
For: **EMPLOYERS**
Dosage: **MORE PARTICIPATION**

of their workers' health care. Employers would pay 80% of whatever an average health-insurance plan would cost.

PROMOTE CHOICE By requiring that all Americans be offered a greater variety of health-insurance programs at different levels of price and service, ranging from traditional fee-for-service medicine from an individual doctor to less costly participation in health-maintenance organizations (HMOs).

SIMPLIFY BILLING By relieving consumers and health-care providers of complex medical billing and insurance claim forms through a simplified universal form and, ultimately, electronic processing.

PROMOTE CHOICE BY STATES By allowing individual states flexibility in choosing among various health-care programs.

CAP COMPANY CONTRIBUTIONS By capping employers' contributions to health insurance at 7.9% of payroll, thus providing financial relief for companies that spend the most on health care by.

AID SMALL EMPLOYERS By subsidizing the health-care premiums of small businesses that employ low-income workers.

SUBSIDIZE MORE COSTS By providing new federal underwriting for prescription drugs and new benefits for long-term care of the elderly.

ultimate passage. Clinton's credibility on the issue was further damaged when he finally backed off from the May deadline, which was first extended to June, then finally pushed to the fall.

Still, most Americans listened with an open mind when Clinton finally presented his proposal to Congress. In a speech that was hailed as the most effective of his presidency, he announced a plan whose sheer size, audacity and intrusiveness into personal and business decisions was startling. The President's plan would push Americans away from private doctors and into less expensive group medical practices such as health-maintenance organizations. It would hold down the income of many doctors, hospitals, insurers and drug manufacturers through stringent federal cost controls. It would dramatically cut health-care costs for many large, high-wage companies such as automakers. But it would increase costs for many mom-and-pop businesses that had generally paid nothing toward their workers' health insurance, and now would be forced to do so under Clinton's proposal.

Overall, the President's plan would cost a budget-boggling $700 billion over five years, half of which represented new spending. Clinton proposed to cover the cost mainly through a new $1-a-pack tax on cigarettes and savings in existing federally funded health-care programs, mainly Medicare and Medicaid. The President claimed his plan would reduce the bewildering mountains of paperwork generated by the current insurance process. He even declared that it would garner $91 billion in savings to apply against the federal budget deficit; later that number was cut almost in half.

At the core of the President's plan was the concept of universal coverage. Brandishing a card that resembled a credit card, the President declared that under his system all Americans would be issued a National Health Security Card that would guarantee them medical coverage throughout their lives, "health care that is always there."

As Congress and special-interest groups began probing the plan after the speech, its political strengths and vulnerabilities began to emerge. Among the President's allies were major lobbies for the elderly, who liked the new benefits for drugs and long-term care. Big Business favored the plan because it would limit employers' expenses for covering work-

The Clinton Health Plan
PRESCRIPTION
Dr: **C L I N T O N**
For: **ALL AMERICANS**
Dosage: **UNIVERSAL COVERAGE**

ers, which amount to as much as 19% of the payroll at General Motors, to 7.9%. Small businesses, however, were frightened by the plan's requirement that all employers pay at least 3.5% of their total payroll for health insurance. After months of coy hand holding, the American Medical Association, the most powerful doctors' lobby, broke with Clinton and criticized the plan, unveiling a $7 million effort to fight it.

In Washington, Clinton's proposed cuts in Medicare and Medicaid drew fire from liberals, while Republicans and conservatives criticized the plan's creation of a new National Health Board that would place caps on both health-care provider charges and insurance premiums. For his part, Clinton continued to speak in terms of conciliation and cooperation; over and over his aides claimed the plan was "not graven in stone." At least for the moment, his stance kept the debate over the bill from descending into partisan bickering.

Though the President followed up his triumphant speech by flying to Florida for an effective town meeting on health care that was broadcast on ABC's *Nightline*, his attention was soon diverted by the struggle to pass NAFTA. It was not until late October that Clinton finally delivered his health bill—which weighed in at 1,342 pages—to Capitol Hill. It included some revisions to his original proposal: the reduction in Medicaid expenditures was lowered, as were the projected savings to be applied against the federal deficit. The new version of the bill also included a complex system of premium and subsidy caps intended to help more families and small businesses to pay for health care without draining the treasury.

In the vacuum that followed the President's September speech, though, more serious challenges to his plan began to emerge. Many Republicans favored the market-oriented Heritage plan, proposed by Utah Senator Orrin Hatch, which was based on a successful program offered to government workers. Liberal Democrats liked the single-payer system employed in Canada, where the government paid everyone's health-care bills through tax revenues. That plan, offering more savings than Clinton's, would assure

The President unveils his proposed national health card before Congress.

universal access to care, but would also require rationing of services and would place more of the system under government control.

The most prominent alternative plan was created by a Democrat, Tennessee Congressman Jim Cooper. Cooper's plan appealed to conservatives by shunning the Clinton requirement that all employers pay 80% of workers' health premiums. It appeased moderates by trimming employers' tax deductions on health-insurance premiums. And it mollified free marketeers by doing away with Clinton's proposed caps on health premiums. "We're the only bipartisan approach," Cooper maintained. "We're true to managed competition." Cooper's plan did not, however, provide for universal coverage, which the Clintons saw as fundamental to any system of reform. The battleground for the 1994 push was starting to take shape.

As Congress adjourned for the year just before Thanksgiving, the sense on Capitol Hill was that legislation would be enacted in 1994 to create a new system of American health care. But even in the Oval Office, few were willing to bet on how closely the final law would reflect the plan presented by Bill Clinton on that memorable September night. ∎

AT THE CENTER OF POWER

She's clearly cornered the clout. Now Hillary Rodham Clinton wonders if she can get a life.

HILLARY RODHAM CLINTON KNEW LIFE HAD changed forever when her daughter Chelsea got sick one night during their second month in the White House and asked her mother to fix one of her favorite dishes. No sooner had the First Lady padded down the hall to the kitchen on the second floor of the family quarters, opened the refrigerator and begun cracking eggs than a steward appeared magically at her elbow. He wanted to help by whipping up an omelet. At the risk of hurting his feelings, the most influential woman in America explained that the eggs had to be scrambled and that she had to scramble them.

Such were the days and nights of Hillary Rodham Clinton. Like other First Ladies before her, she saw all the practical considerations of daily living removed—whether she wanted them to be or not. Yet, having assumed the most ambitious and powerful role of any President's spouse, she was in a position no First Lady had ever experienced. As the icon of American womanhood, she was the medium through which the remaining anxieties over feminism were being played out. She was on a cultural seesaw held to a schizophrenic standard: everything she did that was soft was a calculated

cover-up of the careerist inside; everything that wasn't was a put-down of women who stay home and bake cookies.

In her first year in the White House, Hillary Clinton redefined the role of First Lady in America more than anyone would have imagined before her husband's election. Most notably, she chaired the task force that delivered the proposal for the largest piece of legislation since Social Security, a health-care plan that would affect one-seventh of the American economy. Hillary was the first First Lady to have a major assignment by which she could—and would—be judged. As leader of the task force, backed by a staff in excess of 500, she traveled across the country, held more than 150 congressional hearings and met with everyone from nurses to Native American spiritual healers.

To millions of women, Hillary Clinton's career-and-family balancing act was a symbolic struggle. Never mind that she had plenty of help, including more top officials on her staff than Al Gore had. Hillary still had something in common with women everywhere: a day that contained only 24 hours, and responsibilities that extended way beyond the office. Family duties fell primarily to her, from attending soccer games and helping Chelsea with her homework to organizing birthday parties. She also had to cope with the illness and death of her 82-year-old father, Hugh Rodham, in April. Her plea was familiar to any working woman: "We are trying to work it out that we have some more time just for ourselves. The job eats up every spare minute."

VOICE OF AUTHORITY: The First Lady impressed Congress with her sure grasp of the details of health-care reform.

The President's wife played an up-front, active part in the White House, from domestic affairs to political strategy to speech writing, bringing to the table two decades of experience and no apologies. In all but foreign affairs, she emerged as First Adviser. She was also responsible for the traditional duties of a President's wife. Ceremonial events, like dinner for the country's Governors or tea with the King and Queen of Spain, did not stop because there was a deadline on managed competition. Paint chips and fabric swatches also fell under her jurisdiction. Though her redecoration of the formal rooms on the second floor of the White House seemed overly Victorian and stuffy to some, she renovated the private quarters to suit her informal style, which favors quilts and rocking chairs.

Hoping to re-create a down-home Arkansas atmosphere at the White House, Hillary moved a table and white wicker chairs into the kitchen upstairs so that the family could eat breakfast and dinner in a cozier manner than the imposing dining room would permit. And she had bedside phones installed that did not require going through a switchboard. "He sleeps here and has his phone," she said, indicating one side of the queen-size bed. "And I sleep there and have mine." She furnished her husband's private study next to the Oval Office with a stand-up desk, a CD player, framed campaign buttons and a large portrait of herself.

The solarium in the family quarters sometimes substituted for the huge kitchen in Little Rock where most of the Clintons' entertaining had been done. Here overnight guests gathered for breakfast. When Norman Lear came for dinner, the President wore sneakers and dinner was chicken enchiladas. One night when Arkansas Senator David Pryor was over he urged Clinton to go off to bed, only to have the President try to drag him downstairs to view Steve Martin's *Leap of Faith*. Dressed in leather jackets and jeans, the Clintons went out with the Gores one evening to a Virginia bar to hear Jerry Jeff Walker and drink Molsons. On Valentine's Day the First Couple had a "date," seeing the movie *The Bodyguard* and dining alone afterward in a Washington restaurant.

In her role as First Mom, Hillary hoped to preserve some part of the prosaic quality of life so Chelsea would not grow up believing that food just magically materializes on her plate. One day after Hillary picked up Chelsea from school, they went to a grocery store together to buy peanut butter and cereal, only to find that they had insufficient cash and no checkbook. During a

HOSTESS: Sharing a laugh with referee and First Mate Bill Clinton at the annual Easter Egg Roll at the White House.

POLITICIAN: Visiting the Hill, she touts health-care reform to Senators Nancy Kassebaum and Ted Kennedy.

blizzard in March, Hillary stayed in the White House family quarters with Chelsea on her day off from school. They organized her room, made lunch, watched a movie and played with Chelsea's Game Boy, to which Hillary promptly became addicted. But aside from a refreshing vacation in August on Martha's Vineyard, such days were few during the Clintons' first year in Washington.

Consumed by her project, Hillary's performance on her health-care road show was reminiscent of the 1992 presidential campaign. She seemed to be everywhere: at round, oval and U-shaped tables, with black briefing books, white papers and discussion points. At symposiums morning, noon and night, she presided with brow furrowed, lips pursed, sometimes speaking, sometimes listening, always taking notes. At hearings when 1,000 seats were available, gymnasiums had to be set up with closed-circuit TV to accommodate the overflow. In a field where there was little drama, she interjected some, picking fights with her designated bullies of the system, the doctors and drug companies that have been making

huge profits. There seemed to be no fact that she, ever the best girl in class, had not memorized. The minutiæ of the Veterans hospital regulations? She cited section and subsection. The incidence of diabetes among Indians in Montana? Forty percent, and there wasn't a dialysis machine for hundreds of miles.

The First Lady initially earned grudging respect on Capitol Hill, in part because she made house calls. During her first visit, 30 Democratic Senators listened carefully, although most of them would rather have been having gum surgery. Her every misstep was discussed, from an overly familiar manner to her middle name, but she won points for her preparation and willingness to meet endlessly. Minority leader Bob Dole disputed press reports that she blundered by calling him Bob. "Last time I checked," he said, "that was my name." And he called her Hillary. By the time she went to brief the Senate Finance Committee at the end of April, she had learned the ropes. There is a rule on the Hill that if you can't explain it, you can't pass it. When she briefed the Senators, the clarity of her pitch opened a few eyes. Said committee chief of staff Lawrence O'Donnell: "I haven't been in the company of anyone that made me suspend my disbelief on health care until today. I'll come to my senses, but for the moment she was in the room, I believed she could do it."

DIPLOMAT: Looking over Kabuki actors during a relaxed moment at the Group of Seven economic summit in Japan.

When she journeyed to the Hill in September to present the health plan to congressional committees, she was a star. Her appearance sent a silent but devastating rebuke to the cartoonists. This was not Hillary as overbearing wife, Hillary as left-wing ideologue, even Hillary as mushy-headed spiritual adviser to the nation. This was Hillary the polite but passionate American citizen, strangely mesmerizing because of the way she matched the poise and politics of her delivery with the power of her position. For her interrogators, no amount of obsequiousness seemed excessive. They praised the First Lady with such words as "brilliant" and "remarkable." By the time the hearings had ended, at least one poll found that 40% of Americans believed Hillary was "smarter" than her Rhodes scholar husband, and 47% thought she was qualified to be President.

Outside her health-care mission, there was probably no title that could convey the scope of her role, although counsellor to the President was batted around for a long time. As always, she was her husband's most trusted confidant, best friend, toughest critic and most ardent

TRAVELER: Receiving an old Indian blessing from Burton Pretty, a Native American healer, in Billings, Montana.

SPEAKER: In conference with Governor Ann Richards of Texas before giving a speech on the "politics of meaning."

cheerleader. When the presidential door closed, Hillary was behind it if she wanted to be. "The President sits in the middle of the table, the Vice President right across from him, and Hillary wherever she wants," said an aide. "And the refrain we have all gotten used to is, 'What do you think, Hillary?'" Another aide said staff policy went like this: "A speech that needs a rewrite, get Hillary. A speech that needs to be given, get Hillary. The President has a problem he wants to chew over, get Hillary. The point is, you never go wrong getting Hillary."

When the First Lady went about her work she acted like any other professional with a demanding, brain-crushing job. Her office was one of the least imposing in the West Wing of the White House, furnished with a sofa striped in blue, beige and red; a table submerged in paper; a small desk; and a window looking out on a red tile roof. Hillary wrote her own notes, had a cellular phone glued to her ear and made many of her own calls. She went through paperwork quickly, scribbling in the margins of the mail, trying not to touch the same piece twice. Said her deputy, Melanne Verveer: "I'm efficient,

and she makes me look like a daydreamer." In the office Hillary pressed coffee and bagels on the staff, and frequently sent them home to bed and for holidays. Her style was collegial, and she didn't stand on ceremony. Even so, some people are scared to death of her. One aide said the problem came in mixing up "formidable" with "frightening." Still, White House political consultant Paul Begala said staff members went to her when they had a problem: "I've never seen her lose her temper, and you can tell her anything."

The closest she came to losing her temper was when she angrily went before reporters just before Christmas to defend her husband against charges of philandering. Reacting to an article in a conservative magazine that alleged Clinton used Arkansas state troopers to shield sexual affairs during his tenure as governor, she responded defiantly, accusing the accusers of a political conspiracy. "I find it not an accident," she said, "that every time he is on the verge of fulfilling his commitment to the American people and they are responding, out comes yet a new round of these outrageous, terrible stories that people plant for political and financial reasons." Though she had claimed during the Clinton's grueling campaign for the White House in 1992 that she was no Tammy Wynette, she followed the country singer's advice: she stood by her man. ■

MOM: On an August vacation on Martha's Vineyard, a rare opportunity to enjoy a casual outing with Bill and Chelsea.

Tales From the Arkansas Woods

Yuletide was glum at the White House as charges from the past surfaced to haunt the Clintons

CHRISTMAS AT THE WHITE HOUSE, 1993: AFTER A turbulent but ultimately productive first year, polls were showing that the President's approval rating had jumped to a gratifying 58%. White House aides, looking forward to a long-overdue breather, had lined up a series of Yuletide photo ops and year-end interviews that would let the President and Mrs. Clinton focus on the budget victory, the come-from-behind NAFTA triumph and the upcoming 1994 campaign on health care.

Instead, Christmas week brought forth two painful blasts from the past, one about sex, the other about money. The twin controversies prodded back to life old campaign questions about Bill Clinton's judgment, character and trustworthiness. "We've been having acid flashbacks," groaned an Administration official.

The potentially most damaging problem involved new suspicions that the Clintons, as First Couple of Arkansas, had somehow acted improperly while a real estate partner, James McDougal, ruined Madison Guaranty, a savings and loan institution that eventually cost taxpayers $47 million to bail out. Clinton had joined with McDougal and the two men's wives in a partnership to develop land along the White River. The Justice Department was investigating the now defunct S&L and the Clinton partnership to see whether money from the thrift was diverted to support faltering real estate schemes, including the Whitewater development company in which the Clintons had invested, or to finance politicians, Clinton among them. The President prom-

ised to give Justice all personal documents related to Whitewater, possibly satisfying investigators for the moment. But the potential conflicts of interest in the case were sure to invite further scrutiny: Hillary Clinton had done legal work for the failed thrift, and a Clinton friend served as chief thrift regulator.

Though it was among the largest investments in their portfolio, the Clintons had described their involvement in Whitewater Development as mostly passive, with McDougal making all the decisions. Based on a campaign lawyer's report prepared in early 1992, the Clintons claimed to have made no return on their investment of at least $68,900 in the partnership. Said Clinton: "We were clearly losing money, and we never knew, until obviously the accountant closed the books out, exactly how much we had lost." Whether the Clintons actually lost their entire investment, however, remained unknown.

As the Justice Department stepped up its investigation into Madison Guaranty's collapse, one question its agents wanted answered was whether the failed thrift received favorable treatment by Arkansas state regulators, including Beverly Basset Schaffer, head of the State Securities Department, who was appointed by Clinton. As state documents indicate, though, Schaffer was as tough on Madison as the federal regulators who had the real ability to shut the thrift down. "I may not be Beverly's biggest fan, but she's getting a bad rap," said Lee Thalheimer, her predecessor and a Republican appointee. Still, that line of pursuit also produced questions for Hillary Rodham Clinton, who as an attorney represented Madison in its bid to launch an adventurous stock scheme at a time when Clinton was Governor. Even by the clubby standards of Little Rock, her appearance before state regulators in a petition for the stock issue had all the marks of conflict of interest.

The disclosures brought trouble from Capitol Hill, where Republicans charged that Democrats were dragging their feet on the investigation. Attorney General Janet Reno rejected calls to appoint a special counsel to take over her department's investigations into Guaranty. She explained that since anyone appointed by her would still be seen as her operative, it would be better for experienced department inves-

A TANGLED WEB (clockwise from top left, against the Clintons' deed for Whitewater land): a prospectus for the Whitewater Development; White House legal aide Vince Foster, a suicide in the summer; a show house at Whitewater; the Clintons just before Christmas; the magazine story alleging Bill Clinton's sexual improprieties; Arkansas State Trooper Roger Perry; a notice posting the Whitewater property.

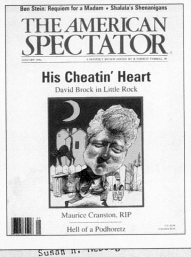

WHITEWATER

Ben Stein: Requiem for a Madam • Shalala's Shenanigans

THE AMERICAN SPECTATOR

JANUARY 1994   A MONTHLY REVIEW EDITED BY R. EMMETT TYRRELL, JR.

His Cheatin' Heart
David Brock in Little Rock

Maurice Cranston, RIP

Hell of a Podhoretz

tigators to carry on. With Reno's blessing, Justice officials picked a prosecutor with impeccable Republican credentials—Donald Mackay, a fraud-section lawyer who was once a Nixon-appointed U.S. attorney—to direct the criminal investigation of Madison and Whitewater.

The more titillating charges from the past came to light in an article in the conservative monthly *The American Spectator* written by David Brock, author of the best-selling attack biography *The Real Anita Hill.* Brock portrayed Clinton as an obsessive womanizer who used state troopers to arrange trysts with a variety of women even after the presidential election.

The article, long on damaging detail but short on corroboration, was based largely on interviews with two Arkansas state troopers, Larry Patterson and Roger Perry, who were assigned to Clinton's security detail in the 1980s. It was followed by an article in the Los Angeles *Times,* which alleged that, as Governor, Clinton had been a prodigious caller of at least one of the women the troopers identified as his sexual partners. By far the most inflammatory charge in the *Times,* however, was Trooper Perry's claim that President Clinton, in exchange for the two troopers' silence, had offered them federal jobs through a third trooper, Danny Ferguson. At the request of the White House, Ferguson issued a signed affadavit in which he insisted that no such offer had been made. As time went on, the sex stories proved impossible to verify and the two troopers turned out to have unsavory personal records.

Would the two scandals continue to dog the President? Many believed that the sexual imbroglio might blow over. After all, Americans knew that Clinton, by his own admission, had caused "pain in his marriage," but they elected him anyway. The financial morass surrounding Madison Guaranty was another matter, however, because it bore on how Bill Clinton operates in the halls of government. In Little Rock in the roaring 1980s, when Clinton was Governor, the environment was apparently clubby and murky enough to keep investigators busy for some time to come. ∎

A Parade of Contradictions

BILL CLINTON IS A STUDY IN PARADOX. A NOTORIous night owl, he often indulges in an afternoon nap. Fiercely competitive at card games, he doesn't like to keep score when he golfs. He runs brisk eight-minute miles—but never more than three at a time. He has a volcanic temper, but his eruptions pass quickly. He's an expert communicator, but his tendency to talk too much sometimes causes problems. And his biggest asset during a turbulent year in office—his ability to focus on problems with an astonishing single-minded intensity—often turned out to be the source of a lot of the turbulence.

The parade of contradictions helps explain why Clinton turned in such a mixed performance in his first year as President. He scored two big legislative victories—on his budget and the North American Free Trade Agreement—but eked them out only by the narrowest of margins. While he won praise for nudging his party to the political center, he was flanked repeatedly by Southern and Western moderates who believed he wasn't centrist enough. Although he paid scant attention to foreign policy, he showed that, when he did concentrate, he could be successful there as well. Clinton also learned that he could not do everything himself. "I tried to do so many things at once," he said in mid-December, "that I didn't take enough time to do one of the President's most important jobs, and that is to consistently explain to the American people what we were doing and why."

Indeed, what was most striking about Clinton after a year in office was the degree to which he had decided to face—rather than run from—the country's problems. He had scribed a high and unusually risky arc for his presidency, dedicating himself to tackling budget deficits, spiraling health care costs, mushrooming welfare rolls, an explosion in crime, sagging national incomes, stagnant job growth and even the growing divisions of race and class. And that was his docket just for the first two years. If he tended to sugar-coat the cost of fixing these problems, he did not shrink from describing them in detail. After 12 years of denial from Presidents, this was truly the "change" that Clinton had promised.

But, like the evolving baby-boom generation from which he hails, Clinton emerged as a much more complex figure than he seemed during the campaign. The energy he brought to his job was often unfocused and undisciplined, forcing him to scramble to play catch-up at almost any given moment. At his best, doing what top advisers refer to as "teaching and preaching" on issues like health care and crime control, Clinton seemed like an open book, a stirring leader who was determined to do well by doing good. At other times, though, Clinton could be darkly private and moody; when he had lost his footing, he could sound bitter and resentful. He often got visibly angry in public, something that Americans accustomed to cool commanders in chief had not seen since Richard Nixon.

One explanation was that Clinton, a lifelong overachiever, may have been embarrassed by his erratic performance during much of his first year. Elected with a broad but vague mandate for change, the new President quickly discovered just how difficult change can be. Though he rallied his White House staff to fight hard against "the way things work in this town," he did not realize that Washington is not much like Little Rock; that he could not twist the arms of a handful of people and make things go his way; that Democrats could be as truculent as Republicans, and sometimes even more so; that the national press corps was not as docile as the one he was accustomed to in Arkansas. He immediately ran up against special interests and a Congress that was often as averse to change as the forces he had defeated a year before.

Some of Clinton's weakness as a President derived less from inexperience than from his rudderless management style. Though he has a well-organized mind, capable of delivering astonishingly cogent, hour-long speeches from memory, he is not a well-organized executive. He had arranged his White House team like a quality circle rather than a hierarchy. Life there is a continuous fire drill, with dozens of aides reporting directly to Clinton himself, often at the same time, rather than to a strong doorkeeper. The President's desire to control everything, even down to minute details of his personal schedule, often led him to control very little. Problems with follow-through, accountability and planning plagued the White House.

Clinton too easily got lost in process. He invited his Cabinet to Camp David during the winter for a day-long group therapy session where, over cocoa and popcorn, they were expected to retell their worst childhood memories. Clinton favored long soul-searching meetings over quick-decision-making sessions. He was literally "restless": aides said he got by on a few hours of sleep a night and often tried to work on the phone, watch TV and do crossword puzzles at the same time. And he surrounded himself with people who shared his weaknesses rather than compensating for them. The result was a White House where strategic planning was thinking one day ahead. "This," said Lloyd Bentsen, "is the meetingest bunch of people you ever saw."

It often seemed as if Clinton was constantly on TV talking about *something*. His basic stump speech lasted nearly an hour, and both his State of the Union message in February and the nationally televised health-care talk in September went on for even longer. He rarely went anywhere outside of Washington without holding an equally long "town meeting" with everyday people, roaming through the audience like a Donahue or a Geraldo. He surprised even his closest aides one morning in October by giving a rousing speech to black Baptist preachers in Memphis on what Martin Luther King would make of America today. Clinton delivered the talk largely off the top of his head. But most news organizations missed the speech, easily his best of the year, because no one on the White House staff knew it was coming.

Still, for all Clinton's faults, the system of designed chaos produced some successes. Clinton did win congressional approval of his budget, his national service plan and the North American Free Trade Agreement. Trade Representative Mickey Kantor called the Administration's near-death, come-from-behind, 11th-hour victories "Clinton landslides." By year's end, his approval ratings approached an all-time Clinton high of nearly 60%. As Hillary Clinton put it, "It's the end of the first quarter and we're in the game." But the high was short-lived. Christmas week at the White House was dominated by new allegations regarding two old scandals: Clinton's alleged womanizing as Governor of Arkansas and the couples' dealings in the 1980s with a real-estate partner who ruined a savings and loan institution that had to be bailed out with $47 million in taxpayers' money.

If George Bush found foreign policy more "fun" than domestic affairs, Clinton saw it the other way around.

Part of the emphasis is vocational: Clinton is uncomfortable with his role as leader of the free world. He was nervous before his first outing at the G-7 summit in Tokyo in July, and he still mangles foreign policy pronouncements. Yet Clinton was surprisingly unfazed by his foreign policy ratings. After all, he took on a foreign policy team that was designed to be chiefly custodial (though he released Les Aspin in December when the shambling Defense Secretary's indecision proved too much even for Clinton). And even during the worst of the Somalia crisis in October, political aides at the White House could point to public opinion surveys and remind the President that Americans believe they elected him to fix America's problems first, not the world's.

Clinton turned to Al Gore as a kind of designated hitter. It was Gore who took on Ross Perot over NAFTA and proposed, later to his regret, that Clinton name Bobby Ray Inman to replace Aspin. The hyperbolic $105 billion in savings claimed by Gore in his "Reinventing Government" report came just when Clinton was in trouble for being a big spender. Clinton reassigned Gore to the foreign policy beat after Somalia, when polls began showing that Americans believed the President lacked expertise in that area. The two men, policy wonks to the core, formed a partnership like few others in presidential history.

BUT THE BIGGEST CHALlenge Clinton faces in his second year in office is defining just what kind of Democrat he is. Though he promised during the campaign to steer a moderate course, he spent much of the first six months veering hard to the left, trying to create new entitlements, appointing liberals to key positions, and generally misjudging the moderate mood of the electorate. When the public responded by sending his approval ratings to historic lows for a new President, Clinton began to tack back, bringing in moderate counselor David Gergen, moving forward on a sidetracked plan to reform welfare, and focusing more on cutting spending and improving health care.

It is probably a mistake to try to pigeonhole someone who never met his father but had thought seriously about being president since high school. Yet perhaps Clinton's continued tacking between left and center is the key to understanding him. Clinton may prove to be neither a "new" Democrat nor an old-fashioned one but something of a hybrid, a transitional president straddling a party in flux. That sounds like another paradox, but it might just work. As one Clinton aide put it, "It's not either/or. It's both." ■

APOCALYPSE

With his Ranch Apocalypse consumed by flames, "messiah" David Koresh made martyrs of the Branch Davidians—and bungling federal agents shared the blame

DAVID KORESH—HIGH-SCHOOL DROPOUT, ROCK musician, polygamist, preacher—built his church on a simple message: "If the Bible is true, then I'm Christ." It was enough to draw more than a hundred people to join him at an armed fortress near Waco, Texas, to await the end of the world. The same message tempted Koresh to entertain a vision of martyrdom for himself. He would die in a battle against unbelievers, then be joined in heaven by the followers who chose to lay down their lives for him.

On April 19 a gigantic fireball consumed the compound Koresh had named Ranch Apocalypse, and his vision was granted. Along with more than 70 members of his congregation, including at least 17 children, Koresh perished in the fire—a fire that in all likelihood was set by his followers at his command—as federal agents stormed the compound with armored vehicles. The conflagration, broadcast live on television, put an end to a 51-day siege by the Bureau of Alcohol, Tobacco and Firearms. Months later came the final, bitter denouement: a report on the tragedy showed that the deaths on both sides could have been avoided.

The grisly saga of David Koresh and his Branch Davidian followers was a tragedy played in three acts. A first bungled raid on the Waco compound in February left four federal agents dead. An uneasy hiatus followed, while ATF officials laid siege to the compound and attempted to convince Koresh to surrender. In the final fiery act, the government attacked the compound yet again, leading to the immolation that Koresh seemed to have desired all along.

THE RAID: Agents from the Bureau of Alcohol, Tobacco and Firearms were first attracted to the small cult in Waco when it began receiving frequent large shipments of firearms: the ATF claimed that over nearly a year and a half the cult had acquired 8,000 lbs. of ammunition and enough parts to assemble hundreds of automatic and semi-automatic weapons. In early 1992, one package addressed to the compound split open before it could be delivered by the United Parcel Service. The contents: hand grenades. Allegations of child abuse also dogged Koresh, who maintained a "women's dormitory" for 18 "wives" in La Verne, California. To monitor his actions, ATF agents acquired a house near the Waco compound and placed a spy within the cult.

On Sunday morning, Feb. 28, following months of

CATACLYSM: "Oh my God, they're killing themselves!" an FBI agent cried as the compound exploded in a fireball.

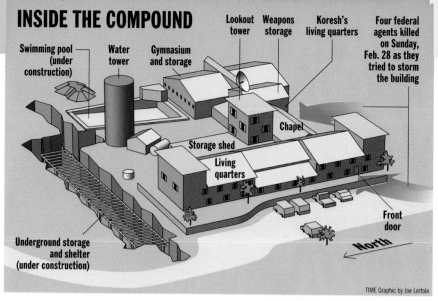

INSIDE THE COMPOUND

Swimming pool (under construction)

Water tower

Gymnasium and storage

Lookout tower

Weapons storage

Koresh's living quarters

Four federal agents killed on Sunday, Feb. 28 as they tried to storm the building

Chapel

Storage shed

Living quarters

Underground storage and shelter (under construction)

Front door

North

TIME Graphic by Joe Lertola

TIPPED OFF: Federal agents remove a wounded colleague after the failed first raid. Alerted in advance, the Davidians were ready and waiting for the "surprise attack."

grabbed his hand and said, "Good luck, Robert."

When the shooting stopped after an hour, four agents lay dead and 16 were wounded; inside the compound six cult members had died, including, Koresh claimed, a two-year-old girl, one of many children that Koresh fathered by his numerous wives.

After the agents withdrew, Koresh eventually let 21 children—none of them his own—and two elderly women leave the compound, but he remained holed up inside with 90 adults and 17 children. He claimed to be wounded, but two days later he sounded remarkably fit as he broadcast a rambling end-of-the-world message across the airwaves in exchange for a promise to surrender. He never did.

THE SIEGE: The bloody initial raid was followed by a 51-day siege, a nerve-grinding standoff with a surreal edge. With four agents dead and Koresh still uncaptured, the ATF was heavily criticized for its conduct of the attack. Critics charged that Koresh had been tipped off, that the ATF agents were outgunned and improperly prepared, that bloodshed could have been avoided if Koresh had been nabbed on the frequent occasions when he left the compound to jog, shop or eat in local restaurants. ATF director Stephen Higgins denied the charges.

Meanwhile, 200 federal agents surrounded the compound and media from around the world kept a gruesome deathwatch while Koresh—whose vanity seemed to feed on the attention—exasperated negotiators with endless, fruitless phone conversations in which he held forth on the Scriptures. At first the federal agents tried conciliatory tactics, delivering milk and medical supplies to the compound. The good-cop tactics got 37 people out, including the 21 children, before it stopped working. So the agents began to play bad cop, launching a campaign of harassment. After dark, high-intensity spotlights were directed into the compound; at times a helicopter circled overhead, playing a mobile searchlight into windows. During the day, the agents bombarded the fortress with Tibetan death chants, the piercing sound of a phone left off the hook and irritating songs played at high volume. Among the selections: Nancy Sinatra's *These Boots Are Made for Walkin'*.

planning, more than 90 law-enforcement agents charged the compound, search warrant in hand, only to be met by an explosion of gunfire. Koresh had already been tipped off to the raid. An ambulance company hired by the ATF agents had leaked word of "Operation Trojan Horse" to a local TV station; one of their cameramen asked a postman, David Jones, for directions to the compound and told him about the raid. Jones was David Koresh's brother-in-law.

Koresh was leading a Bible session when he got the news. In attendance was Robert Rodriguez, the undercover ATF agent. Koresh was already suspicious of Rodriguez; now, in a dramatic confrontation, Koresh, looking agitated, dropped his Bible and muttered the words "the kingdom of God." Then he said, "Neither the ATF team nor the National Guard will ever get me." Looking out the window, he said, "They're coming, Robert. The time has come." Rodriguez immediately made an excuse to leave in order to warn the ATF team that all hope of surprise was lost. As he left, Koresh

In the Grip of a Psychopath

EQUIPPED WITH BOTH A CREAMY CHARM AND A cold-blooded willingness to manipulate those drawn to him, David Koresh was a type well known to students of cult practices: the charismatic leader with a pathological edge. He was the most spectacular example since Jim Jones, who committed suicide in 1978 with more than 900 of his followers at the People's Temple in Guyana. Like Jones, Koresh fashioned a tight-knit community that saw itself at odds with the world, plucked sexual partners from among his cult and formed an élite guard of lieutenants to enforce his will. And like Jones, he led his followers to their doom.

The son of a single mother, Koresh was born Vernon Howell in Houston in 1959. Growing up in the Dallas area, he was an indifferent student—he dropped out of school in the 9th grade—but an avid reader of the Bible who prayed for hours and memorized long passages of Scripture. He also played guitar, using rock music as well as his magnetic preaching to recruit followers. Raised in the mainstream of the Seventh-Day Adventist Church, he found comfort as a young man in the teachings of an obscure offshoot, the Branch Davidians, which was a mutation of an earlier Adventist splinter group. The Davidians traced their roots to Victor Houteff, a Bulgarian immigrant who was expelled from a Los Angeles Adventist church in 1929 and established a splinter congregation in 1935 on the outskirts of Waco, Texas.

Following Houteff's death, leadership of the sect passed to his widow Florence, then to Benjamin Roden, a preacher who styled himself the successor to King David of Israel. Howell joined them in 1984, after he was expelled by a conventional Seventh-Day Adventist congregation. Following a power struggle with Roden's son George, who then headed the sect with his mother Lois, Howell became undisputed leader of the Branch Davidians in Waco, completing their transition from congregation to cult. In 1990 he changed his name legally to Koresh, Hebrew for Cyrus, the Persian king who allowed the Jews to return to Israel after their captivity in Babylon. His apocalyptic theology converged with secular survivalism, and Koresh transformed the

Waco settlement, a collection of cottages scattered around 78 acres of scrub pasture, into a compact fort equipped with an underground bunker and an armory—conveniently adjacent to the chapel.

Once in the cult, Davidians surrendered all the material means of personal independence, like money and belongings, while Koresh seemed to have unlimited funds, much of it apparently from his followers' nest eggs. Daily life in the compound was a harsh mix of work and Bible study. Men labored at construction, while the modestly dressed women did chores and schooled the children, who were rarely taken off the grounds. Television was for-

STAIRWAY TO HEAVEN: Koresh's brand of salvation mixed rock with religion.

bidden, and children's birthdays were never celebrated.

Having convinced his followers that he was the messiah, Koresh went on to persuade them that because his seed was divine, only he had the right to procreate. Even as Koresh bedded their wives and daughters—some as young as 11—in his comfortable private bedroom on the second floor, the men were confined to a dormitory downstairs. Beer, meat, air conditioning and MTV, taboo for others, were available to the leader. In Koresh's mangled theology, he was Jesus Christ in sinful form, whose indulgences of the flesh allowed him insights that the first Messiah had lacked. Behind the mind games lay the threat of physical force. Offenders might be paddled, or forced down into a pit of raw sewage, then not allowed to bathe. No amount of adulation seemed to satisfy Koresh. "I AM your God," he wrote the FBI, "and you will bow under my feet. Do you think you have the power to stop my will?" ■

Every morning they even provided Koresh with the sound of a trumpet blasting reveille.

Koresh replied with mind games of his own, repeatedly hinting at a mass surrender, but failing to follow through. Three times negotiators seemed to be at the verge of a breakthrough, only to have Koresh balk at the last moment. It seemed at times that he was toying with them, even putting children on the phone to the agents: "Are you coming to kill me?" a tiny voice would ask. Increasingly frustrated, FBI officials began to develop a plan to put an end to the stalemate.

THE END: As critics around the country assailed the government's handling of the case, the pressure landed on a figure new to national office: Janet Reno, the Miami prosecutor who had come to Washington to head the Justice Department after President Clinton's first two nominations failed. Only one month into her job, Reno confronted a disaster she had done nothing to create. The drama in the Texas prairie began as she was still awaiting the Senate's confirmation. Now she was in charge, and on Monday, April 12, the FBI came to her with a plan to storm the compound, laid out in a wine-colored briefing book. That started a week of meetings, briefings, phone calls and more meetings in which Reno probed the bureau's plan.

The officials had come to believe that time was no longer on their side. Their rationale: Koresh had broken one deal after another, and they believed he was growing more menacing. Meanwhile, their agents—and the snipers who had kept their sights trained on the windows of the compound for 50 days—were tiring. The plan they presented to Reno was to pump gas into the compound and create enough chaos to distract anyone intent on either firing back or orchestrating a mass suicide. The FBI believed that many of the Davidians want-

ed to come out, but Reno had to balance conflicting reports that they were prepared for mass suicide. A children's advocate, Reno was strongly swayed by accounts of Koresh's mistreatment of children within the compound, including chilling reports of sexual abuse.

After consulting with the army's élite Delta Force on the feasibility of the plan, Reno received the President's approval to proceed, along with his promise to support her decision. On Sunday, an armored vehicle towed Koresh's black Camaro away from the compound. On Monday morning, April 19, the agents moved in.

Before the sun came up, state troopers went door to door to the houses near the compound, telling people to stay inside. Over their loudspeakers, the tired negotiators called one last time for Koresh and his followers to surrender peacefully. Then they got on the phone and told him exactly where the tear gas was coming, so he could move the children away. The compound phone came sailing out the front door.

A few minutes after 6 a.m., an armored combat engineer vehicle with a long, insistent steel nose started prodding a corner of the building. Shots rang out from the windows the moment agents began pumping in tear gas. A second CEV joined in, breaking windows and nudging the buckling walls as though moving the building would move those inside. "This is not an assault!" agent Byron Sage cried over the loudspeakers. "Do not shoot. We are not entering your compound." Koresh left his apartment on the top floor and stalked the halls. "Get your gas masks on," he told his followers. Once equipped, people went about their chores: women did the laundry, cleaned, or read the Bible in their rooms, even as a tank crashed through the front door, past the piano, the potato sacks and the propane tank barricaded against it.

ASHES TO ASHES: Federal agents search the compound for bodies after the conflagration.

AFTERMATH: Attorney General Reno took full responsibility; ATF boss Stephen Higgins resigned under pressure.

By now 30-m.p.h. prairie winds had sent the flames gulping through the compound. The fire raced through the big parlor, feeding on the wooden benches and the stacks of Bibles kept by the door. The chapel crackled as flames consumed hundreds of thousands of dollars' worth of equipment from the messiah's rock-'n'-roll band and the wooden pew-like bleachers for his audience. Table after table in the cafeteria burned, and rows of children's wooden bunk beds upstairs, as the flames spread, through the attic that ran the length of the building like a wind tunnel. The structure burned fast because it was built on the cheap, a tar-paper, yellow-pine and plasterboard crematorium. By the time the fire fighters went into the compound, only ashes and bones were left, and questions.

THE REPORT: Attorney General Janet Reno had no answers to the questions; even so, she won the nation's admiration by standing tall after the raid, going on television to take full responsibility, in stark contrast to President Clinton, who maintained a conspicuous distance from the tragedy. But by the fall, some of the questions were answered. First the Treasury Department released a devastating 220-page critique of the ATF's conduct of the initial raid. Evidence that top officials had mismanaged the attack and attempted to cover up their mistakes were found in their own records and in the accounts of more than 60 agents in the field. After the report was released, Treasury Secretary Lloyd Bentsen announced the replacement of the agency's top management. Stephen Higgins, who knew the findings would be harsh, had announced his resignation three days before.

Once the shooting started, the agents abandoned their plan to target the gas where it was least likely to hurt the children. The vehicles exhaled gas through the entire building, punching hole after hole through the walls as the rounds of bullets rained down. Fleeing the gas, women and children clustered on the second floor, from which there was no exit. Then suddenly the firing stopped, and a white flag emerged from the front door. Koresh's chief lieutenant retrieved the telephone, and the agents felt a moment of hope. But the firing began again.

A few minutes past noon, FBI snipers say they saw a man in a gas mask cupping his hands, as though lighting something. An explosion rocked the compound, then another and another as ammunition stores blew up. The building shuddered, like the earthquake Koresh had foretold. A man appeared on the roof, his clothes aflame, rolling in pain. Agents moved toward him, but he waved them off. He fell off the roof, and the agents ran over, tore off his burning clothes and got him safely inside the armored vehicle.

Bentsen also removed from active service the five ATF agents in charge of the raid. A later Justice Department report did not fault Reno's supervision of the second raid, but showed that her accounts of child abuse within the compound were unfounded.

In the end, though, even the ATF's fiercest critics could not deny that it was Koresh who placed children in harm's way, who preyed on people who were weak and lonely and hungry for certainty. In the weeks following the raid, a dozen Branch Davidians found shelter at a hotel near the Waco Convention Center. They took comfort in a shared belief that their fallen leader would return. No resurrection has come. ∎

Truth, Justice And the Reno Way

SHE CAME LATE TO WASHINGTON, A third-choice candidate without a long-standing friendship with the President or his wife, without national stature, but with natural allies. She came alone, moved into an apartment furnished right down to the ironing board and the coffeepot, and set to work on an experiment in alchemy. But would it work? Would the most celebrated Cabinet member to storm the capital in years be able to turn raw personal popularity into hard political power?

There was one person in Washington in Janet Reno's early days who seemed to think so. On the 100th day of his presidency, as his star was flickering and hers ablaze, Bill Clinton came to the Justice Department for the first time since the Branch Davidian debacle in Waco, Texas, and addressed the ranks in the courtyard about his vision for a just society. Afterward he went up to Reno's small inner office and gazed at the picture near her desk of Bobby Kennedy walking alone on the beach. "One day," Clinton told his Attorney General, "people will look at your portrait this way."

Reno is pure oxygen in a city with thin air, and at first she went to its head. Senators said she was Clinton's most impressive Cabinet member by far; the New York *Times* called her "a prized asset." No one could have predicted that the most popular member of an Administration saturated with lawyers would be a lawyer herself, that she would surface from a process that barbecued two other prominent female attorneys. But if Clinton had had the luck and prescience to pick Reno first, he wouldn't have got her; back in November of 1992, when the President's staff was shuffling résumés, she was at the bedside of her mother Jane, an indestructible force in her life, who was dying of cancer. Had the President called, Reno wouldn't have come.

From the day three months later when Clinton and Reno first met and he offered her the job, their styles were, to put it politely, complementary. Where Clinton was twice shy, having been charred by his earlier nominations, Reno was blunt, irrepressible. White House officials tried to coach this daughter and sister of journalists on how to dodge reporters' questions gracefully.

> Standing tall and talking straight, **Janet Reno** is a self-described "old maid" whose chief concern is America's kids

Abortion, for one, she was urged to avoid. "What the President of the United States told me as we started into the Rose Garden on Feb. 11, 1993," she recalls, was, " 'Don't blow it.' "

So the question on abortion came. And Reno, being Reno, hedged as much as she was capable. "I'm pro-choice," she said flatly. End of coaching.

Reno's popularity took her by surprise, but she had not spent much time in the capital before. It is a city that loves a character, and the early profiles of her Florida upbringing invited an instant mythology. Here she came, trailing swamp stories and reptiles, a self-described awkward old maid with a sensible name and big, sensible shoes, a bracing contrast to the precious professionals that the city seasonally absorbs. "I can be impatient," she told reporters, preferring to skewer herself rather than let them do it for her. "I do have a temper. My mother accused me of mumbling. I am not a good housekeeper. My fifth-grade teacher said I was bossy. My family thinks I'm opinionated and sometimes arrogant, and they would be happy to supply you with other warts."

Reno's maternal grandmother Daisy Sloan Hunter Wood was a genteel Southern lady who lost her own mother and two sisters to tuberculosis and instilled in her children and grandchildren a passionate commitment to duty and family. In World War II, her daughter Daisy became a nurse, landing with General Patton's army in North Africa and marching on Italy. Another, Reno's Aunt Winnie, joined the Women's Air Force Service Pilots, an élite corps of civilian flyers who tested combat aircraft, towed targets for ground artillery practice and trained male pilots.

Reno's mother Jane, coming of age during the Depression, took a bachelor's degree in physics and at 24 was about to go to graduate school at Columbia when she met and married Henry Reno, a 36-year-old police reporter for the Miami *Herald*. Tired of having his Danish surname, Rasmussen, mispronounced, he had picked his last name off a map of Nevada. The couple built a house out of cypress logs in the woods of rural Dade County; 43 years later, it survived Hurricane Andrew

without losing more than a couple of shingles. In addition to the now legendary alligators, there were cows, beagles, macaws, raccoons, goats, geese, ponies, pigs and skunks (not descented), all welcome members of the famously unorthodox Reno household. Such a colorful personal history guaranteed that Janet Reno would arrive in Washington and become, instantly, a cartoon. Friends who have known Reno since her days as a chemistry major at Cornell, or as one of 16 women in a class of 500 at Harvard law, or as a powerhouse prosecutor in Miami, are amused at the caricature. "Everybody thought she was this li'l gal from the swamp," says longtime Miami friend Sara Smith. "I chuckle because they underestimated Janet."

Not anymore. Such was the power of her personal geometry that Reno towered above the countless new arrivals to the city. The last time such a crop of eager young technocrats arrived to take over the capital, Sam Rayburn surveyed the bushy-tailed crowd and told Lyndon Johnson, "Well, Lyndon, they may be just as intelligent as you say. But I'd feel a helluva lot better if just one of them had ever run for sheriff."

Reno ran five times, and kept winning by vast margins. That she managed to do so running as a liberal-minded, pro-choice Democrat in a deeply conservative county without hiding her principles carried a lot of weight in the city of perpetual pandering. But Washington is also the city of perpetual reassessment, and by the fall Reno's halo was beginning to tarnish. News stories questioned her judgment in the Waco tragedy and her competence in running the Justice Department, while admitting that Reno continued to receive hundreds of admiring letters from the public each week.

Yet even Reno's fiercest critics acknowledge her ethical hygiene. Here is a public servant who pays list price for a new car to avoid any charge of getting a sweet deal. In a department under fire for being deeply politicized and ethically challenged, employees consider her their best chance at redemption.

If her popularity has a bleeding edge, it may be that it dates to one of the worst days of her life. On that April afternoon when Reno went before the cameras to explain the disastrous finale in Waco, the peculiar laws of politics ensured that she would get all the credit for taking all the blame. The first image Americans held of their brand-new Attorney General was of a stern, sad, certain woman describing a terrible tragedy and using none of the greasy legal language that would have shielded her from blame.

Her performance won her the lasting loyalty of her own department. "She stood up and took a bullet for us," a veteran FBI agent says. But Reno paid a political price.

"I do have a temper. My family thinks I'm opinionated and sometimes arrogant, and they would be happy to give you other warts."

Much was made at the time of the contrast between her mea culpa and that of President Clinton, who vanished for hours before surfacing to claim responsibility. Further strains with the White House arose over her support of Lani Guinier after Clinton abandoned her and over the FBI's role in the botched firing of the White House travel department.

Friends say Reno has no regrets about not being part of Clinton's inner circle. Lacking her own power base, she spends much of her time campaigning for the issues she cares most about. Wedged into her busy days are speeches to government and community groups whose help will be crucial to building the consensus she needs. She is fighting hardest on two fronts: children's issues and cooperation among government agencies. "We spend more money trying to determine whether people are eligible for services than we do in serving them," Reno says. "We've got to figure out how to take the federal bureaucracy and weave it together as a whole, so that we can reweave the fabric of society around our children."

Reno has never married and has no children. Yet her life is filled with them. Children seem to sense a powerful friend in Reno, and she is everyone's favorite honorary aunt. In her years as a prosecutor, Reno saw firsthand the link between a miserable child and a vicious adult. She fought for better children's services, from health care to day care to preschool education, all on the grounds of crime prevention. She was one of the first prosecutors around to come down hard on scofflaw spouses who skipped out on child support, prompting a disgruntled father to scrawl threatening graffiti on a sign near her home. Some critics charge that in her zeal she goes too far. In 1984 her office came under fire for forcing confessions and railroading defendants in a high-profile child-abuse case. Testifying before a Senate hearing on TV violence in October 1993, she warned that if the television industry didn't do something to curb violence in its programs, government regulations would be "imperative."

Reno's prescriptions go well beyond the legal realm. She has advocated workdays that end at 3 p.m. so that parents can be home when their children get out of school. "There are children who, after school and in the evenings, are unsupervised and adrift and alone and fearful," she said in a speech to the Women's Bar Association. "And they are getting into trouble, and they are being hurt." Reno draws on the lessons of her own family. "It was my mother, who worked in the home, who taught us to bake cakes, to play baseball, to appreciate Beethoven's symphonies," she says. "She spanked us hard, and she loved us with all her heart. And there is no child care in the world that will ever be a substitute for what that lady was in our life." ∎

■ INVESTIGATIONS

Fallout of Secrets

Disclosures revealed the U.S. used civilians as unsuspecting guinea pigs in radiation tests

ONE SPRING DAY IN 1950, U.S.. SCIENTISTS PERFECTing techniques for tracking Soviet atomic tests packed a conventional bomb with radioactive material—probably lanthanum-140—and exploded it in the atmosphere near Los Alamos, New Mexico. No injuries were reported—but the radioactive fallout reached populated areas at least 70 miles away.

The Los Alamos test was only one of many similar experiments described in a congressional report released in December. The tests dated back to the early days of the atomic age, when the government often learned about the effects of radiation the quick and dirty way: by exposing unsuspecting civilians.

When the first reports of such experiments appeared in the 1980s, in a congressional study titled *American Nuclear Guinea Pigs*, the Energy Department had been less than forthcoming. This time, Energy Secretary Hazel O'Leary said the Clinton Administration's policy would be to "come clean" about the tests. On December 7 she called upon the government to lift the shroud of secrecy surrounding radiation experiments conducted from the 1940s through the 1970s, and ordered the most thorough investigation ever into them. The Energy Department also promised to declassify millions of pages of documents related to past activities of the nuclear-weapons industry.

Among the frightening array of nuclear experiments that came to light were large-scale medical tests involving hundreds of patients. A series published in the Albuquerque *Tribune* detailed one experiment in which 18 people received a high concentration of plutonium, apparently without their full consent. In another test, 800 pregnant women were exposed to radioactive iron in order to investigate its effects on fetal development. The testicles of 67 inmates at an Oregon state prison were exposed to X rays to determine how radiation might alter sperm production.

In Tennessee, the local press dug up a series of nutritional experiments conducted in the 1940s at Vanderbilt University's free prenatal clinic in Nashville. Funded in part by the Tennessee Department of Health, the tests involved feeding more than 800 women a "cocktail" laced with a mildly radioactive iron isotope to chart how the iron was absorbed. A followup study in the 1960s found a "small but statistically significant increase" in cancer among children born to the women. University officials said they did not know if the women's consent was obtained. At least one woman, Emma Craft, 72 in 1993, said she was never told of any experiments.

As a battle began to take shape over government liability, the question of informed consent emerged as the core issue. Many scientists and doctors argued that Americans should keep in mind the context of the cold war tests. Standards for human experimentation were less stringent back then, they argued, and the long-term effects of radiaton were not yet known. But O'Leary refused to accept those positions. On December 28 she promised compensation to some victims of the tests, which department officials estimated might produce liability claims totaling anywhere from $1 million to $300 million. But as allegations of secret tests mushroomed in the final weeks of the year, it appeared the worst of the disclosures might be yet to come, and the estimate of the compensation due to America's unsuspecting nuclear guinea pigs might be low. ■

Terror

TARGETS THE TOWERS

After a massive bomb rocked New York City, a radical Muslim cleric and his followers were charged with a wide-ranging conspiracy against the U.S.

A MERICANS WERE NOT ACCUSTOMED TO what so much of the world had already grown weary of: the sudden, deafening explosion of a car bomb, a hail of glass and debris, the screams of innocent victims followed by the wailing sirens of ambulances. Terrorism seemed like something that happened somewhere else—and somewhere else a safe distance over the horizon.

And then, in a single instant on a snowy Friday afternoon in February, the World Trade Center in New York City became ground zero.

At 12:18, as workers were preparing for lunch, a massive explosion rocked the foundation of the Twin Towers of the Trade Center in lower Manhattan—the second tallest buildings in the world and a magnet for 100,000 workers and visitors each day. The bomb was positioned to wreak maximum damage to the infrastructure of the buildings and the commuter networks below. It blew out a crater 200 ft. by 100 ft. across and seven stories deep. Floors collapsed into one another with an impact that caused the ceiling of the PATH subway line that links Manhattan and New Jersey to come crashing down, showering chunks of concrete onto commuters waiting on the platform. In the same moment, the 110-story Twin Towers swayed visibly as the force of the blast shuddered upward. Lobby windows exploded onto the plaza and marble slabs fell from the walls. As fractured steam pipes launched jets of hot mist into the air, the first victims stumbled out of the buildings, bloodied and in shock.

More than 1,000 workers were treated for smoke inhalation, minor burns and shock.

Fires quickly broke out, launching thick, acrid smoke up scores of stairwells and elevator banks. In both towers the electricity went out, including emergency backup systems. Even on the highest floors, workers were stunned by the speed at which smoke flew upward. David Deshane, 25, was on the 105th floor when he felt the explosion. "All the computers shut down, then all the phones shut down," he said. "Then all of a sudden we saw smoke everywhere." He ran to hit the fire-emergency button. "Nothing happened." In a panic, some people broke windows to admit air, sending daggers of glass raining onto the crowds below and creating a chimney effect that drew smoke upward even more quickly.

Six people died in the blast, four of them employees of the Port Authority of New York and New Jersey, which owns and operates the giant structures. The employees' work areas were located on the lower levels, which sustained the worst damage. The fifth victim, a salesman who was walking in the garage when the bomb exploded, suffered a fatal heart attack after being rescued; the sixth, an employee of the Trade Center's Vista Hotel, was found under the bomb rubble in the parking garage. More than 1,000 were injured. But the toll was less severe than first feared. Though some suffered major injuries, most of the victims were treated only for smoke inhalation or minor burns.

In the wake of the explosion, bomb threats forced the evacuation of the Empire State Building and Newark Airport, and police checked 19 phone calls claiming responsibility for the blast. Around the country, airports and other facilities stepped up security. The blast was a reminder of the vulnerability of most American office buildings, shopping malls, airports and railway stations.

Even as the rescue effort was in progress, intelligence agencies mobilized. The news from New York sent federal agencies to Code Red, their highest state of readiness. The FBI, CIA and Bureau of Alcohol, Tobacco and Firearms (ATF) all mobilized their counterterrorist teams. Experts speculated about the bombers' identity and affiliation; their early list included various Balkan factions, Russian nationalists and a host of Middle Eastern groups, from Palestinians to Iraqis, Iranians and Libyans.

To the nation's relief, the answer came with surprising swiftness. The search for the terrorists began late in the afternoon of Sunday, February 28—a bare two days after the blast. Ten investigators began picking their way down a ramp leading to what had been the garage's second parking level, shining flashlights on the mangled remains of cars and trucks that had been blown to bits. "Hey, look at this," said Joseph Hanlin, a bomb expert from ATF, picking up a thin, charred, twisted bit of metal about 18 inches long. "This is something that we need to take."

That piece of metal led investigators across the Hudson River to a Jersey City mosque of Islamic fundamentalists, where a frequent guest preacher was a blind Muslim cleric from Egypt who had long advocated holy war. In a nearby apartment agents found electronics manuals, wiring and other bomb-making material. By week's end authorities had two men in custody. One, Ibrahim El-Gabrowny, an Egyptian, had dunked his hands into a toilet to foil any testing for traces of explosives, a prosecutor charged at his arraignment. The other, Mohammed Salameh, an illegal immigrant from Jordan, had rented the van that apparently carried the bomb into the Trade Center garage. In a scene that no

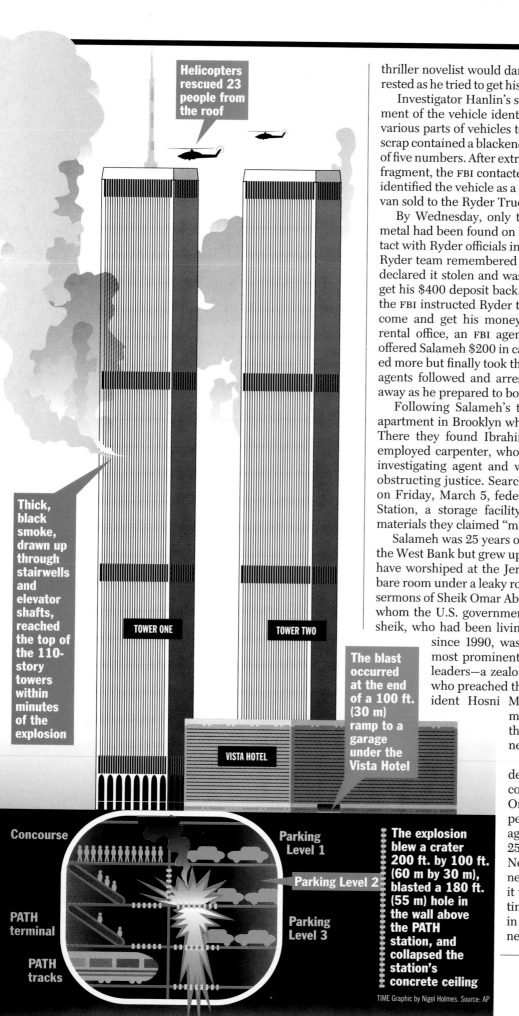

Helicopters rescued 23 people from the roof

Thick, black smoke, drawn up through stairwells and elevator shafts, reached the top of the 110-story towers within minutes of the explosion

TOWER ONE

TOWER TWO

The blast occurred at the end of a 100 ft. (30 m) ramp to a garage under the Vista Hotel

VISTA HOTEL

Concourse

Parking Level 1

Parking Level 2

PATH terminal

Parking Level 3

PATH tracks

The explosion blew a crater 200 ft. by 100 ft. (60 m by 30 m), blasted a 180 ft. (55 m) hole in the wall above the PATH station, and collapsed the station's concrete ceiling

TIME Graphic by Nigel Holmes. Source: AP

thriller novelist would dare dream up, Salameh was arrested as he tried to get his $400 van rental deposit back.

Investigator Hanlin's scrap of metal included a fragment of the vehicle identification number stamped on various parts of vehicles to help police trace them. The scrap contained a blackened but decipherable sequence of five numbers. After extrapolating the full VIN from the fragment, the FBI contacted the Ford Motor Co., which identified the vehicle as a yellow Ford Econoline E-350 van sold to the Ryder Truck Rental Co.

By Wednesday, only three days after the piece of metal had been found on the ramp, the FBI was in contact with Ryder officials in Jersey City, New Jersey. The Ryder team remembered the renter of the van: he had declared it stolen and was making a pest of himself to get his $400 deposit back. Mounting a sting operation, the FBI instructed Ryder to call the renter, Salameh, to come and get his money. When he returned to the rental office, an FBI agent posing as a Ryder official offered Salameh $200 in cash; Salameh loudly demanded more but finally took the money and walked out. FBI agents followed and arrested him a block and a half away as he prepared to board a bus.

Following Salameh's trail, FBI agents went to an apartment in Brooklyn where Salameh had once lived. There they found Ibrahim El-Gabrowny, 42, a self-employed carpenter, who allegedly tried to punch an investigating agent and was arrested on a charge of obstructing justice. Searching for bomb components, on Friday, March 5, federal authorities raided Space Station, a storage facility in New Jersey, removing materials they claimed "may be linked to Salameh."

Salameh was 25 years old, an Arab who was born on the West Bank but grew up in Jordan. He was known to have worshiped at the Jersey City mosque—actually a bare room under a leaky roof—where he heard the fiery sermons of Sheik Omar Abdel Rahman, the blind cleric, whom the U.S. government was trying to deport. The sheik, who had been living in New Jersey on and off since 1990, was considered one of Egypt's most prominent and radical fundamentalist leaders—a zealous voice of Islamic holy war who preached the violent overthrow of President Hosni Mubarak's Egyptian government. Yet in these first weeks there was no evidence to connect the sheik to the bombing.

But in surprisingly short order, the pieces of the puzzle continued to come together. Only a week after the first suspects were arraigned, federal agents arrested Nidal Ayyad, 25, at his home in Maplewood, New Jersey. A chemical engineer, Ayyad was a Kuwaiti who, it was discovered, possessed a timing device commonly used in terrorist bombs. His business card had been found in

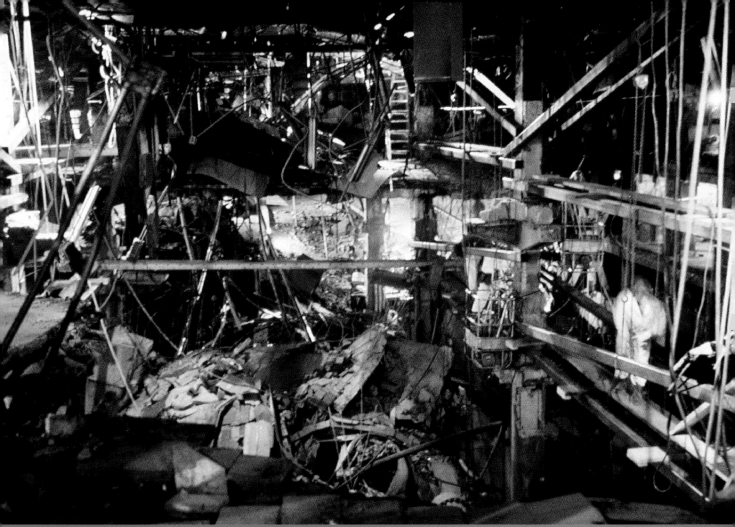

Entering the bomb crater, inspectors anticipated a lengthy, painstaking search for clues. Instead, shortly after beginning their inquiry, they found the metal fragment with the vehicle identification number that led them to the culprits.

Salameh's pocket. Although Ayad was from Kuwait and Salameh was from Jordan, both men were of Palestinian descent and had been friends for more than a year. The federal complaint against Ayyad stated that on February 25, the day before the blast, Salameh made several trips to the storage shed in New Jersey where he kept his bombmaking materials. Four times that day he phoned from a nearby booth to Ayyad's office at Allied-Signal, calls that Salameh's lawyer insisted concerned "a family matter." Perhaps most intriguing, the two men shared a joint bank account at the branch of the National Westminster Bank located near Al-Salam Mosque, where, investigators said, the men placed several deposits of less than $10,000. Federal agents said at least $8,000 was transferred to the account from Germany in 1992 and was withdrawn by Salameh.

The two men did not fit the profile of the typical terrorist bomber. Ayyad's relatives depicted the chemical engineer as a devout Muslim who had achieved the American Dream since immigrating from Kuwait in 1985. In 1991 he became a naturalized citizen, earned a bachelor's degree from Rutgers University and began work at AlliedSignal. A year later, his mother arranged for him to marry a Middle Eastern woman.

Salameh, by contrast, was a drifter, never settling into a permanent home or regular job. His grades in school were so mediocre that he could not get into university law or science programs; his only option was to attend the University of Jordan's college of religious law, where one professor recalled that Salameh was involved in fundamentalist student activities. Back in the Jordanian city of Zarka, his father and brothers wept openly as they spoke of the many letters they had received from Salameh praising America as a free and democratic society.

By the third week of March the investigation had already yielded three imprisoned suspects, a cache of bombmaking chemicals, and the beginnings of a money trail. Yet, despite the eerie ease of the initial arrests, police still had not nabbed a ringleader, someone not quite "the John Gotti of this group," as a New York sleuth told New York Newsday, but "the guy who runs the crew." Then on March 25, authorities in Manhattan arraigned the alleged mastermind: Mahmud Abouhalima, a 6-foot, 4-inch redhead who in the late '80s had fought with Islamic fundamentalists to liberate Afghanistan and who was close to Sheik Omar. Shortly before Salameh's arrest, Abouhalima had taken flight, making a pilgrimage to Mecca and then Medina, Saudi Arabia, before being picked up by Egyptian police at 2:30 one morning at his parents' house in Kafr El Dawar on the Nile delta. Once in the hands of the Egyptians, he was hustled off to parts unknown and, his lawyer later charged, "strung up like a shish kebab" for torture for 10 days. The Cairo government denied the torture. The FBI learned of Abouhalima's capture from his brother Mohammed, who also lived in New Jersey, during a five-hour interrogation. After a round of intense and delicate negotiations, Egypt turned Mahmud over to U.S. authorities.

WITH THE KEY SUSPECTS APPREHENDed so quickly, the nation's attention turned to other news. Then, on June 24, a SWAT team of FBI agents and New York City police burst into a garage in the borough of Queens at 1:30 a.m., and caught five men hunched over 55-gal. barrels, swirling wooden spoons to mix fertilizer and diesel fuel into an explosive paste. The alleged bombmakers were hauled into court, some still wearing overalls splotched with what the local FBI chief called a "witches' brew." They and three others nabbed in raids on apartments, all described as Muslim fundamentalists, were charged with conspiracy to carry out a new series of bombings and were held without bail.

The agents had foiled a grandiose plot that would have sent bomb blasts spreading fire and smoke through United Nations headquarters, the New York offices of the FBI, and the Holland and Lincoln tunnels under the Hudson River, all timed to provide America with a ghoulish kind of pre-Fourth of July fireworks display. The alleged ringleader, Siddig Ibrahim Siddig Ali, boasted to an FBI informant inside the ring that the message of the bombing was "We can get you anytime!" The scheme was thwarted thanks to the work of the informant, Emad Salem, 43, a former Egyptian military officer. Salem was said to have turned informant partly for money, but largely because he thought terrorist killings were betraying, not furthering, the cause of Islam. With Salem's help, the FBI and New York City police had been keeping close watch on the conspirators, even setting up concealed television cameras in the Queens warehouse where the bombing brew was being mixed.

The second bomb ring seemed at first to be only tangentially connected to the Trade Center group, mainly through the figure of the one man whose preachings seemed to underlie both plots, but whose fingerprints could not be placed on a bomb: Sheik Omar. The informant Salem, it turned out, had also been part of the inner circle around the sheik. As the radical cleric's involvement with both groups became known, calls increased for the government to arrest him, but for weeks Attorney General Janet Reno refused, saying she lacked evidence to bring a case. When New York politicians protested the sheik's continued freedom, the best Reno could do was have him arrested on a charge of violating immigration laws.

Behind the scenes, though, the FBI was assembling a case. Finally, in late August, federal prosecutors declared that both bomb plots, as well as the 1990 murder of prominent Zionist

Mahmud Abouhalima is led into FBI headquarters in New York City.

A Student and His Master

MAHMUD ABOUHALIMA, ALLEGED MASTERMIND of the gang that planted the powerful bomb at the World Trade Center, is one of a new breed of militant Muslim. His fundamentalist faith led him from an impoverished village in Egypt to the war in Afghanistan, where he received a CIA-bankrolled education in violence, and to the teachings of the radical Sheik Omar Abdel Rahman, whose calls for a holy war against the Western world were eventually charged with sparking the bombing.

Abouhalima and his fellow conspirators epitomize Islam's dark side, which shows its face in violence and terrorism intended to overthrow modernizing, more secular Islamic regimes and harm the Western nations that support them. Its influence far outweighs its numbers. The Islamic revival that has swept the Middle East in recent years is primarily a movement for a return to religious purity. But where desperation is greatest, a small number of radicals have resorted to military action to impose Islamic ideology. For the most part, they are not members of some grand conspiracy, but loosely organized, grass-roots militants who use similar terrorist methods and get money and weapons from the same like-minded sources. Violence inspired by radicals determined to topple President Hosni Mubarak killed 200 people in Egypt between 1991 and 1993. In Algeria the toll was at least 1,200. Hamas, the Islamic Resistance Movement, was the greatest danger to the peace process in the Middle East.

The emotional wellsprings of Islamic extremism lie in the social displacement and alienation of the modern Arab world. Discontent runs deep in Muslim countries where poverty is endemic, unemployment keeps growing, prices soar. Poorly educated, poverty-stricken peasants are obvious recruits to fundamentalism. So,

Under heavy guard, the militant Sheik Omar Abdel Rahman was flown from prison to his arraignment in Manhattan.

Rabbi Meir Kahane in New York, were part of a single terrorist conspiracy led by Sheik Omar. A grand jury in New York City indicted him and 14 others on sweeping charges that they had plotted "to levy a war of urban terrorism against the United States."

On August 26 all 15 defendants were marched, handcuffed and in single file, into a courtroom in lower Manhattan, where they entered pleas of not guilty. In the months to come, they would join the defendants in the World Trade Center bombing and the Fourth of July conspiracy in trials that would seek to find them guilty of a massive plot to undermine the U.S. government. The catalog of charges against them, according to New York University law scholar Stephen Gillers, amounted to "the gravest allegations to come out of any American court in this century." ■

increasingly, are younger members of the middle class who find themselves without a viable future.

Like Mahmud Abhouhalima. He was born in 1959 into a struggling family in Kafr al-Dawar, a Nile delta town 15 miles south of Alexandria. Rebellious as a youth, he began to hang around with members of the outlawed fundamentalist Islamic Group as a teenager; their spiritual guide was the blind Sheik Omar. In 1981, in the same month that Egyptian President Anwar Sadat arrested 2,000 Islamic fundamentalists who opposed him, Abouhalima left Egypt for Germany. A week later Sadat was killed. Abouhalima became a force in Munich's Egyptian immigrant community, then moved with his German wife to America in 1985. He settled in Brooklyn and drove taxicabs in New York for the next five years. But his attention was focused on the Islamic jihad, or holy war, in Afghanistan. Between 1988 and 1990 he made several trips to Pakistan, where he was trained for combat; Sheik Omar was also in Pakistan during this heady period for militant Islamists. During the 1980s an estimated 20,000 Arabs from 50 nations rallied to the Afghan jihad, and for many it was a transforming experience. Ironically, since they opposed the Russian-backed regime in Afghanistan, the militants were armed and trained partially with financial support from the CIA.

When Abouhalima returned to the U.S., he became part of Sheik Omar's inner circle. The controversial cleric had long been suspected of giving religious approval for bloodshed. The sheik had been arrested, imprisoned, then acquitted in Egypt for encouraging the 1981 assassination of Anwar Sadat. U.S. and Egyptian officials suspected him of issuing *fatwas*, religious death warrants, in the 1990 slaying of Jewish militant Rabbi Meir Kahane and the 1992 Brooklyn murder of an Egyptian named Mustafa Shalabi. Cassette tapes of his messages of sedition were smuggled abroad from the U.S. for circulation in Egypt and for broadcast on a Lebanese radio station. Egyptian security officials also blame Sheik Omar and his 10,000 hard-core disciples in Egypt for 20 attacks against tourist targets. One, a TNT explosion that killed four in a Cairo café, came just 75 minutes after the Trade Center explosion.

Sheik Omar's name had been on the State Department's list of suspected terrorists since before the assassination of Sadat, and FBI agents had been monitoring the cleric and his followers long before the Trade Center bombing. Still, despite a storm of criticism, agents waited for frustrating months after the bombing and the foiled summer conspiracy, assembling the strongest possible case against the sheik before arresting him. ■

SWEPT AWAY:
70,000 people were left homeless as roiling floodwaters broke through the levees along the Mississippi and its tributaries.

The Great Flood

NO PROPHECIES were uttered when it all began, when the wind blew and the rain descended on the plains. No dire predictions augured the disaster; no omens hinted at a catastrophe of epic proportions. But for months the sky fell, bit by bit and drop by drop, and the waters gathered on the face of the earth to flow into the river; and then the river rose up and rolled onward like an ocean on the march, capturing farmland and township, bridge and barge.

And when it was over, when the river finally retreated from its conquered territory, the great flood on the Missouri and upper Mississippi basins had moved beyond mere awe and tragedy to the realm of mysticism, to top almost every means of measure, verbal and mathematical.

A FEW GOOD MEN: An army of volunteers, including children and prison inmates, fought to contain the rising waters.

> **❝**None of us is ever going to forget how the rains came in the summer for the first time, out of nowhere. And we will never feel the same about our place on earth.**❞**
>
> **VICTOR LESPINASSE, Illinois**

In the "500-year flood," as much as 10 times the normal rainfall was flung over eight states for the better part of two months, killing 50 people, immersing 13.5 million acres of land, bursting federal levees in 12 places and private levees in nearly 800 spots, and causing an estimated $12 billion in damage.

The flood did not discriminate. Among its detritus were picnic tables and automobiles, tree stumps and deer. Its waters flowed over the enduring emblems of America's heartland: the barnyards and barbecues, the fields and fence posts. The barges that usually command the waterway were rendered helpless and inert, tethered to a vanished shore. Crops were submered under inches, even feet, of water. Said a dairy farmer in Wisconsin: "We deal with Mother Nature all the time, but this is hurting us more than people can take."

It began with the rains. The precipitation in St. Louis in the first six months of the year was more than twice the amount in the same period in 1992; those months were the wettest in Iowa in 121 years of record-keeping. On July 13 an inch fell in only six minutes at Papillion, Nebraska. The floods followed. On the night of July 15 in Fargo, North Dakota, the Red River, engorged by a daylong deluge, rose 4 feet in six hours, rampaging into town and causing sewage to back up into homes and Dakota Hospital. On July 16 the Missouri River poured over the top of a railroad embankment being used as a levee in St. Charles County, Missouri, northwest of St. Louis. Its waters mingled with those swirling south from the Mississippi 20 miles upriver from the two rivers' normal junction, forcing several hundred people to join the 7,000 who had already evacuated their homes. That evening the Mississippi broke through a sand levee at West Quincy, Missouri, forcing the closing of the Bayview Bridge— the last span that was open over a 200-mile stretch of the river where it separates Missouri and Illinois.

Much of the drowned land is normally among the most fertile acreage on earth. Prospective crop losses were spectacular: $1.5 billion worth of soybeans in Illinois, $1 billion worth of corn in Iowa. Farmers took it hard. For all the urban pretensions in bigger towns like St. Joseph and Des Moines, the river region was geared to nature's rhythms, a verdant land of quilted green and slow streams with such names as Skunk and Nodaway. The Flood of '93 stole some of its innocence and trust. Bob Plathe, who farms 800 acres of soybean and corn in Lu Verne, Iowa, echoed the region's lament. "There

BUCKET BRIGADE: "Our arms are six inches longer," said one of the 250,000 Iowans left waterless.

WATER HAZARD: The Raccoon River has the right of way near the water-treatment plant it crippled in Des Moines.

ROW-ME STATE: A little water didn't keep customers from dropping into a convenience store in Missouri.

> **"I don't mean to be irreverent, but the Mississippi has a presence in life. When I think of it, I think about God almighty himself."**
>
> **SHELBY FOOTE, Tennessee**

aren't a lot of farmers around anymore who can take a hit like this and survive. It's pretty hard for a third-generation farmer to lose his grandpa's farm."

Some lost great-grandpa's farm. For 160 years Nick Goederis' family had tilled 150 acres of rich farmland along the Mississippi near Quincy, Illinois. Repeatedly, the river had reached out to destroy the crops; each time, the family had returned to replant and prosper. This flood was different. The river, recalls Nick's wife Crystal, "was like something possessed." For weeks in July the Mississippi occupied their five-bedroom home. Like many others, they had no flood insurance; now their dreams had been set back for a generation. "The kids know that someday they are going to return to a farm," said Crystal. "They just don't know it is not going to be this one."

Hard times. Yet as the flood crest rolled from Minnesota down through Iowa and on to Missouri and Illinois, Midwesterners showed remarkable resilience, a neighborly spirit and stunning good humor. The resilience was especially notable in the Iowa capital, Des Moines, which was possibly harder hit than any other big city. A flood along the Raccoon River on July 11 knocked out the city's water-treatment plant. Residents had to line up for water trucked in from outside and dispensed at 100 different locations (limit: 2 gallons to a customer). Even so, as a chain of about 100 people heaved sandbags to protect the water-treatment plant in West Des Moines from further flooding, the atmosphere was downright festive and jokes flew. At Iowa Methodist Medical Center, president David Ramsey explained why trauma cases were down: "People are helping out and are not out on motorcycles drinking beer and acting crazy."

Downriver the story was the same. Mayor Chuck Scholz of Quincy, Illinois, was touched to find two girls who looked to be a mere eight to 10 years old clutching shovels and waiting to board a bus carrying volunteers to a nearby sandbagging site. At Ste. Genevieve, Missouri, south of St. Louis, volunteer inmates from the Farmington Correctional Center heaved sandbags side by side with people from the neighborhood.

The suffering and loss were also eased because the Federal Emergency Management Agency moved with uncharacteristic speed. Under its energetic new administrator, James Lee Witt, FEMA swiftly set up offices in eight flooded states. Witt's boss Bill Clinton also moved fast. In mid-July he cut short a Hawaiian vacation to fly to Des Moines, where someone held up a sign reading ALOHA, BILL. WELCOME TO THE OTHER BIG ISLAND.

Clinton returned to the area a few days later with nearly half his Cabinet to talk about the regions' needs.

Lake Superior

MICHIGAN

MICHIGAN

Lake Michigan

MINN.

S. DAK.

St. Croix River

WISCONSIN

Minneapolis

St. Paul
5.2 ft. on June 26

Minnesota River

Winona

Mississippi River

Estherville
8.4 ft. on June 30

Prairie du Chien
5.9 ft. on June 30

Dubuque
6.8 ft. on July 1

Rockton
2.4 ft. on June 30

Sioux City

IOWA

Cedar River

Des Moines River

Raccoon River

Iowa River

Davenport
7.6 ft. on July 9

Rock River

Chicago

NEB.

Missouri River

Des Moines
11.3 ft. on July 9

Van Meter

Rock Island

INDIANA

Omaha

Ottumwa

Nebraska City
9.2 ft. on July 23

Quincy
15.2 ft. on July 13

ILLINOIS

Hannibal

KANSAS

Kansas City
16.9 ft. on July 28

Jefferson City

St. Louis
19.6 ft. on Aug. 1

Ohio River

KENTUCKY

St. Paul
5.2 ft. on June 26

River crest above
official flood level

Flooded river

Area affected
by flooding

MISSOURI

Cairo

Source: National Weather Service;
Climate Analysis Center, NOAA

ARKANSAS

TENNESSEE

> **"I'm not going anyplace. This is my home. My father lived here. You learn to contend with the river. But I never heard of a 500-year flood before."**
>
> **FLOYD "SHORTY" HUTSON, Illinois**

VENICE, U.S.A.: "Except for the fact that the streets are quiet," goes a saying attributed to Mark Twain, "there's really nothing good to say about a flood."

Transportation Secretary Federico Peña roamed the riverbanks overseeing plans to get barges, trucks and rail traffic moving as soon as possible. Later Clinton pushed a recalcitrant Congress into approving more than $3 billion for flood relief, scolding Capitol Hill for political bickering that delayed approval of the measure.

By August 9, the crisis had passed as the flood spared St. Louis, cresting 2½ feet below the top of the city's 52-foot-high flood wall. With the vast inland sea receding, the region turned to the flood's messy leavings, and the great cleanup began. The removal of the stinking residue with shovels and hoses plainly did not produce the heady bonding among neighbors that the sandbag brigades had developed. When the treatment plant was fixed and Des Moines officials first appealed to citizens to keep their water turned off so that pressure could build in the pipes, the effort failed. Too many cheaters.

The receding waters left behind all manner of wreckage: chicken coops and tree branches, lumber, ice chests and garbage cans. Beneath the junk there was mud. Tons and tons of mud. Denizens of the river valley who had endured previous temper tantrums of the Mississippi were all too well acquainted with the thick, claylike layers of earth that coated the inside of houses, barns and machinery, delaying repairs and driving up the cost of recovery. The old-timers have an appropriate term for the primordial ooze. They call it gumbo.

The flood left a further legacy. Even before the rains stopped and the rivers crested, questions were raised about the financial and environmental costs of a program that relied on man-made structures to contain the mighty river. Over the past seven decades, the U.S. Army Corps of Engineers has spent billions of dollars constructing an elaborate flood control network, including 7,000 miles of levees, along the Mississippi and its tributaries. But many environmentalists believe that the effect of levees is to raise the level of the river, moving its flow faster downstream, and making the possibility of a backup more likely. They cheered in late August when Agriculture Secretary Mike Espy declared that the Administration was considering proposals to convert entire towns and some large tracts of farmland to wetlands rather than rebuild levees to hold off the river.

The epic song claims that "He don't say nothin.'" But with the great flood of 1993, Old Man River spoke, and with such volume that even Washington decided it might be best to let him just keep rolling along. ∎

HOMELESS: Encircled by floodwaters, the 488 residents of Portage des Sioux, Missouri, became island-dwellers.

YUCK! The initial emergency fostered a strong sense of community as people banded together to buttress the levees; the cleanup exiled them to solitary toil, mopping up a postdiluvian muck of sand, flotsam and mud.

An I.R.A. terrorist: Would his kind finally renounce violence?

A Plan for Irish Peace

After years of deadlock, a breakthrough seemed at hand in Ireland. In March the Irish Republican Army and the British government began a secret exchange of messages aimed at opening peace talks to end the "troubles" that had rent Northern Ireland for 25 years and left thousands dead. In November a newspaper uncovered the secret talks. Although many Britons were delighted, others were shocked that their government had been dealing with terrorists. But Prime Minister John Major argued he would have been remiss had he not responded to the I.R.A.'s overtures.

In mid-December, Major and Prime Minister Albert Reynolds of Ireland announced a "framework for peace" for Northern Ireland. The plan called for the people of Northern Ireland eventually to decide their fate: whether they would remain part of Britain or join the Irish Republic. And the plan offered a carrot to the the I.R.A.: if the militant group forswore violence for three months, its political wing would be offered a place at the bargaining table.

Clean Hands and Dirty Deeds

The Italians called their long-running probe of bribery and corruption among politicians and business leaders Operation Clean Hands. But it seemed that everyone it touched got dirty. In April 263 members of Parliament, 852 local officials and 1,487 business people were under investigation, and 1,356 arrest warrants had been issued.

Italy's problems sadly multiplied in late June, when a terrorist car bomb exploded near Florence's Uffizi Museum, one of the world's greatest storehouses of art, killing five but sparing the most famous of its paintings and sculptures. Authorities suspected that the Mafia, beleaguered by ongoing investigations, had set off the bomb.

Canada's Historic Upset

Canadian voters handed the reigning Progressive Conservatives the worst election defeat in the country's history. In October 25 balloting,

Chrétien: Canada's voters turned over a new leaf.

they reduced the party's House of Commons strength from 155 seats to a rock-bottom two. At the same time, they handed Liberal Jean Chrétien, derided by Conservatives as "yesterday's man," a comfortable 177-seat majority. Prime Minister Kim Campbell lost her seat and the leadership post she had assumed from Brian Mulroney and held for only three months.

Soaring into the vacuum left by the imploding Conservatives, two new regional parties gained substantial power, dragging with them the perennial issue of Canada's political survival. The Bloc Québécois, devoted to independence for Quebec, won 54 seats. The western-based Reform Party, which opposed special deals to keep Quebec in the union, won 52 seats.

> "What is happening in Serbia shows the need for a United States of Europe. There is no other political reality than that."
> —VICTOR HUGO, 1876

The Child Killers

February in Liverpool, England: Denise Bulger, 25, was buying meat at the butcher in a mall when she looked down to find that her high-spirited son James, two, had vanished from her side. Only a few minutes later, as she frantically searched for him, James was walking off with two 10-year-old boys, his hand trustingly in theirs. The scene, captured in a hazy film on mall security cameras, was shown at the trial of the two boys, whose names were withheld. The trial, at which 27 witnesses testified against the two schoolboy truants, revealed that they had dragged the now distraught James more than 2½ miles to a railway siding, where he was kicked, stoned, and beaten on the head with bricks and a metal rod until he died. Both boys pleaded innocent; in private, claimed the prosecutor, each blamed the other. The jury found them guilty of the senseless murder and, despite their age, sentenced them to prison for an indefinite term.

Captured on tape, James Bulger's abduction shocked Britain.

Bhutto's Return to Power

After a bitter name-calling campaign, Benazir Bhutto returned to power in October elections in Pakistan. Her Pakistan People's Party gained 87 seats in the National Assembly to the 72 won by her rival Mian Muhammad Nawaz Sharif, leader of the Pakistan Muslim League. But while Bhutto reveled in her return to the power she had lost

The wreck of the _Braer_ in January fouled Scotland's Shetland Islands with 619,000 barrels of oil.

990, her failure to win a majority suggested there might be no quick end to the political crisis that paralyzed the nation for much of the year. The concern only deepened when Bhutto, the daughter of executed Pakistani leader Zulfikar Ali Bhutto, engaged in a very public quarrel with her mother Nusrat Bhutto and her jailed brother Murtaza Bhutto at the end of the year. The pair charged the Prime Minister with squeezing them out of power.

Japan's Struggle for Reform

After years of paralysis and rule based on kickbacks and bribery, change came at last to Japan's political system. In July the reform movement headed by Morihiro Hosokawa overturned the 38-year reign of the L.D.P. and the government of Kiichi Miyazawa. Hosokawa, the telegenic scion of an aristocratic landowning family, appeared to solidify his revolution in November. Aided by crossover votes from L.D.P legislators, he pushed legislation through Japan's Lower House that promised to open up the political system, reduce the number of parties, stanch corruption and shift power from rural voters to city dwellers—if the Upper House followed suit.

Later, Hosokawa took on the farmers again, ending Japan's long-standing ban on foreign rice imports as the price of signing the GATT agreement. That still left him a mighty challenge: Japan's once widely envied economy continued to stumble; between August and December the Nikkei stock market declined in value by 17%.

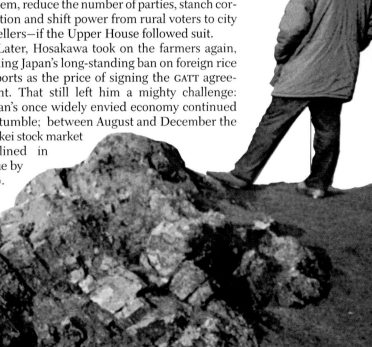

Red October

Hard-line communists waged their last battle with Boris Yeltsin in the streets of Moscow

CIVIL WAR
Monday: Troops loyal to Yeltsin opened fire on the rebellious Deputies in the White House early in the morning; by Tuesday, jubilant Muscovites were calling it "the Black House."

FOR MUCH OF 1993 RUSSIA WAS A HOUSE DIVIDED, as Boris Yeltsin's reform government vied for power with the conservative parliament. Elected before the collapse of the Soviet Union in December 1991 and led by Chairman Ruslan Khasbulatov, a former Yeltsin protégé, the Congress of People's Deputies was filled with communists who viewed Yeltsin as a traitor. After a constitutional crisis in the spring, the two sides settled into an uneasy truce and a summer of paralysis. (*See following story.*)

Finally, after dropping broad hints that September would be "a month of battle," Yeltsin struck. On Tuesday, September 21, he announced he was disbanding the legislature and calling new parliamentary elections for December. In a hastily convened session, a rump Congress of angry Deputies denounced the move as a coup d'etat, impeached Yeltsin and set up its own government, led by Vice President Alexander Rutskoi, the Afghan war hero who had been Yeltsin's ally during the failed coup attempt in August 1991. Yeltsin responded by establishing a perimeter around the parliament building, called the White House. Then he turned up the pressure, cutting off telephone lines and food supplies, and finally turning off the electricity.

Many Deputies slipped away. But a hard core of them, some 150 out of 1,033, remained loyal to Rutskoi and Khasbulatov and refused to leave the White House. Their stand inspired their followers. On Sunday, October 3, a gang of hard-liners, fascists, communists and nationalists rampaged 10,000 strong through the streets of Moscow, braving a hail of rubber bullets and tear gas from troops loyal to Yeltsin. Breaching police lines, the demonstrators recaptured the plaza behind the barricaded White House. Then, after a fiery address from Rutskoi commanding them to "stand up, take positions . . . and attack," they grabbed shields and guns from their opponents, commandeered military vehicles and seized control of Ostenkino, the national television broadcasting center.

Yeltsin, who had left Moscow for an afternoon in the country, rushed back by helicopter to direct the counteroffensive. He held the superior hand: the army refused to join Rutskoi and Khasbulatov. At 7:30 a.m. on Monday, soldiers loyal to Yeltsin began lobbing shells at the White House from their T-80 tanks. The building began to burn, black smoke spiraling into the Moscow sky. Inside, Rutskoi, clad in combat fatigues, prowled the halls while a shaken Khasbulatov was reported to exclaim "I have known Yeltsin for a long time, but I never expected anything like this from him!" After brief cease-fires allowed some Deputies to surrender, Yeltsin's troops burst into the building late in the afternoon. Rutskoi and Khasbulatov were arrested and hauled off to prison.

The toll of the street riots and final assault: more than 170 dead, 900 wounded and nearly 1,300 arrested. Then, in a last gesture of contempt for his communist enemies, Yeltsin stripped Lenin's Tomb of the honor guard that had goose-stepped there around the clock since the founder of the Soviet state was buried in 1924. ∎

MOB RULE
Sunday: A ragtag army of hard-liners and drunken hooligans ruled Moscow, breaking through a police cordon to reach the White House.

CORNERED
Monday: Inside the White House, Rutskoi made a futile call for help.

Old Woes, New Foes

Yeltsin ousts his enemies, only to face a fresh one

BORIS YELTSIN MADE A FATEFUL DECISION IN OCtober 1993: in order to save Russia's fledgling democracy, he found it necessary to destroy it. Suspending the Soviet-era Congress of Deputies and squashing a last revolt by the hard-line communists who had fought his government's every attempt at reform, Yeltsin assumed dictatorial powers, outlawed opposing parties, even shut down the newspapers. Yet his victory was short-lived. Two months later, even as Russians voted to grant Yeltsin vast new powers as President, they elected another parliament poised to oppose him, handing a surprisingly high share of their votes to a neofascist party led by 47-year-old lawyer Vladimir Zhirinovsky.

Yeltsin's roller-coaster year reflected his monumental task: to transform a nation with a history steeped in despotism into a multiparty democracy with a market economy. So far, the President and his team of shock therapists had produced few successes and much turmoil and anxiety. As the pain mounted, Parliament's Chairman Ruslan Khasbulatov and Yeltsin's other conservative antimarket, anti-Western rivals muttered and threatened, then finally acted. Meeting suddenly just weeks before an April 25 national referendum on whether Russians favored a parliamentary or presidential republic, the Congress voted to put Yeltsin and the Kremlin under its control. The President struck back by announcing a period of "special rule" in which he would govern by decree until the referendum. Khasbulatov talked of impeaching Yeltsin, then backed down.

In the referendum Yeltsin commanded majority support for both his political and economic reforms. Yet he failed to earn enough votes to force early elections for the new parliament. An exultant Khasbulatov declared that the vote had "brought no losers or winners." Yet there had to be a winner and loser. Finally, in late September, Yeltsin forced the issue by disbanding the Congress. That set off a revolt by the conservatives that was quelled only when tanks rolled into the streets of

TOASTING: While an exultant Zhirinovsky hails his surprising clout in the new Duma, a shaken Yeltsin feels the heat.

Moscow and shelled the parliament building, where Khasbulatov and Vice President Alexander Rutskoi had taken refuge with their backers. Like so many before them who had quarreled with the Kremlin, the two ended up in Moscow's infamous Lefortovo Prison.

A victorious Yeltsin quickly acted to consolidate his power. He suspended the Communist Party and banned 15 opposition newspapers. He also declared that the early parliamentary elections would be held as scheduled on Dec. 12; later he reneged on an earlier offer to stand for re-election early and said he would serve out his full term, which ends in 1996.

The December elections provided yet another surprise. Ultranationalist Zhirinovsky, a goldentongued demagogue who has been compared to Adolf Hitler, swept up enough votes to establish a powerful bloc for his party in the State Duma, the lower house of the new Russian parliament. Zhirinovsky had campaigned against Yeltsin's reforms, and his calls to restore the Russian empire touched a deep chord among citizens who felt humiliated by the country's plunge from a great power to global beggar. A classic rabble-rouser, he cultivated the military, blamed Jews for anti-Semitism and offered up foreigners as scapegoats for Russia's problems.

Yeltsin reaped what he had sowed. Choosing to stand above the electoral fray, he endorsed no party, not even the Russia's Choice group led by his disciples. Instead he threw his energies into the constitutional referendum. His popular clout brought in a 58% vote of support for the measure, which granted him sweeping powers, among them the right to disband the parliament. But instead of producing a majority of legislators for reform, the elections assured Yeltsin would face a parliament perhaps as belligerent as the one he had dissolved. This time, however, Zhirinovsky enjoyed the electoral legitimacy the President once claimed as uniquely his own. ■

> **"Apparently we must deal with [minorities] as America did with the Indians and Germany did with the Jews."**
>
> **—VLADIMIR ZHIRINOVSKY**

Restless Republics

Russia calls the shots in the "near abroad"

TIME Map by Paul J. Pugliese

RUSSIANS CALL THE NEWLY INDEPENDENT REPUBLICS along the highly combustible southern rim of the old Soviet Union "the near abroad." Here Moscow's hardline nationalists and military leaders continue to play power games that hark back to more than two centuries of Russian imperialism. The goal: to restore Moscow's influence by weakening its neighbors and making them ever more dependent on Russia.

Azerbaijan

Firing on Armenian rebels.

IN AZERBAIJAN THE RUSsians exploited the political aspirations of the Armenians, an ethnic minority that, with the aid of countrymen in the neighboring state of Armenia, has been waging a war of secession for its enclave of Nagorno-Karabakh against the Muslim government of Azerbaijan. Russia apparently provided guns to a rival of Azerbaijan's Prime Minister Abulfaz Elchibey, who is considered by many to be one of the most anti-Russian leaders in the old Soviet Union. Then the Russians withdrew their troops, paving the way for the rival, Geidar Aliyev, a former KGB man, to take power. In line with Moscow's plan, Aliyev demonstrated his gratitude by asking that Azerbaijan be readmitted to the Commonwealth of Independent States (C.I.S.), the post-Soviet confederation that is dominated by the Russians.

Georgia

Flight from fallen Sukhumi.

SINCE ASSUMING LEADERship of Georgia in 1992, Eduard Shevardnadze has struggled to hold the new nation together. But the former Soviet Foreign Minister has battled on two fronts, fighting both an ethnic rebellion in the province of Abkhazia and a guerrilla-style insurgency waged by the country's former President, Zviad Gamsakhurdia, who was deposed in a popular coup in 1992. Russia indirectly supported the rebels in Abkhazia, where a small minority of ethnic separatists were fighting for an independent state. Under pressure from Moscow, the Abkhazians endorsed a cease-fire in July. But at that time, Gamsakhurdia launched an offensive in the west of Georgia, and with Shevardnadze's attention diverted, the Abkhazian rebels broke the truce and launched a ferocious attack on Sukhumi, Abkhazia's capital city. Shevardnadze set up headquarters in Sukhumi and vowed to stay, but finally returned, vanquished, to his capital, Tbilisi. Shortly afterward, Sukhumi fell; Abkhazia had effectively won its independence. Russian weapons enabled the Abkhazians, who make up only 17% of their province's population, to outgun the Georgians. Exploiting Shevardnadze's weakness, Gamsakhurdia continued his attacks in the west. Desperate, Shevardnadze agreed to join the C.I.S. in exchange for Russian troops and weapons, which helped him prevail at last over Gamsakhurdia. With Abkhazia free and Georgia in the C.I.S., Russia seemed the real winner.

Tajikistan

Tajiki rebels scorn Moscow.

SUPPORTED BY AFGHANistan and Iran, Islamic militants and pro-democracy rebels continued to wage a bloody civil war against the ex-communist rulers of this Central Asian Muslim republic. Some 20,000 people have died since the rebels captured President Rakhmon Nabiyev, the former Communist Party boss, in May 1992. Moscow supported the regime, pouring troops and men into the republic to fight the rebels. With Russian soldiers everywhere and Russian aid dominating the economy, Tajikistan has become a client state. Mindful of Russia's 20 million Muslims, and of the threat of infiltration of Islamic militancy, guns and drugs from Pakistan and Afghanistan, Boris Yeltsin has declared that Tajikistan's borders "are effectively Russia's." ∎

"To Get Rich

In Asia's booming giant, the Me generation replaces the Mao generation

IT WAS CALLED THE MIDDLE KINGDOM, A SELF-absorbed and xenophobic empire. Its massive indifference to the outside world remained in place for millenniums, through dynasties and revolutions. Until suddenly the communists in Beijing cast aside their Marxist zeal and set their country on the road to capitalism. Only 15 years later, China—which has a fifth of the globe's population—is a candidate superpower, more involved in international life than ever before. The impact of its emergence is so profound that scholars are predicting relations between China and the U.S. will shape the world in the 21st century.

President Bill Clinton's meeting with Chinese President Jiang Zemin in Seattle in November, the highest-level contact between the U.S. and China since the massacre of pro-democracy demonstrators in Beijing in 1989, underscored the importance the Clinton Administration places on improving relations with the People's Republic.

China's leap forward is still hampered by its rigid politics—and the prospect that the system could soon change dramatically. The man who was not there in Seattle but who figuratively sat in on all the meetings was Deng Xiaoping, China's senior leader and chief reformer. Deng, 89 in 1993 and very frail, is China's last emperor, the tail end of the charismatic generation of military and political leaders who held power alone. And he is not likely to rule China much longer.

As Deng slips away—"going to meet Marx," he jests—the key question is whether his economic reforms will remain in place or be overturned by elderly hard-liners who survive him. Can the Communist Party, with waning legitimacy and faith, provide the stability to keep the vast country on track and under control? So convincingly has Deng left his stamp on the country that many Chinese will find it difficult to envision a China without him. After the ruinous years of the Cultural Revolution and the death of Mao Zedong, Deng consolidated his power. In 1978 he dropped Marxist orthodoxy and began economic reforms to make China a "socialist market

FROM PROPHET TO PROFIT: Young Chinese chase Western status symbols, while a statue of Mao, right, becomes a backdrop for ad slogans.

economy," an oxymoron his disciples interpret as "socialism with Chinese characteristics." While they cling to such slogans to bolster their positions, in practice they are producing capitalism with Chinese characteristics.

The effects of Deng's revolution are astounding. In Mao's time, leveling was the rule, and everyone aimed at a drab, fanatical egalitarianism, dressing in rumpled blue tunics that made it difficult to tell men from women. Today Chinese society is brazenly materialistic, roaring through cycles of boom and bust that have made millions rich. In the 15 years since Deng abolished the agricultural communes and opened the door to cooperative business and private enterprise, China's economy has mushroomed, growing an average of 9% a year. Though per capita income is still only about $380, by some calculations of purchasing power China has the third largest economy in the world (after the U.S. and Japan) and could become No. 1 in two decades.

Some provinces are even more gung-ho for growth than the bosses in Beijing. Hainan in the far south plans to build itself into another Hong Kong. Guangdong and Shandong hope to catch up with such Asian powerhouses as South Korea and Singapore by 2015. In the southern city of Guangzhou bustling construction sites and rows of town houses, factories and shopping centers line the road through the Pearl River delta. In Shanghai, China's New York City, shop windows are crammed with chic imports, electronic pagers and fancy cuts of meat. Nearby in the Pudong economic zone, modern highways, bridges, and office buildings are taking shape.

Individual lives have been similarly transformed. "It used to be that Communist Party membership was important," said Wang Zhixiong, a Guangdong researcher. "Now people's tastes favor money, professional rank and appearance." More than a million Chinese have become *dakuan*, or dollar millionaires, and as much as 5% of the population is affluent by Chinese standards. In 1978 Li Xiaohua was a cook in a Beijing restaurant. Today he is a business tycoon who owns two Mercedes-Benz and a red Ferrari. Wang Guoqing quit his job at the Bank of

"It used to be that Communist Party membership was important. Now people's tastes favor money, professional rank and appearance."

发扬首钢人的开拓情
神创造新的世界之最

A WORD FROM OUR SPONSOR: Socialism remains the official party line, but here, outside Beijing, as in the rest of China, the big wheels are capitalists.

China in Xian three years ago and is now a multimillionaire retailer and real estate developer who wears Pierre Cardin suits and a $2,000 Swiss watch.

Deng says, "To get rich is glorious." That is undoubtedly true for people like Li and Wang, but for the vast Chinese nation getting rich is a mixed blessing. The rigid discipline of the party is slipping, and crime is on the increase. Corruption—payoffs and connections—is the rule at every level. Wealth is growing unevenly: very fast in the special zones, in big cities and along the seaboard, but slowly in the great agricultural interior. While perhaps 200 million coastal dwellers are prosperous, and tens of millions of township and village enterprises are thriving, 90 million hamlet dwellers in the interior are still stuck in subsistence farming and near feudal conditions. At least 100 million peasants have left the land to search for quick riches, and are floating rootlessly from job to job in the cities, increasing the crime rate and the profits of resurgent drug rings.

Like Russia, China is trying to create a market-based economy out of one that had been planned and commanded from the center for decades. Beijing is running into some of the same problems Boris Yeltsin and his reformers have encountered, including a shortage of capitalist institutions and a surplus of recalcitrant bureaucrats. Because leaders have not institutionalized capitalist tools like interest rates and money supply to control growth and inflation, the country repeatedly goes through periods of fast growth followed by frantic clamps on credit to slow inflation. Beijing's ability to control the country is far more limited than it was a few years ago. Those who take over from Deng will face two immediate challenges. They will have to make sure his reforms and the growth they bring survive, and they will need to hold the country together while the economic revolution is completed.

In November a Communist Party Central Committee plenum adopted a 25-page, 50-point reform outline called "a program of action to restructure the economy." The plan focuses on two central problems: the inefficient state-held factories and the chaotic fiscal and monetary systems. It calls for turning some enterprises into stock corporations and allowing competition to drive some out of business. And it lays out the need to reform both the tax system, which now shortchanges Beijing and weakens its hand with the provinces, and the central-banking operation, which is essentially unregulated. "China suffers not from too much central control but from too little," says Richard Margolis, corporate finance director of Smith New Court Ltd. in Hong Kong.

The men who will have to carry out this plan will lack the personal authority Deng has exercised for so long, and they could be forced into a collective leadership or even a wrenching power struggle. President Jiang, 67, is Deng's choice as successor, and he already heads the party as well as the government. But many experts do not expect him to hold on to his position. Hard-line Premier Li Peng, 65, is still a contender, but he has been ill. If Jiang self-destructs, the leading role could go to either Vice Premier Zhu Rongji, 65, the economic policy chief and a committed and pragmatic reformer, or National People's Congress chairman Qiao Shi, 68, a former overseer of the intelligence and security services who is known as a fence straddler but leans toward reform.

Even if succession were assured, there are many other uncertainties. No former communist state has subsequently managed a full emergence into a market economy. Certainly none has made the journey while under a government that still calls itself communist. Chinese officials sometimes say, without irony, that their ambition is to achieve the authoritarian and wealthy status of tiny Singapore. China's history of strongman rule goes back 3,800 years. So, with a Communist Party drained of Marxist ideology, perhaps it no longer matters what the rulers call themselves. Their subjects are united behind the central plank of their political platform: the glory is in getting rich. ∎

War of Nerves at The Nuclear Brink

The United States talks and talks in seeking atomic compliance from a secretive regime

As 1993 DREW TO A CLOSE, 40 YEARS AFTER THE KOrean War, American and North Korean diplomats were back at the negotiating table, once more laboring over matters of life and death. This time Washington was intent on stopping Pyongyang's march toward building an atomic bomb, while North Korea was trying to head off the sanctions that its atomic ambitions would inevitably prompt.

The dispute heated up through the last months of the year. Hans Blix, head of the International Atomic Energy Agency, told the U.N. in early November that in addition to blocking inspections of two secret sites to which the IAEA had demanded access last February, Pyongyang was now refusing to allow even routine monitoring of five declared nuclear sites at Yongbyon, 65 miles north of the capital, and at two other locations. At a 5-megawatt power reactor whose fuel core could be mined for plutonium to make bombs, IAEA inspectors were not being allowed to reload spent surveillance cameras.

Blix had the right to refer the dispute to the U.N. Security Council, which can punish a nuclear miscreant with sanctions that can range from a reprimand to an embargo, and ultimately to war. But the West decided instead to keep negotiating with Pyongyang. The reason: fear of driving North Korea into a corner from which it would fight its way out. Pyongyang had threatened to resume its atomic-weapons program if the U.S. broke off talks over the stalled inspections, and North Korean diplomats said privately that any pre-emptive attack on their nuclear facilities would trigger an invasion of the South. China refused to support sanctions, and U.S. analysts feared a violent response if an oil or trade embargo were imposed. The U.S. also worried that an attack on the plants might spread a radioactive cloud over the region.

At meetings in New York City in the fall, Washington promised some carrots: the possibility of diplomatic ties, and even economic aid—tempting to a country where many people could afford only one meal a day and soap was a luxury.

In Pyongyang Kim Il Sung, 81, remained the ultimate power, but the last Stalinist had spent nearly 20 years building a base for his son, Kim Jong Il, 51, to be his successor. Their only hope for reversing continuing economic decline rested with opening the country to foreign investment and trade. But the Kims seemed hesitant to take any steps that might weaken their grip over North Korea's 22 million people.

In the final weeks of December the North Koreans declared that a meeting at the U.N. had produced a "breakthrough." Officials in Washington said only that the U.S. had "moved closer" to its goals. Meanwhile, a classified CIA study concluded that there was a "somewhat better than even" chance that North Korea had already built one or two atomic weapons. With President Clinton vowing, publicly and unequivocally, that the U.S. would not allow the North Koreans to acquire nuclear weapons, Pyongyang was playing a dangerous form of nuclear roulette. ■

KIM IL SUNG: The "Great Leader" and son Kim Jong Il want the bomb.

■ THE BALKANS

No Way Out

The world agonized at a distance
while Serbs, Croats and Muslims
held peace at bay in Bosnia

OR THE HATE-FILLED NEIGHBORS IN THE RAVAGED
republics of the former Yugoslavia, 1993 began
and ended in war. The conflict, which had been
raging since 1991, soaked Bosnia and Herzegovina in blood—and seared the conscience of
the world. At times it seemed as if the warriors
might grind to a halt from sheer exhaustion, if
not from the outside world's attempts to stop them. But
the killing never ceased, nor did the deliberate starvation, the mass rape, the shelling of innocent civilians, the
destruction of cultures.

One hard fact emerged from the rubble: the out-
numbered, outgunned, predominantly Muslim government of Bosnia and Herzegovina had lost the war to
rebellious Serbs and Croats within their own borders.
The rebels declared their right to major portions of the
two republics, demanding that those areas be "ethni-
cally cleansed" of Muslims. With overwhelming support from their kinsmen in Serbia and Croatia, the
neighboring republics of the former Yugoslavia, the
two factions continued to swallow Bosnia and Herzegovina. By the spring 70% of Bosnia was under rebel
control; by the summer 90%. Still, the besieged Muslims held out in enclaves like Sarajevo and Mostar, Srebrenica and Gorazde.

"Do something—anything!" cried Nobel laureate Elie
Wiesel, and the world echoed his cry. But those outside
feared commitment to a quagmire, and those inside rejected peace as surrender. The result: the U.S., its European allies and the U.N. continued to debate the wisdom
of intervention—without intervening. Peace plans were
drawn up, then voted down. New boundaries were
mapped, but not agreed to. The U.S. was going to bomb
the Serbs; it didn't. NATO was going to tighten the pressure; NATO backed down. Meeting in Geneva, the warring parties were ready to declare peace; they did not.

The story of the war became
the story of the besieged Muslim
enclaves. Among the most desperate as the winter of 1992-93
ended were the towns of eastern
Bosnia, near the frontier with
Serbia. In Gorazde, where 70,000
people were surrounded by Ser-

SEARCH PARTY
In the genocide
that a watching world
has come to know
as ethnic cleansing,
two Croat gunmen
track down Muslims
in Mostar.

KILLING HISTORY

Destroyed: the 16th century Old Bridge in Mostar, a superb example of Ottoman design and a symbol of ethnic harmony before the war.

bian guns, a murderous route over the mountains was the only lifeline to food and supplies. In March the U.S. dispatched C-130 transport planes from Germany to drop supplies to Gorazde and other towns; several people were stabbed in struggles over the bundles.

Later that month, General Philippe Morillon, French commander of the U.N. peace force in Bosnia, surprised the world by standing with the besieged Muslims in Srebrenica. Arriving there, he had found that refugees from captured towns had swollen the population from 9,000 to as many as 80,000. A ferocious assault on the town by Serbs was halted only by a cease-fire brokered in Sarajevo at the last minute.

Just as the bloodshed seemed to taper off between Serbs and Muslims, a second theater of war emerged: Croats attacked Muslims along the boundary line between Croatia and Herzegovina. Like the Serbs before them, the Croats subjected Muslims to ethnic cleansing, systematic rape and cold-blooded murder; there were reports of Muslim atrocities as well. In the fall the Croats besieged the former Herzegovinian capital city of Mostar and obliterated its celebrated bridge.

Sarajevo, the Bosnian capital, refused to succumb despite its encirclement by Serbian artillery. But within the city death became a way of life. In November heavy shelling killed 17 people in one day, including several children in a school.

In a different kind of enclave, the fate of the region was debated by diplomats and ministers. Meeting in Geneva throughout the year, the U.N., the U.S., Russia and the NATO allies struggled to fashion a way out of the carnage. The plan to partition the country among the three warring forces, proposed by former U.S. Secretary of State Cyrus Vance and Lord Owen of Britain and so long denounced as rewarding Serb and Croat aggression, finally seemed the only way to end the warfare. But each time the Serbs, Croats and Bosnian Muslims seemed ready to sign the plan, it was derailed. The allies continued to apply trade sanctions that put severe stress on all the parties, yet seemed only to increase their defiance. In 1993, for the ravaged people of the Balkans, peace was nowhere, war was everywhere, and there was no way out. ∎

THE HUNTED

Muslim refugees, above, on an 8-hour journey through enemy lines. Serb forces surrounded Srebrenica in eastern Bosnia and blocked delivery of a U.N. convoy carrying relief supplies. After the trucks were finally allowed through, they carried the refugees out to Tuzla. Seven died en route.

THE HUNTERS

Bosnian Serb irregulars on patrol near the Drina River. When the political leaders of the Bosnian Serbs agreed to sign the Vance-Owen partition plan in May, the zealous militia leaders refused, claiming they would never give up land they had bled for. "Let them bomb us," said a defiant soldier.

BLEARY-EYED AS THE clock ticked past midnight on November 18, negotiators continued to bargain over final details. At last, nine hours beyond their deadline, 19 men ascended the podium in the cavernous convention center and, one by one, signed a draft constitution conferring equal rights on South Africans of every color. The last-minute delay was nothing to South Africa's blacks, who had waited generations for this moment. "We have reached the end of an era," declared a triumphant Nelson Mandela, leader of the African National Congress. President F.W. De Klerk agreed: "South Africa will never be the same again."

The new law of the land was a package of compromises designed to bring full democracy and a long list of fundamental rights to 28 million increasingly impatient blacks, while assuring 5 million apprehensive whites that black rule would not threaten their jobs and livelihoods.

Birth of A Nation

The bastion of apartheid moves to give blacks equal rights, equal votes and a majority role in government

Dress rehearsal for the future? Young white students listen to Nelson Mandela, who would seek the presidency in April 1994.

Its signing capped a year in which South Africa moved inexorably away from its legacy of apartheid. In June black and white political leaders declared that every citizen would be able to vote to choose a government in elections scheduled for April 27, 1994. In September the two sides agreed to create a 20-member, multiracial, multiparty transition council—with blacks in the majority—to supervise the existing government until the elections. Following that announcement, the A.N.C. called for an end to the international sanctions that had isolated the country from the world community, some for as long as 30 years. Mandela and De Klerk, the chief architects of the new South Africa, were awarded the Nobel Peace Prize in October.

Under the compromise plan, following the April 1994 elections the country will be governed by a two-house parliament—one elected by proportional representation, the other by nine new provincial legislatures—that will write a permanent constitution. The President, chosen by the winning party, will oversee a Cabinet of 27 ministers, including representatives from any party that wins 5% of the vote. A powerful constitutional court will back up the guarantees of equal treatment for all.

The fear is that this interim constitution, which puts in place a government of national unity for the next five years, will not fulfill its promise of a reasonable balance of power for those who distrust Mandela and the A.N.C. De Klerk called the draft "a product of compromise" that could be either "a charter for peace" or "a prescription for powermongering." Ominously, the Zulu-based Inkatha Freedom Party and several white separatist groups—which had rejected the negotiations, threatened to boycott the elections and even hinted at armed resistance—stayed away from the signing. Both continued to insist that regions with strong ethnic composition be granted the right of autonomy or even total independence.

To clinch the deal, De Klerk had to abandon demands for ironclad guarantees that whites and other minorities would share power indefinitely. He had sought a system in which whites would in effect have a permanent veto in such vital affairs of state as defense, foreign policy and the economy. But he finally gave up his insistence that the coalition Cabinet could act only with a two-thirds vote. Instead the President will be required merely to consult the Cabinet in a "consensus-seeking" spirit.

Concessions were made by the other side as well. Mandela's A.N.C., a strong advocate of centralized government, agreed to a system that will provide a share in decision making to the nine provincial legislatures and police forces. And despite intense pressure to place A.N.C. supporters in government jobs, Mandela agreed not to throw 1.2 million employees of the white-dominated civil service out on the street.

The interim constitution was a heartening milestone in South Africa's bloodied march toward democracy. At least 12,000 died in factional violence in the four years after Mandela was released from prison and De Klerk lifted the ban on the A.N.C. But shared power is not a South African tradition. With the A.N.C. enjoying a commanding lead in the pre-election polls, die-hard supporters of racial separation or ethnic self-determination would have to decide whether to accept the new government as a legitimate institution or work to undermine it. ■

The shake seen 'round the world: Palestinian women applaud as Rabin and Arafat seal the pact at the White House.

HISTORY IN A HANDSHAKE

Burying past enmities, Israel and the P.L.O. agree to work toward a durable peace

HISTORY IS OFTEN THE RESIDUE OF TANKS AND armies, of victors and vanquished. Sometimes it is the work of paper and pens. But when veteran antagonists Yasser Arafat and Yitzhak Rabin clasped hands in front of a beaming Bill Clinton on the White House lawn on September 13, 1993, history was forged in a handshake. Caught in the click of hundreds of cameras, the seemingly unbelievable scene was beamed to millions of people in a world nurtured for 45 years on a diet of hate and death in the arid lands of the Israelis and Arabs. This, more than the Declaration of Principles signed by the peacemakers, was the affirmation of a new era in which its witnesses could believe, an era thrust upon an unsuspecting world with stunning swiftness. The parchment they signed was a framework for interim Palestinian self-government, as well as a document meant to bind Israel and the Palestine Liberation Organization to further constructive deliberation.

The handshake was the culmination of months of secret negotiations between emissaries of the Israeli Prime Minister and the chairman of the P.L.O. Ironically, the Declaration of Principles was not the product of the formal Middle East peace talks, which had been going on for almost two years, but of free-lance peacemakers whose first meeting was in a hotel in central London. There Yair Hirschfeld, a Middle East history professor at Haifa University, first broke Israeli law by talking to Ahmed Kriah, head of the P.L.O.'s economics department. That first meeting in London would lead to more than a dozen secret sessions in Norway that would not only surprise the world but produce the biggest breakthrough in Middle East negotiations since Anwar Sadat made peace with Menachem Begin in 1979.

Ever since the Labor Party regained power in Israel in 1992, Rabin's government had pursued the peace process with new vigor. Foreign Minister Shimon Peres had already tentatively explored the possibility of opening back-channel talks with the P.L.O. with the help of Thorvald Stoltenberg, then Norway's Foreign Minister. The link would prove fortunate; with the aid of the Norwegian government, the unofficial Israeli and Palestinian representatives met 14 times in and around Oslo, over a period of eight months beginning in January 1993. With their hosts keeping the atmosphere intimate—the negotiators feasted on Norwegian salmon and wandered together in nearby woods—both sides by May had produced a draft of a peace treaty that brought senior Israeli diplomats to the table.

Arafat and Rabin by now had realized that the process was more fact than fantasy. Their deputies went through countless revisions of the accord that kept the negotiators haggling for uninterrupted stretches of 24 and even 36 hours. On August 20, Peres himself witnessed the initialing of the Declaration of Principles in Oslo. On the 27th, he flew to California to brief Secretary of State Warren Christopher.

Amazed by what he heard, Christopher swiftly telephoned President Clinton, who expressed immediate support for the agreement. Washington had been aware since the outset that secret talks were taking place, but had little idea of their pace and scope.

The 17 articles and four annexes of the Declaration of Principles indicated that they were firmly intended to lead to some final political settlement. The plan came in two parts. The first was a framework for interim Palestinian self-rule of the Israeli-occupied West Bank and Gaza Strip, the hotbeds of discontent that had given birth to the Palestinian revolt, or intifadeh. The second was still being negotiated when the first was announced: it called for mutual recognition and an end to warfare between Israel and the P.L.O. Agreement on the subject of recognition was sought by all sides, but proved hard to put into precise language.

The Declaration specifically provided for Israeli withdrawal from the 140-square-mile Gaza Strip, with its 770,000 Palestinians, and from Jericho, an ancient, somnolent Jordan Valley town of about 20,000, a thin sliver of the 1 million Palestinians who live in the West Bank. On December 13, Palestinians were to take over the administration of those two places, with Israel retaining responsibility only for their external security and the protection of Jewish settlers. At the same time, the West Bank would move toward what was called "early empowerment," a kind of preliminary self-rule in education, health, social services and taxation.

Israeli occupation authorities and soldiers would remain for about nine months, until a Palestinian Interim Self-Government Authority could be elected to govern the whole of the territories. At that point Israeli security forces would withdraw and a "strong" Palestinian police force of several thousand would take over. This interim deal would last no more than five years; after two years the Israelis and Palestinians would begin negotiating for the future of the areas, which might conceivably include total independence for a new Palestinian state.

Why peace now? Ironically, it was probably sired by the P.L.O.'s weakness rather than its strength. Fed up with the P.L.O.'s failures, young Palestinians had been radicalized, many embracing the militant Islamic fundamentalism of Hamas, the organization born in the late 1980s at the beginning of the intifadeh. Hamas claimed support by a majority of Palestinians in the Gaza Strip and at least 40% of West Bank Arabs. Conversely, Arafat was compelled toward moderation after the Soviet Union's demise deprived him of a superpower patron, and even more when his allegiance to Iraq over Kuwait cost him his bankroll from the gulf states. Without money or visible progress in the formal peace talks he had endorsed, fundamentalism's rise threatened to make him irrelevant. So the man seen by most Israelis and much of the world as a symbol of terrorism surprised his rivals by accepting a little instead of all-or-nothing.

Since its founding in 1948, Israel had been a garrison state, devoting its energies and capital, and aid from foreign governments and Diaspora Jews, to building and maintaining a military establishment that would crush its Arab enemies. The expense had deprived Israel of funds needed for the enjoyment of an even better life and more vibrant economy. The squalid Gaza Strip, seized by Israel in the Six-Day War in 1967, had been the orphan no one wanted; certainly not the Israelis, whose policing of the turbulent slums had become a shame and burden. In reaching out to Arafat to resolve the festering problems in the Gaza Strip and West Bank, Rabin saw an opportunity for Israel to be a normal nation, doing business and living well.

Once the Declaration of Principles was revealed to the world, the peace process took on an inexorable life

MORE QUESTIONS: Would the Declaration lead to a Palestinian state? Would Israel's other Mideast enemies seek peace?

The Declaration called for Israeli soldiers to withdraw from Gaza and Jericho by December 13, but a series of bloody incidents forced them to stay on.

of its own. The second portion of the Declaration, left unresolved in Oslo, was agreed upon. In letters signed by Arafat at his headquarters in Tunis, and in Jerusalem by Rabin, each party formally recognized the other's right to exist, actually putting on paper the idea that generations of Palestinian and Israeli leaders, themselves included, had vowed never to entertain.

Then it was on to Washington, where, at the request of both sides, President Clinton arranged the historic White House ceremony that would seal the agreement in memorable fashion before the eyes of the world. Some 3,000 guests assembled on the White House lawn in a high state of excitement. Bill Clinton claimed he spent the night before reading the Book of Joshua from the Bible, unable to sleep. Arafat, from the moment he appeared silhouetted against the White House, in sharp-pressed khakis and trademark black-and-white kaffiyeh,

could not stop smiling. This was the arrival on the world stage he had always dreamed of. Rabin was plainly of a different mind, uncomfortable and stiff. His body language throughout the ceremony—the cocking of his head, the eyes cast toward the sky, the ground, anywhere but Arafat—gave away just how uneasy he was.

Time for a handshake was worked into the 26-page script meticulously prepared for the occasion. Clinton was to act as stage manager. He would reach for the hand of Rabin at the crucial moment, turn next to shake the hand of Arafat, then step back half a pace and enfold the two in a wide and gentle extension of his arms with the expectation that the weight of history would bring their two hands together. It did. First Arafat reached out, then after what seemed like endless minutes, Rabin responded. Simple, shattering.

The world celebrated, but it also wondered whether the promised peace could ever be achieved. A host of questions remained unanswered: Could Arafat control the militants in the occupied territories? Could Arafat guarantee his own safety? Could the Israelis accept the "strong" armed police force of Palestinians promised in the pact? Would the Declaration lead to a Palestinian state? Would Syria, Jordan and Lebanon, Israel's other enemies, join the peace process?

Within days after the signing in Washington the answers began to be written in the Mideast, in blood. In both the Gaza Strip and the West Bank, Israeli Defense Forces clashed with Palestinian extremists; there were deaths on both sides. When five Palestinian suspects arrested for slaying a Jewish settler in October admitted that they belonged to the P.L.O., Rabin and Clinton demanded a public condemnation from Arafat. Arafat complied and appealed for an end to the violence; it was the first time the P.L.O. chairman had ever spoken out against a specific attack on Israelis by Palestinians in the occupied territories. In late November Israeli soldiers wounded 37 Palestinians who were protesting in the Gaza Strip over the Israeli killing of a Hamas leader. Concerned about security arrangements, the two parties agreed that Israel would not withdraw its troops from Gaza and Jericho by the December 13 deadline agreed to in September. By the end of the year, they were still working to agree upon a realistic date to begin the transition.

After the secret negotiations, after the historic handclasp, after the raising of hopes around the world, a single nagging question lingered that only the passage of time would answer: Could the ancient enemies, so schooled in hatred, live with a victory for peace rather than for Israel or Palestine? ∎

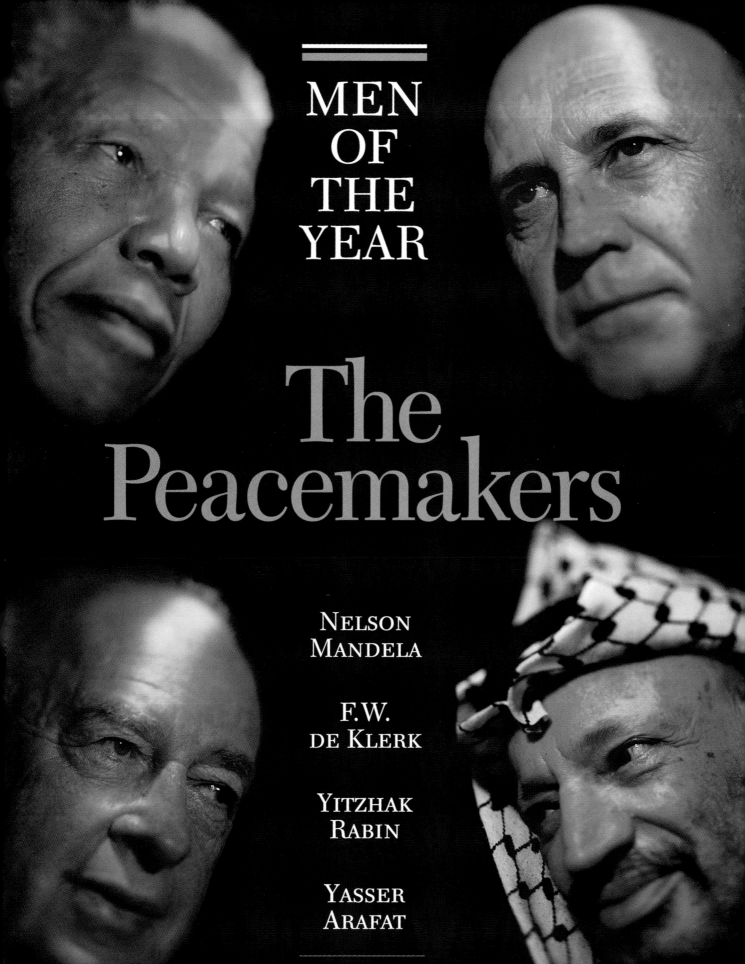

MEN OF THE YEAR

The Peacemakers

NELSON
MANDELA

F.W.
DE KLERK

YITZHAK
RABIN

YASSER
ARAFAT

Ready to Conquer the Past

For years conflicts ravaged the Middle East and South Africa like terrible local beasts, with histories of deep hatred and the potential to erupt into wider violence—even, in the case of the Middle East, into nuclear war. These struggles were not ideological, like the standoff of the superpowers. South Africa and the Middle East worked at a nastier level, closer to bone and gene and skin. They had, over the years, arrived at stalemate, a no-exit of chronic hatred. The struggles (whether to liberate one's own people, or to suppress the dangerous other tribe, or simply to survive in the moral airlessness) became prisons.

The Men of the Year of 1993—Yitzhak Rabin and Yasser Arafat, F.W. de Klerk and Nelson Mandela—did nothing more and nothing less than find a way to break out.

By tradition, TIME's Men and Women of the Year are those who have most influenced history, for good or ill, in the previous 12 months. By that standard, Rabin, Arafat, Mandela and De Klerk might be perceived as odd choices. Neither of the two peacemaking deals they brought forth in 1993 was complete. Extremists on all sides threatened to destroy the arrangements, which looked at times like fragile shelters being nailed together in a high wind. The regions seemed just as violent later as they had before Arafat and Rabin shook hands on the White House lawn and before Mandela and De Klerk locked into their collaboration toward a new South African constitution.

And yet . . .

Peacemaking, like warmaking or courtship, depends upon exquisitely balanced, mysterious and usually unpredictable combinations of context, timing, luck, leadership, mood, personal needs, outside help and spending money. Certainly one of the forces behind the movement toward peace in both the Middle East and South Africa was what one observer called "a biological compulsion" in all four men to reach a settlement as a capstone to their careers. Mandela was 75 in 1993, De Klerk 57, Rabin 71 and Arafat 64.

Beyond that, they were impelled, or at least strongly encouraged, by new historical realities. The cold war left Arafat without a Soviet patron; backing the wrong side in the Gulf War cost him his wealthy oil-state sponsors. The Israelis were growing weary of the economic and moral costs of the endless occupation. In South Africa the white minority faced a catastrophe: a main

achievement of apartheid had been to inflict near fatal damage on the country's economy. As for Mandela's African National Congress, it foresaw a descent into chaos and civil war that might destroy any nation worth its inheriting. And so on.

Some thought South Africa and the Middle East proved what might be called the Exhaustion Theory of

The Middle East: WHEN ISRAELIS TOOK JERUSALEM, ABOVE, PALESTINIANS FACED AN EXILE THAT LASTED FOR DECADES.

Peacemaking, which arises from the cynical, and accurate, observation that peace is the last resort when all else has failed. True: if either side had been able to conquer, it would have let victory dictate the peace.

Yet the settlements-in-the-making in the Middle East and South Africa were hardly involuntary, and they were far from inevitable. Without Rabin and Arafat, the Israelis and Palestinians would have continued down the same bleak, violent road they have followed since 1948. Without Mandela and De Klerk, blacks and whites would have descended into the bloodiest race war in history. In 1993 Rabin and Arafat, Mandela and De Klerk all rose to the occasion before them. Their common genius was that they saw in the convergence of circumstances a ripeness of moment—and that they acted.

They worked in pairs at their two separate projects, even though something inside each man came to the rendezvous reluctantly, uncomfortably, as if history had given him no choice. Each needed his other, absolutely, in order to succeed—and each knew it. Each of the men was putting himself at enormous personal risk in the en-

1960

South Africa: THE SHARPEVILLE MASSACRE, ABOVE, IGNITED A MOVEMENT TO END APARTHEID THAT SUCCEEDED 33 YEARS LATER.

1993

terprise, not now from his long-sworn enemy but from those on his own side who would cry betrayal. But each had the armor of his record in the struggle. Only men with the longevity in their conflicts of Rabin, Arafat, De Klerk and Mandela had the credibility to make peace.

None of the men much liked his partner. They were bound together, two by two, as if in an impossible combination: they became each other's steptwins. Their negotiations at times resembled nothing so much as the conflict they were trying to resolve. Mandela and De

Klerk were at each other's throats even as they accepted the Nobel Peace Prize together. Rabin could barely stand to shake Arafat's hand on the White House lawn. Each of the settlements-in-progress shows that peacemaking is often as difficult and dirty, in its own way, as warmaking. The Men of the Year sometimes seemed to be elaborating on Churchill's thought about democracy: peace is the worst mess, except for the alternative.

For all that, these four men reasserted the principle that leaders matter, that an individual's vision, courageously and persuasively and intelligently pursued, can override the rather unimaginative human preference for war. No one can quantify a negative, but it seems obvious that the absence of leadership—the opportunities squandered or unenvisioned—costs the world dearly every day.

War is a profound habit—and sometimes a necessity. It is rich and vivid, with its traditions, its military academies, its ancient regiments and hero stories, its Iliads, its flash. Peace is not exciting. Its accoutrements are, almost by definition, unremarkable if they work well. It is a rare society that tells exemplary stories of peacemaking—except, say, for the Gospels of Christ, whose irenic grace may be admired from a distance without much effect on daily behavior.

It was against all the usual inclinations that these four men took what must be the first step in the metaphysics of peace: they recognized the other's existence. They crossed the line from the primitive intransigences of blood/color/tribe to the logic of tolerance and, farther down the road, of civil society. They asserted the power of the future to override the past, a fundamental precondition of change. Few forces are more intense than tribal memory and grievance, the blood's need for vindication. The past wants revenge, like Hamlet's father's ghost. Peace settlements in South Africa and the Middle East would bury the bloody shirt, shut down the past as an imperative.

The projects of Mandela-De Klerk and Arafat-Rabin are not yet realized, of course. Leaders must bring followers along. Leaders must exercise the visionary's gift. They must tell their people a new story about themselves (in these cases, the story of themselves at peace, to replace their older myth of struggle) and make it plausible. Peace is a way of reimagining the world. Often it must actually be made before people will embrace the idea. We do not know—and may not know for months or years—how good these four will be as storytellers, but their beginning was amazing to behold. ∎

Yasser Arafat And Yitzhak Rabin

Tunis is quiet after midnight, when Yasser Arafat summons visitors to make their way through a gauntlet of steel barricades to a villa in a quiet residential corner of the city. The stucco house is surrounded by young men in jeans, bearing Kalashnikovs, smoking cigarettes. Their job is to keep the Chairman of the Palestine Liberation Organization alive—and they take it seriously. Male guests are patted down, their pockets emptied, wallets searched. Women are scanned with ultrasensitive metal detectors, their purses ransacked.

Over the years Arafat has probably had more people trying to kill him than any other public figure in the world. Closest to succeeding were the Israelis, who might have buried him under the rubble in the Tunis bombing raid that killed 73 people in 1985, had the Chairman not been running late that day. Now Israel wants to keep him alive—to hold him to the pledge of peaceful coexistence that he made with a handshake on a sunny September day in Washington. At that moment, in accepting far less than the independent state he has always promised his people, he became a traitor to many of his own. So now it was the Palestinian extremists who sought to kill him in order to kill the peace accord.

There is an air of bravado in the room this December night as Arafat meets interviewers from TIME. The peace on which he has staked so much is not yet real for those dying in the streets of the

"FOR CENTURIES WE LIVED WITH THE JEWS. WE CALLED THEM OUR COUSINS."

West Bank and the Gaza Strip. Yet the P.L.O. leader gives no sign he is troubled. He is direct and engaging, full of a charm half calculated, half natural as he makes his case. Asked if he has concerns about his own personal security, he chuckles. "I only fear God."

Visitors to Yitzhak Rabin's modest office in western Jerusalem expect their sessions with him to be strictly business. He is known to be abrupt, omitting from such visits so much as a hello or goodbye. Today, the office is hectic. Chants of angry Jewish settlers camped outside to protest the peace agreement fade in and out. A delegation of conservative Knesset members argues against giving weapons to the future Palestinian police force.

But Rabin is calm, almost relaxed. Those who know him well say that since he signed the Declaration of Principles with Arafat, his manner has softened: he smiles more and grimaces less. Though he has taken a great gamble with his country's future, the mission of seeing it through, and the confidence that he has made the right choice, have energized him. As he talks to his guests from TIME, it is clear he has thought deeply about what he wants to get across. "Arafat carried out what I consider to be atrocities," he says. "But I've said more than once, we make peace, or we negotiate meaningful steps toward peace, with enemies. Sometimes bitter enemies."

"I'VE NEVER TRIED TO PUT MYSELF IN THEIR SHOES . . . [OR SEE] MYSELF A PALESTINIAN."

political destruction at the hands of his friends. Rabin's confidence is that of a proven warrior committed to peace—a "carnivorous dove," as Ariel Sharon put it.

Both men were dangerously flanked by extremists. Muslim fundamentalists and other militant factions vowed to break any deal that delivered less than an independent Palestinian state now, this instant. Fanatical settlers and other right-wing Jews swore never to give up one inch of the West Bank soil that is part of what they call Eretz Yisrael, the land God gave to the Jews. The pressure from internal enemies only complicated an already knotty negotiation.

Unlike many Israelis, Rabin has managed to accommodate his view of Arafat as a terrorist and a murderer with the belief that he is a man with whom Israel can do business. "I came to the conclusion that it's in their interest as well as our interest," he says. "It is not based on any feeling of affection or affiliation." Arafat is just as sternly pragmatic. "He is the boss, and without him, the accord will not work. He was my enemy, but he is a man who fulfills his commitments."

While Rabin labored in the shadow of great nation builders—David Ben-Gurion and Golda Meir—Arafat stood alone as a folk hero to his people. The teetotaling vegetarian is conniving, disarming, engaging, and quick with such perfect sound bites as the fact that his favorite cartoon is Tom and Jerry, since the mouse so often wins. He is a master of symbolism: never much of a soldier, he chose a fighting man's khakis and holster for his daily costume. His checkered kaffiyeh helps maintain his mythic stature. The headdress had no special meaning until he draped it to approximate the shape of mandatory Palestine. Then it became an emblem of Palestinian identity.

Peace is not yet a fact between the Israelis and the Palestinians. But Rabin and Arafat were Men of the Year 1993 because they took those meaningful steps from which it will be difficult to turn back. The idea of peace, once planted, is a powerful incentive to two peoples who have lost so many lives, so much time, so much prosperity in bloody wars.

Both leaders proved, against expectations,

that they could grasp the moment. They also shared a confidence in their ability to deliver on their promises. Arafat has the mystical arrogance of the survivor, so often has he cheated death at the hands of his enemies and

It was Arafat who made the intellectual leap to a definition of the Palestinians as a distinct people: he articulated the cause, organized for it, fought for it and brought it to the world's attention as no Kurd or Basque had ever managed. Until 1991, when he wed Suha Tawil, a Christian less than half his age, he was always said to be married to the revolution. Now it would be more accurate to say Suha is married to the revolution.

As a boy growing up in Jerusalem and Cairo, the son of a spice merchant and grocer, Arafat had no revolutionary ambitions. After graduating from Cairo University, he went to Kuwait to make his fortune in construction. By age 30 Arafat was a rich man, driving a Thunderbird,

Arafat in Lebanon, 1982: AS HE RETREATED FROM THE WRECKAGE OF BEIRUT, ISRAELI FORCES HAD HIS HEAD IN THEIR GUNSIGHTS.

moving smoothly through the prosperous circles of Palestinian exiles, and preparing to launch his crusade.

His Fatah organization, which he founded in the late 1950s with other educated, well-to-do Palestinians, eventually became the heart of the P.L.O. During the first few years, he had the most to fear from other Arabs: he came to know his way around the jails of Syria and Egypt; it was Israel that never once held him in prison. By the 1960s, Fatah was divided into two factions. There were the "sane ones," who urged building up the infant group before launching guerrilla attacks against Israel. And there were the "mad ones," already out for blood: Arafat was their leader. Whether he gave the orders or not, his organization has always been linked to some of the bloodiest acts of terrorism in the Arab-Israeli conflict, including the massacre of Israeli athletes at the 1972 Olympics in Munich and the 1974 murder of Israeli schoolchildren at Maalot.

For years the Israelis saw
Arafat as the main obstacle to peacemaking. Even when the Palestinians joined in Mideast peace talks in Madrid in 1991, Arafat was officially kept out. When Rabin came to power in mid-1992, he looked for more moderate leaders to speak for the

Palestinians. But the negotiators made no secret that they took their orders from Arafat and that it would be dangerous to cross him.

Meanwhile, Arafat and his organization were in trouble. Strapped for cash after losing his Soviet sponsors and alienating his rich Arab patrons during the Gulf War, he had to cut back funding for Palestinian schools and hospitals, students' tuition and widows' pensions in the occupied territories, which hurt his popular support. The militant fundamentalists of Hamas were winning converts and beating his candidates in elections for chambers of commerce, labor unions and student organizations.

Bankrupt, dismissed by some U.S. officials as a spent force, Arafat needed Rabin. And in turn Rabin needed the Chairman.

Like Arafat, Rabin had not intended to make a life of soldiering; he, like Arafat, had once wanted to go to the U.S. to become an engineer. But he had earned a reputation as a gifted military commander in the Palmach, the commando unit of the Haganah underground army. On the eve of his country's war for in-

Toward a Middle East Peace

In mid-December 1993 a team of TIME editors and correspondents met separately with Rabin and Arafat to ask about common issues.

RABIN: I've said more than once, we make peace with enemies, sometimes with bitter enemies.

ARAFAT: It was the results of the Israeli election last year [1992] against Yitzhak Shamir's policy that made a deal first seem possible. This was a very important signal that the Israelis were willing to achieve peace.

RABIN: I knew that the key for any meaningful movement toward peace was with either Syria or the Palestinians. Through my explorations, done quietly, I concluded that there would be a better chance to do it with the Palestinians. What we did in recognizing them would have been unheard of four years ago. I believed I had to do something which is not expected.

ARAFAT: The intifadeh motivated the Israelis. There were no signs that it would end anytime soon. There was no military solution, only a political solution.

This superarmy was running after kids and fighting against women.

RABIN: No doubt the intifadeh brought the Palestinian case to the headlines of the world. It created problems for us, and it continues. Now it's less an uprising and much more terror in opposition to the agreement.

ARAFAT: It is very accurate to say there is opposition from some Palestinians. There are 10 Damascus-based organizations supported by the Arab opposition. They have been financed by some Arabs from the gulf states and also by the Iranians. But this opposition does not have the ability to overcome the masses. There must be compromise. I haven't the ability to get what I need. And the other side hasn't the ability to get all it wants.

RABIN: What we are trying to create here is peaceful coexistence between two entities who do not much love each other. Geographically they are mixed up; they crisscross one another daily by vehicles. There is no line that divides. The real problem is to what extent the P.L.O. will have the ability to take over what we are ready to give them and to

dependence in 1948, Rabin was persuaded by his military superiors to
abandon his study plans and join the
battle. He was charged with helping
to break the Arab blockade of
Jerusalem and to keep the road to Tel
Aviv open for convoys.

By age 32 Rabin was a general.
Twelve years later, he became Chief
of Staff and devised the tactics for
Israel's brilliant victory over Syria,
Egypt and Jordan in the 1967 Six-Day
War. Swashbuckling Defense Minister Moshe Dayan took most of the
credit, an injustice that rankles Rabin
to this day. Nonetheless, Rabin always subscribed to the Labor Party
doctrine that one day Israel would
have to trade back territory for peace.

The general first became

Prime Minister in 1974 after a stint
as ambassador to Washington. His
tenure cut short in 1977 by a scandal over a small but illegal U.S. bank account he maintained with his wife, he
retreated to Labor's back bench until 1984, when the national unity government of Shimon Peres, his bitter rival within the Labor Party, turned to him as Defense

Rabin and Moshe Dayan, 1967: CELEBRATING VICTORY AFTER THE
SIX-DAY WAR, WITH RABIN TYPICALLY IN DAYAN'S SHADOW.

Minister. Rabin seemed just the man to suppress the intifadeh, the uprising against Israeli rule in the occupied
territories that began in December 1987.

Tough and unrelenting toward the protesters, Rabin
is said to have told his troops to "break their bones,"
also ordering deportations and the
destruction of Palestinian houses.
Yet he was quicker than many to
grasp the import of the uprising.
As early as February 1988, Rabin
was telling Labor Party activists,
"I've learned something in the
past 2½ months, among other
things that you can't rule by force
over 1.5 million Palestinians." An-
nexing the occupied territories
would dilute the Jewish character
of Israel, he believed. But military
rule would mean endless war.

In the 1992 elections, Rabin
campaigned as the man who
could bring the country peace
with security. But to succeed,
Rabin told Israelis, they would
have to relinquish a central part
of their identity: their sense of
fearful isolation.

The Prime Minister has a keen
sense of history; Arafat is no less
aware—and no less the engineer—
of the historic role he is enact-
ing. "This is my destiny," he says.
"No one can escape his destiny."
And so these two old soldiers, so
wounded by history, resolved to
put history to death. ■

---

fulfill their commitments. The P.L.O. has
never been responsible for running the
life of a large community.
ARAFAT: The P.L.O. is responsible for
the whole life of our people. We have a
parliament representing Palestinians
everywhere; no revolution ever had a parliament. We have democracy. We have
established universities, schools and hospitals. We have a political department,
one of the strongest in the Arab world.
RABIN: Let the Palestinians run their
affairs, create a situation in which no
Israeli soldier will have to maintain public
order, whether in Gaza or the West Bank.
Let's give it to the Palestinians, as long
as there is security for us. No more
occupying another people.
ARAFAT: What is important for me is to
fix my people on the map of the Middle
East and not to be like those who have
been canceled out in international
agreements, like many communities after
World War I and II. It is the continuous
tragedy of my people that I cannot
forgive. We have paid a very high price.
RABIN: I don't pretend that I can imagine myself as a Palestinian. I understand
their desire for their own entity, but at
the same time I can't understand why
they missed so many opportunities that

could have prevented much bloodshed,
at certain moments in which we were
ready for compromise. I hope that Arafat
learned a lesson, as I learned the lesson,
that you have to be more forthcoming.
ARAFAT: I have many dreams: a Middle
East without wars and violence and
oppression; a Middle East that cooper-
ates, that is prosperous, that could contribute to the new world order. I will
design my own house—not in Jericho but
in Jerusalem. I remember living there
with my uncle, near the Wailing Wall.
The house was demolished. I imagine a
future Jerusalem as a capital of two
states, without a Berlin Wall.
RABIN: Jerusalem is a different issue
from others. For us it's the symbol.
Jerusalem is a living city, but also the
heart, the soul of the Jewish people and
the state of Israel. We understand that
Jerusalem is holy to Christianity and
Islam. We believe that we have to secure
free access for the believers of the other
religions. We believe the administration
of the holy shrines, not the holy city,
should be by them.
ARAFAT: Things will work out, if not this
time, the next time. There is no other
alternative. Wars are an impossibility for
everybody.

Nelson Mandela And F. W. de Klerk

Two days before receiving his Nobel Peace Prize, African National Congress President Nelson Mandela entertains visiting interviewers from TIME at the Grand Hotel in Oslo, Norway. Tall, exquisitely tailored, he dispenses soft handshakes and his world-famous smile. The 27 years he spent in South African prisons seem somehow to have left him younger than his 75 years; he looks well rested and benign.

Gradually, as Mandela begins to talk of how his fellow Peace Prize winner, South African President F.W. de Klerk, has "disappointed" him during their long, tortuous negotiations toward a new, free, just South Africa, his sunny demeanor fades. His voice rises; the smile becomes a scowl. Blacks have been killing other blacks in gruesome ways and growing numbers back in his country, and Mandela says he knows who is partly to blame: "There is no doubt that the National Party is involved in violence; we have got very solid evidence."

Two days after the Nobel ceremony, De Klerk, 57, sits in an ornate suite in another Grand Hotel, this one in Rome, where he awaits an audience the next day with Pope John Paul II. For someone who has just been heralded and laureled as a peacemaker, he falls into moods that border on the bellicose. The President, who is smaller, more delicately featured than he appears in photographs, cannot resist complaining.

"I WAS DISAPPOINTED BY HIM BECAUSE HE DID THINGS THAT I DID NOT EXPECT."

He feels Mandela has upstaged him in Norway and maligned him in general, he tells TIME. He, the son and grandson of National Party leaders who helped erect the artifice of apartheid, has traveled further from his heritage than anyone could have predicted. He has dismantled the past and prepared his nation for democracy. And what does he hear from Mandela, the A.N.C. and others? That he is a foot dragger, unconcerned with the injustices and violence suffered by blacks in his land, even, perhaps, secretly instigating such turmoil; that he is not an architect of progress but at times its impediment.

The mutual bitterness and resentments between De Klerk and Mandela are palpable. The two perfectly meet the first precondition of peacemakers: they do not like each other very much. They have been forced into a fascinating pas de deux, coordinating their steps while not so secretly resenting the necessity of their partnership. "Mandela and De Klerk," says A.N.C. spokesman Carl Niehaus, "were delivered to each other by history." Neither one, in the season of their triumphs, seems grateful for the gift of the other.

But those triumphs are immense. These unlikely allies created the conditions for an event the world could not have foreseen only a few years earlier. "Our goal is a new South Africa," De Klerk told the audience at the Nobel awards ceremony. From the same platform,

Thanks to their work, the election scheduled for April 27 would embrace all the nation's citizens, including the previously disenfranchised blacks who, numbering 28 million, make up 75% of the population. Given the stunning majority of potential black voters, Mandela was regarded as a shoo-in. But not by De Klerk, who seemed determined to prove against all odds that he has not negotiated himself out of his job.

Both De Klerk and Mandela are attorneys, skilled in the art of compromise. Both also have stubborn streaks and strong, entrenched opinions, shaped in large measure by their very different South African pasts. For De Klerk, a fourth-generation Afrikaner and hence a beneficiary of white privilege under the old system, change has meant revoking the legacy of his forebears. Still, he was not a born reformer. During his rise through the ranks of the National Party, he allied himself with its *verkrampte*, or "closed-minded conservative," camp. He was a pragmatic politician, eager to press the flesh and do the deal. He proved cautious in his personal life as well. He married and stayed married to his college sweetheart. An earlier generation of South African leaders liked to relax by hunting big game; De Klerk took up golf.

One thing that rankled Mandela's supporters throughout the talks was De Klerk's dogged refusal to condemn the principle of apartheid. De Klerk will admit that the system led to injustices, particularly the forced removals of blacks from places legally declared off limits to them. Even so, he speaks wistfully about "grand apartheid" as a system that might have worked in South Africa had all the nation's diverse ethnic and tribal groups accepted geographic separation voluntarily. Mandela, a child of the oppressed majority, finds this notion hateful.

Mandela proclaimed, "We can today even set the dates when all humanity will join together to celebrate one of the outstanding victories of our century."

That victory was not easily won, and the

mutual enmity between Mandela and De Klerk may be due in part to battle fatigue. (They are not, after two dozen meetings, even on a first-name basis; it is "Mr. Mandela" and "Mr. President.") There was another reason. Both men knew their collaboration would, if successful, lead to political rivalry between them. De Klerk the incumbent and Mandela the challenger were now active candidates for the presidency of South Africa.

It has been the labor of his life to overthrow apartheid, not because it did not do its job but because it was morally repellent.

The Nelson Mandela who walked with such dignity out of prison in February 1990 was not the same firebrand who had been placed there 27 years before. Born into the royal family of the Thembu, a clan of the Xhosa tribe based in the Transkei, Mandela was trained as a boy to rule someday as a chief. Instead he became a lawyer and an A.N.C. militant. It was just a few months after A.N.C. leader Chief Albert Luthuli was awarded the 1960 Nobel Peace Prize that Mandela urged the party leadership to take up arms. Committed to nonviolence,

De Klerk on the rise, 1978: NOT A BORN REFORMER, HE STILL BELIEVES A SYSTEM OF "GRAND APARTHEID" MIGHT HAVE WORKED.

collapsing of its own inherent absurdity. Moreover, the outlawed A.N.C.'s 1984 call to make South Africa "ungovernable" had been answered by a surge of black demonstrations and acts of civil disobedience.

To put down such unrest, the government had to use increasingly brutal police and military actions, many of them filmed by news cameras and televised to appalled viewers around the globe. These ugly spectacles increased international pressure for economic sanctions against South Africa. Whites saw their nation becoming an international pariah. Realizing he needed Mandela, Botha arranged a meeting with him at the presidential residence, Tuynhuys, in Cape Town in July 1989. Mandela had been slipped out of prison for the purpose. The two issued a joint communiqué committing themselves, in general terms, to peace. A month later, Botha, whose authoritarian style had impeded real progress, was nudged out of office by party leaders.

Upon taking over as Botha's successor, De Klerk cautiously began softening his stance on the necessity

Luthuli was deeply ambivalent about the proposition, but allowed Mandela to form a separate group, Umkhonto we Sizwe, to embark on violent actions. As a founder of the armed wing of the A.N.C., the young Mandela clearly participated in such violence. By 1962 he was under arrest, and two years later he was sentenced to life imprisonment for sabotage.

Several interesting changes

occurred during Mandela's long, long incarceration. For one thing, his enforced isolation slowly transformed him into a mythic figure. Incommunicado, without the opportunity to speak out on specific issues, Mandela in his silence became South Africa's most persuasive presence: an inspiration to blacks, a recrimination to whites. What is more, he sensed the moral power his confinement had conferred. Mandela had always been willing to talk; violence was his recourse when the other side would not listen.

One day in 1986 Mandela sat down and wrote a letter to the government proposing a dialogue on the nation's future. This gesture received a secret but surprisingly willing response from President P.W. Botha, a hard-liner on apartheid who nonetheless had begun to sense his country's escalating dilemma. Apartheid was

The Last Days of Apartheid

In mid-December 1993 a team of TIME editors and correspondents met separately with Mandela and De Klerk to explore common issues.

DE KLERK: In prison, Mr. Mandela probably had a perception of leaders of the National Party that was proved wrong when he met us. My first meeting with him in 1989 was fairly relaxed. We came to grips with some fundamental things, basically the need to solve the problem of South Africa through negotiation and recognizing each other as main players who would have to take the lead.

MANDELA: I found Mr. De Klerk very positive, very bright, very confident of himself, and ready to accommodate the views I expressed. I smuggled a message to the A.N.C. leadership in Zambia and said, "I think we can do business with this man." I did not expect that he was going to be so positive.

DE KLERK: I don't believe I am irreplaceable. I don't believe he is irreplaceable. The fact is, we were around, and we were the leaders.

MANDELA: I was disappointed by him

because he did things that I did not expect. Such as the question of violence. I said to him, if there is anything that will create bad blood between us, it is the slaughter of human beings with government connivance. That is the one thing that has created a great deal of friction between me and De Klerk.

DE KLERK: A different approach from the A.N.C. could have prevented much of the grief. Mandela could have started negotiating sooner. They should never have embarked on acts of terrorism, killing innocent civilians; it had a dramatic effect on white public opinion. Sanctions were quite counterproductive. They built a strong sense of nationalism: We will not allow the world to tell us what to do!

MANDELA: When I was sent to jail, my mother got a terrible shock. She had never been to school, and valued education. She had in mind a dignified profession for me. I had to explain to her why I was in the A.N.C. She became so convinced that later she said to me, "If you don't join other children and fight for our liberation, I am going to disinherit you."

DE KLERK: My brother was a very liber-

of preserving apartheid, announcing "Our goal is a totally changed South Africa." In December 1989 he convened a historic *bosberaad*, or bush council, at which he won his Cabinet's authorization to lift the government's ban on the A.N.C. and release Mandela in February the following year.

Then came the hard part.

Shortly before Mandela was freed, he and De Klerk met for the first time, again at the presidential residence in Cape Town. Things went well, both men now recall. Once out of prison, Mandela commended De Klerk as "a man of integrity." Months later, he retracted this judgment. As the intense bargaining between them began, Mandela was outraged to discover that De Klerk was not a meek facilitator of historical inevitability but a tough, grudging opponent.

De Klerk kept attempting to insert into any proposed power-sharing agreement checks and balances that would still give whites some guarantees of a voice in future governments. He flew into rages at the charge that

Mandela speaks out, 1961: A FIREBRAND AND FOUNDER OF THE ARMED WING OF THE A.N.C., HE PARTICIPATED IN ACTS OF VIOLENCE.

he did not care about township violence—as if, Mandela suspected, he could not stand being scolded by a black man. And Mandela's stony reserve sometimes dissolved as well. A Mandela aide commented: "I sometimes feel sorry for De Klerk after the old man bullies him."

al editor of a daily newspaper. He was criticizing us, he was urging us to do what we are doing now. My father [a Cabinet minister in three apartheid governments] would agree with me today; he died in 1979. At dinner, before we reached the sweets we got on to politics. He was a man who always looked for justice. He asked himself, If a plan cannot work, then it becomes immoral to continue something you acknowledge in your own conscience cannot work.
MANDELA: Chief Albert Luthuli [A.N.C. president, 1952 to '67] believed in nonviolence as a way of life. But we who were in touch with the grass roots persuaded the Chief that if we did not begin the armed struggle, then people would proceed without guidance. Armed struggle must be a movement intended to hit at the symbols of oppression and not to slaughter human beings.
DE KLERK: I don't think it was a good idea to tell people where to live and to kick people out of particular townships. It became forced removals. That is where apartheid became morally unjustifiable. As it failed, it became more and more racist and less and less morally defensible. People's dignity was being impaired, and it brought humiliation. I have said time

and again, "We are sorry that happened."
MANDELA: I don't think it is necessary for De Klerk to apologize. It is what a person does to ensure that the most brutal system of racial oppression is completely eliminated from our society.
DE KLERK: I don't want to sound vindictive, but I am relatively satisfied with the agreement. I don't see that we have made any fundamental concessions on principle—practical concessions, yes.
MANDELA: There is no doubt that South Africans, black and white, are coming together. I have been addressing some of the most conservative sectors. Their response is so positive. One of the first questions is, "When did you change your policy?" I say, "This has always been our policy." They say, "It's not true. You have been a terrorist organization." Nobody who hears our policy can fault it.
DE KLERK: Looking back, I wouldn't have done any of the fundamental things I did differently. I achieved thus far almost all the goals I set for myself within these past four years. I would hope that history would recognize that I, together with all those who supported me, have shown courage, integrity, honesty at the moment of truth in our history. That we took the right turn.

Their disagreements became so acrimonious that Mandela and De Klerk at one point broke off all personal contacts, communicating only through letters and public statements. But both had invested too much in the process to let it founder. Shrewdly, they delegated the day-to-day haggling to subordinates, who eventually came through with the crucial compromise: an agreement to establish a government of national unity for five years after the first free elections in April. And then both men, despite private disappointments over details, energetically sold this plan to their people.

Mandela and De Klerk both deny they deserve much individual credit for what they have done so far. They are too modest. If the chain of events they have set in motion leads to the conclusion they both want, then the future will write of them—as it will of Yasser Arafat and Yitzhak Rabin if their vision is realized—that these were leaders who seized their days and actually dared to lead. ■

Peacock Eats Crow

It was a bad patch for NBC News. In February *Dateline NBC* stars Jane Pauley and Stone Phillips delivered a stunning on-air apology for a report on the safety of GM trucks, which showed a pickup catching fire in a test crash—but did not show that incendiary devices had been attached to the vehicle to help ensure a blaze. GM, reeling from a $105.2 million verdict in an Atlanta truck explosion, held a press conference that showed the falsehood in devastating detail, and NBC averted a major lawsuit from the auto-maker with its admission of guilt. A week later, anchor Tom Brokaw expressed his regrets for several aspects of a *Nightly News* report about the environmental abuses on an Idaho river that featured footage of "dead" fish. The allegedly deceased fish turned out to have been only stunned as part of an experiment. Clearly, someone's head had to roll at the network, and the chief rollee turned out to be the top man himself, Michael Gartner, president of NBC News, who chose to resign "voluntarily".

The arrow shows smoke emerging from the truck before the crash.

Ending with a Whimper?

A little more than two years after the shady doings at the corrupt Bank of Credit & Commerce International exploded into the biggest financial scandal in history, the prosecution of the bank and its operators stumbled badly. In New York City a jury acquitted banker and lawyer Robert Altman of four charges relating to his various affiliations with B.C.C.I. Four other charges had been dismissed earlier by the judge; in all, they ranged from bribery to deceiving the government. Clark Clifford, 86, the old-line Washington Democrat also accused in the scandal, was deemed too ill to stand trial. The case was so complex that some jurors fell asleep listening to it. Altman and Clifford faced further suits that could mire them in B.C.C.I. legal proceedings for years to come.

Biting the Hand

In a fundamental power shift in corporate America, boards of directors, once tame and docile, were turning on their masters. In their willingness to take on entrenched management and bloated corporations, the directors became oddly reminiscent of the takeover artists they had feared in the '80s. A long line of executives fell prey to the potent new trend. Among the victims: at American Express James Robinson III was out and protégé Harvey Golub was in; at IBM John Akers was out and RJR Nabisco's Lou Gerstner was in; at Kodak Kay Whitmore was out and Motorola's George Fisher was in. Meanwhile, throughout the land, blue-chip companies continued to slice away at their employee rosters, "downsizing" with a vengeance.

Sorry, Wrong Continent

The Magic Kingdom's spell was finally broken: for the first time since Michael Eisner became chairman a decade ago, the Walt Disney Co. reported a quarterly loss. The $77.8 billion in red ink was attributable to Euro Disney, which lost nearly $1 billion in its first fiscal year. With attendance still below anticipated levels, the theme park 20 miles outside Paris announced it would shed 950 administrative and staff positions, reducing the employee roster to 11,000, down from 19,000 during the park's first summer season in 1992. But Disney refused to swear off amusement parks, instead announcing plans to build an American-history theme park near Manassas, Virginia.

It's Just the Sound That Cannons Make

Even after the biggest one-month drop in the unemployment rate in 10 years, economists, business and government officials resolutely refused to so much as whisper the four-letter word: "boom." Previous spikes in the economy had come and gone, hence the caution. And 8.3 million Americans were still looking for jobs. Still, it looked at year's end as if people might be able to feel the recovery in their wallets. Mortgage rates were holding at their lowest levels in 25 years. Other statistics were strong as well: personal income, consumer spending, factory orders, business profits, you name it. End-of-the-year figures showed them all marching ahead. But no, it wasn't a boom; things were simply "moving in the right direction," according to Bill Clinton.

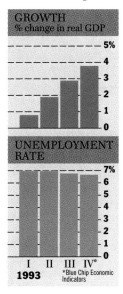

GROWTH
% change in real GDP

UNEMPLOYMENT RATE

I   II   III   IV*
1993   *Blue Chip Economic Indicators

Smoke Damage

In early April, without warning, Philip Morris slashed 40¢ off the price of Marlboro cigarettes, reducing the average cost of a pack to $1.80. Admitting that this aggressive pricing could reduce earnings 40% in 1993, the company said it took the measure to meet the challenge of discount and generic brands. But Wall Street didn't light up: on "Marlboro Friday," Philip Morris shares plunged $14.75, and since the company was among the 30 firms whose stocks are in the

Alors! **When Euro Disney faltered, chief Mouseketeer Eisner gave up his year-end bonus.**

Dow Jones industrial average, that bellwether index plummeted nearly 69 points on the same day.

Expanding Rapidly and Restlessly

Just two years after he was nearly buried beneath a mountain of debt, media mogul Rupert Murdoch, 62, was on a tear, expanding his global empire more rapidly than ever before. For starters, in July he bought 63.6% of Hong Kong–based STAR TV and its potential to reach 3 billion viewers from Tokyo to Tel Aviv. In September he agreed to acquire Delphi Internet Service, a Massachusetts-based computer network whose gateway to the worldwide Internet system provided access to 20 million computer users. Finally, Murdoch unleashed his long bomb, when his Fox TV network outbid CBS to take over the Sunday broadcasts of the N.F.L.'s National Football Conference. Murdoch's whopping bid: $1.58 billion for four years.

Rupert Murdoch stole the ball from CBS.

An End to Talk and Talk

Officially, it was the General Agreement on Tariffs and Trade, but GATT had become known as the General Agreement to Talk and Talk. That's why it was a relief when, after seven long years of talks capped with a 23-hour gabfest between U.S. and European representatives, negotiators for 117 nations approved a new trade pact. Immediately hailed as the most comprehensive in history, the pact would wholly or partly eliminate national tariffs, subsidies, quotas and other forms of protection for dozens of industries. To reach final accord, the U.S. and Europe deferred resolving their differences over film and television markets.

THE WIRING

EVERYBODY KNOWS WHAT THE telephone is for. It rings. You pick it up. A voice is routed down a wire right to your ear.

Everybody knows what the television set is for. You turn it on and let news and entertainment flow into your home.

Now imagine a medium that combines the routing capabilities of phones with the video and information offerings of the most advanced cable systems and data banks. Imagine punching up any item from an encyclopedic menu of choices and having it appear immediately on your TV set or computer screen. A movie? Airline listings? Tomorrow's newspaper or yesterday's episode of *Northern Exposure*? How about a new magazine or book? A stroll through the L.L. Bean catalog? One touch, and it's yours.

Welcome to the information highway, the wildly heralded (and often wildly hyped) revolution in communications that dominated America's business agenda in 1993. Like the railroad, like the automobile, the electronic highway was a new technology that promised to change the way Americans work and play. And like them, its advent reshaped America's corporate landscape, setting off a year-long mating dance of media moguls as they maneuvered to control the new digital frontier.

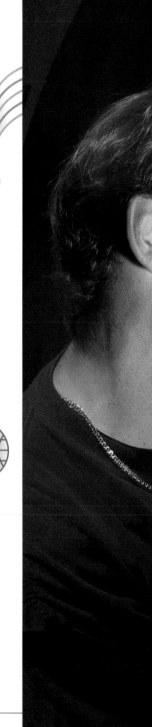

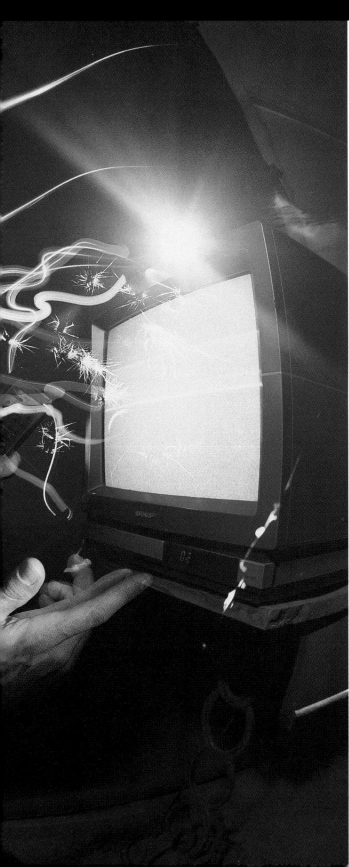

On Line

Building the Information Highway

FOR YEARS SCIENTISTS AND MEDIA executives have envisioned a brave new world of communications. In this world, home TV sets would shrug off the networks and cables that bound them and become interactive gateways to a communicopia of entertainment, information and services. In 1993 this dream came down to earth, and the electronic superhighway began to take shape. Driving the explosive merger of video, telephones and computers were some rather simple technological advances: the ability to translate all audio and video communications into digital information; new methods of storing this digitized data and compressing them so they can travel through existing phone and cable lines; fiber-optic wiring that provides a virtually limitless transmission pipeline; new switching techniques and other breakthroughs that make it possible to bring all this to neighborhoods without necessarily rewiring every home.

Suddenly the brave new world of videophones and smart TVs that futurists have been predicting for decades seemed at hand. The final bottleneck—the "last mile" of wiring that takes information from the digital highway to the home—was broken. Now the only questions were whether the public wanted the new systems and how much it was willing to pay for them.

The prospect of multiplying today's TV listings has launched a furious debate over what a fragmented and TV-anesthetized society would do with 100—or 500—offerings. But to focus on the number of channels would be to miss the point of the revolution. When the information highway comes to town, channels and nightly schedules will begin to fade away and could eventually disappear. In this postchannel world, more and more of what one wants to see will be delivered on demand by a local supplier (either a cable system, a phone company or a joint venture) from giant computer disks called file servers. These might store hundreds of movies, the current week's broadcast programming and news, plus all manner of video publications, catalogs, data files and interactive entertainment. They would also make available virtually all archived entertainment hits from the past: *I Love Lucy, Star Trek, The Brady Bunch*. Click an item on the menu, and it will appear instantly on the screen.

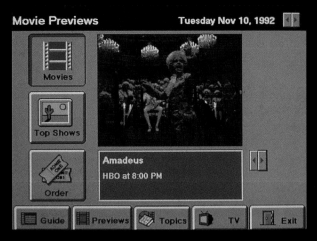

Movie Previews   **Tuesday Nov 10, 1992**

Movies

Top Shows

Order

Amadeus
HBO at 8:00 PM

Guide   Previews   Topics   TV   Exit

CHANNELS?

Soon they will multiply into the hundreds. But ultimately, channels will be an outmoded concept, as interactive technology makes a host of programming and services available instantly at the touch of a button. Microsoft has developed a prototype in which viewers simply scan a menu and make their selection.

COMMERCIALS?

The traditional 30-second spot will be supplemented by more creative hybrids of advertising and information. Car buyers, for instance, may be able to take a 15-minute trip around auto showrooms via home video. Advertisers will be able to target messages to individual homes, but consumers willing to pay for it may be able to enjoy commercial-free TV.

And there's more: this digital highway is a two-way street. Once the storage and switching systems are in place, all sorts of interactive services become possible. The same switches used to send a TV show to your home can also be used to send a video from your home to any other linked TV set, paving the way for videophones that will be as ubiquitous and easy to use as TV. Today's home-shopping networks could blossom into video malls stocked with the latest from Victoria's Secret, Toys "R" Us and the Gap. Armchair shoppers could browse with their remote controls, see video displays of appealing products and charge purchases on their credit cards with the press of a button—a convenience that will empower some people and surely bankrupt others.

In the era of interactive TV, the lines between advertisements, entertainment and services may grow fuzzy. A slick demonstration put together by Microsoft shows how. It opens with a Seattle Mariners baseball game. By clicking a button on a mouse or remote control, a viewer can bring up a menu of options. Click on one, and the image of the batter shrinks to make room for the score and the player's stats—RBIs, home runs and batting average—updated with every pitch. Click again, and you see the Mariners' home schedule. Click yet again, and a diagram of the Kingdome pops up, showing available seats and pricing. Click one more time, and you have ordered a pair of field box seats on the first-base side (and reduced your credit-card balance by about $25).

The key to the entire enterprise is fiber. Fiber-optic cable, made up of hair-thin strands of glass so pure you could see through a window of it that was 70 miles thick, is the most perfect transmitter of information ever invented. A single strand of fiber could in theory carry the entire nation's radio and telephone traffic and still have

room for more. As it is deployed today, fiber uses less than 1% of its theoretical capacity, or bandwidth, as it's called in the trade. Even so, it can carry 250,000 times as much data as a standard copper telephone wire.

In the mid-1980s, AT&T, MCI and Sprint installed fiber-optic cable between major U.S. cities to increase the capacity of their long-distance telephone lines. At about the same time, the Federal Government, spurred by Senator Al Gore, leased some of these lines to give scientists a high-speed data link to supercomputers funded by the National Science Foundation. These two networks, private and public, carry the bulk of the country's telephone and data traffic. In the superhighway system of the future, they will be the interstate turnpikes.

The problem comes when you get off the turnpike onto the roadways owned by local phone companies and cable-TV operators. Some of these are being converted to high-bandwidth fiber optics. But at the end of almost every local system—that "last mile" that goes from the local-service provider to the house—you run into the electronic equivalent of a bumpy country road. In the phone system, the bottleneck is the very last bit of copper wiring, which seems far too narrow to admit the profusion of TV signals poised to flow through it. In cable TV, the roadblocks are the long cascades of amplifiers that run from the company's transmission headquarters to the home, boosting the signal every quarter-mile or so. These amplifiers are notoriously unreliable and generate so much electronic noise that two-way traffic in a cable-TV system is all but impossible right now.

It has long been assumed that nothing was going to change much in telecommunications or television until fiber was brought all the way to the home, a Herculean

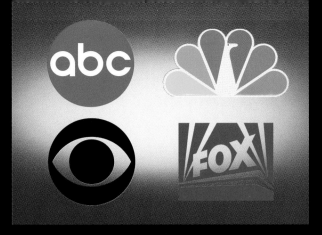

NETWORKS?

Near term: Though perhaps diminished, they will remain the pre-eminent providers of mass-audience fare in a sea of narrowcasting. **Long term:** With video on demand, the prime-time schedule may become a thing of the past, and the networks might survive only as brand-name suppliers of news and other programming.

YOUR BILL?

It could get bigger as pay-per-view options multiply along with such services as games and videoconferencing. Though many are likely to remain advertiser-supported and thus "free," your monthly bill may one day resemble today's phone bill, with viewing time and use of services totted up like message units.

task that was expected to cost $200 billion to $400 billion and take more than 20 years to complete. The breakthrough that is bringing the info highway home much sooner than expected is the discovery, by both the phone companies and the cable industry, that it is possible to get around the bottlenecks in their respective last miles without replacing the entire system.

For the cable-TV companies, the key insight came in the fall of 1987, when cable engineers demonstrated that coaxial wire could carry extensive information quite effectively over short distances; in fact, for a quarter-mile or so, it has almost as much bandwidth as fiber. By using fiber to bring the signal to within a few blocks of each home and coaxial cable to carry it the rest of the way, the cable companies could get a "twofer": they could throw away those cranky amplifiers and get two-way interactivity almost cost-free.

For the phone companies, the breakthrough came in 1990 when scientists at Bellcore, the research arm of the Baby Bells, found a way to do what everybody had assumed was impossible: squeeze a video signal through a telephone wire. The technology, known as asymmetric digital subscriber line, has some drawbacks. It cannot handle live transmissions, and the picture it produces is not as clear as that provided by a well-tuned cable hookup—never mind the high-definition TV signals expected to come on line before the end of the decade. Bellcore researchers say they have already improved the quality of the picture and that with further compression they may be able to accommodate several channels of live video.

With the final technological barriers broken, the question becomes: what shape will the highway take? The answer depends to some extent on who ends up

building it. The cable companies tend to think in terms of entertaining mass audiences. Their emphasis is on expanded channels, video on demand and video-shopping networks. They admit the possibility of more special-interest programming—such as MTV, the Discovery Channel and Black Entertainment Television—but only if they can be convinced that the demographics are sufficiently attractive.

The phone companies, with their background in point-to-point switching, focus on connectivity and anything that will rack up message units. They emphasize services that will generate a lot of two-way traffic, such as videophones, videoconferencing and long-distance access to libraries. The computer users see the information highway as a glorified extension of computer bulletin boards that would do for video what those boards did for print: make it easy for everyone to publish ideas to an audience eager to respond in kind.

The new technology makes all these things possible. And with the rush of mergers and deals that realigned telephone companies, cable concerns and computer outfits during 1993, the old barriers separating them appear to be as dated as the Berlin Wall.

In the end, how the highway develops and what sort of traffic it bears will depend to a large extent on consumers. As the system unfolds, the companies supplying hardware and programming will be watching to see which services are favored by the early users. Consumers will in effect be voting with their remote controls. If they don't like what they see—or if the tolls are too high—the electronic superhighway could lead to a dead end. Or it could offer more—much more—of what we already have. Just as likely, it could veer off in surprising directions and take us places we've never imagined. ■

The Battle For the Electronic Frontier

The promise of the Information Highway rocked America's telecommunications industry

IN 1993 AMERICAN BUSINESS LOOKED INTO THE FUTURE and saw the information highway, a technology that promised to force the merger of television, telecommunications, computers, consumer electronics, publishing and information services into a single interactive industry. With visions of empowered couch potatoes dancing in their heads, America's media moguls set out to control the highway, launching a series of corporate courtships that revived the mega-mergers and hostile takeovers of the '80s and sent longtime enemies scrambling to make love, not war.

Cable-TV operators and telephone companies turned from years of competition to a frenzy of top-this deals as they raced to control the "last mile" of wire that would feed information into the home. Computer companies such as IBM, Hewlett-Packard and Sun vied to build the huge file servers that would act as video and information libraries. Software companies like Microsoft and Apple contended to build the operating systems that would serve as the data highway's traffic cops, controlling the flow of information to and from each viewer's screen.

"Make no mistake about it," said Vice President Al Gore, who was talking about information highways long before they were fashionable. "This is by all odds the most important and lucrative marketplace of the 21st century." Former Apple Computer chairman John Sculley estimated that the revenue generated by this mega-industry could reach $3.5 trillion worldwide by the year 2001—quite a sum, given that the entire gross national product of the U.S. in 1993 was about $6.4 trillion.

The first deal out of the gate was the alliance of cable, publishing and entertainment giant Time Warner (TIME's parent company) with phone company U S West, one of the seven "Baby Bells" spun off by court order from AT&T in 1984. In a deal that surprised Wall Street, still accustomed to cable-TV operators and telephone companies behaving like jealous rivals, the two companies announced a strategic alliance in which U S West would supply technological savvy (and an infusion of cash) in return for 25.51% worth of Time Warner Entertainment, a subsidiary of Time Warner that includes the film and TV properties of Warner Bros., HBO and Lorimar, but not the parent company's music and publishing operations.

The matchup between cable and telephone was so compelling because each had something the other needed. The TV operators had extensive networks of coaxial cable with enough information-carrying capacity to broadcast hundreds of TV channels simultaneously. The phone companies badly needed that cable to replace their narrow copper wires; in return, they offered sophisticated switching and billing systems that the cable companies would have had to build from scratch. Time Warner officials said the deal would reduce the waiting period for information-on-demand services to be rolled out to the company's cable subscribers.

The deal promised to shatter whatever solidarity still remained among the Baby Bells, which had enjoyed a monopoly on local telephone service, billing phone companies in towns and cities in their regions hefty fees for connecting them to customers outside the region. Through its new alliance, U S West would, in theory, be able to provide local phone service to Time Warner cable subscribers outside the Western states, threatening

PARTNERS: AT&T and McCaw Cellular Communications.
PLAYERS: Robert Allen and Craig McCaw.
DEAL: A merger in which AT&T bought McCaw for $12.6 billion in stock and Craig McCaw joined the AT&T board.
PLAN: AT&T gets local, creating new customized services by linking its long-distance grid with McCaw's cellular phone network.

PARTNERS: Bell Atlantic and TCI.
PLAYERS: Raymond Smith and John Malone.
DEAL: Bell Atlantic acquired cable TV leader TCI in a stock transaction valued at $21.4 billion.
PLAN: Add Bell Atlantic's phone switches to TCI's cable networks to hot-wire the electronic superhighway.

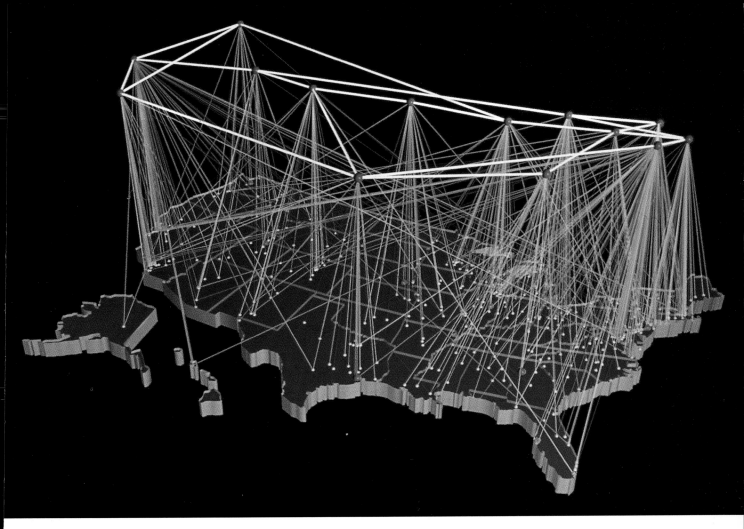

A computer rendering of the Internet, the largest U.S. on-line service and a prototype for the future of communications.

to grab a share of the long-distance connect charges that accounted for a quarter of the Baby Bells' revenues and half their profits. "You can bet every major cable operator is talking to every phone company right now," said a cable-industry insider.

They were, as it turned out. But the next big deal was an incestuous matchup of two giants in the telephone family: in mid-August AT&T agreed to acquire McCaw Cellular Communications. In the fifth largest buyout in U.S. corporate history, the largest U.S. telephone company obtained the No. 1 provider of cellular service for $12.6 billion in stock. In the process, visionary McCaw chief Craig McCaw became a billionaire and his three brothers centimillionaires. Although the merger was praised at the time by consumer groups because it might lead to lower phone rates and innovative products, many analysts accurately predicted that it would bring on even more industry turmoil as it reduced the boundaries sep-

arating long-distance and local telephone service. It would also bring AT&T into close competition with local telephone carriers, including the Baby Bells.

AT&T and McCaw Cellular were expected to strengthen each other's hold on their respective markets. By linking its own computerized telephone grid with McCaw's advanced cellular network, AT&T hoped to develop a broad menu of customized services, including the bundling of telephone handsets, long-distance and cellular service in a single package. Some believed McCaw could turn out to be the Trojan horse that would let AT&T into the rigidly fortified local telephone business, bypassing local networks completely to provide long-distance cellular service directly to customers. That would sharply reduce the access fees it paid local carriers for the right to hook up with them, which totaled $14 billion in 1992 alone.

PARTNERS: Time Warner and U S West.
PLAYERS: Gerald Levin and Richard McCormack.
DEAL: $2.5 billion investment by U S West for "strategic alliance" with Time Warner Entertainment, a subsidiary.
PLAN: U S West's telecommunications savvy meets Time Warner's copyrights, cable connections, HBO and Warner production power.

PARTNERS: Viacom and Paramount (or QVC).
PLAYERS: Sumner Redstone, Marvin Davis (and, unexpectedly, Barry Diller).
DEAL: Viacom hoped to acquire Paramount for $8.2 billion, until QVC intervened with a higher, hostile bid.
PLAN: Link Paramount's copyrights and entertainment holdings to Viacom's MTV and cable network.

"This [AT&T/McCaw buyout] is going to set off another round of deals as everybody scrambles to find a dancing partner," said Peter Huber, a telecommunications consultant in Washington. Even as he spoke, other former rivals were pitching woo. On September 12 Sumner Redstone, 70, the chairman of MTV-owner Viacom Inc., announced that he had engineered an offer to acquire Paramount Communications, the film, publishing and TV powerhouse. The proposed nuptials looked like a marriage made in heaven. But the bride didn't reach the altar. Instead, Barry Diller's QVC home shopping cable channel made a strong counter-offer for Paramount, and the ensuing battle developed into a long-running soap opera that transfixed business-watchers throughout the end of the year. (*See box.*)

Yet, fascinating as the protracted battle for Paramount turned out to be, it was soon dwarfed in size by the announcement of the largest communications deal in U.S. history. On October 13, chairman Raymond W. Smith of Philadelphia-based Bell Atlantic said it would acquire John Malone's TCI, the world's largest operator of cable-television systems, in a stock transaction valued at $21.4 billion. That would make the deal second in size only to the $25 billion purchase of RJR Nabisco by buyout barons Kohlberg Kravis Roberts in 1988. The new giant would boast 28 million cable and phone customers across the U.S. and combined revenues of more than $16 billion, making Bell Atlantic by far the largest of the seven Baby Bells.

The proposed marriage would face months of scrutiny from Washington regulators, Justice Department attorneys and state and local agencies. The key question: whether it would violate antitrust standards. That issue was not expected to be decided until well into 1994. Meanwhile the business world wondered whether the tough-talking, imperious king of cable, Malone (who was once compared by then Senator Al Gore to Darth Vader), could peacefully coexist with the studious Smith.

Like a tremor that follows a great earthquake, the year ended with a final media marriage, as Southwestern Bell Corporation, another Baby Bell, announced on December 7 that it would form a $4.9 billion joint venture with Cox Cable of Atlanta, the nation's sixth largest operator of cable television systems. As with the year's earlier mergers of former rivals in telephone and cable, the deal was founded on the belief that the information superhighway would usher in a golden age of new technologies and new markets. Only the passage of time would reveal whether the great battle for the electronic frontier was waged in pursuit of vast new treasures, or of fool's gold. ∎

communications brought back memories of the '80s, with its shifting alliances, boardroom intrigue, and cast of swaggering "players." Under the initial deal, Viacom would acquire Paramount for $8.2 billion, paying $69.14 a share in cash and stock, to create a new company to be called Paramount Viacom. The plan was to unite Paramount's film and television studios with Viacom's cable systems and networks. Result: a global giant with annual revenues totaling

SUMNER REDSTONE: The Boston mogul wanted more than his MTV, and Paramount seemed just the ticket.

$6.1 billion, primed to compete with Time Warner, cable monster Tele-Communications Inc. and Rupert Murdoch's News Corp.

Since Sumner Redstone's Viacom would hold 70% of the voting stock of the combined company, the deal would give him majority control of more movies, books and television shows than any other U.S. media mogul. Redstone was a rags-to-riches tycoon from Boston who built his father's drive-in movie firm into National Amusements, Inc., an 800-theater chain. In 1987 he acquired Viacom, which owned the nation's 10th largest cable system, as well as MTV, Nickelodeon and The Movie Channel. But as soon as the new deal was announced, other suitors began circling the Para-

BARRY DILLER: The "Killer" was initially mocked for leaving Fox for an in-home cable shopping service.

mount building. CNN guru Ted Turner, TCI chief John Malone and former Fox TV boss Barry Diller, now the chairman of the home shopping network QVC, were most frequently mentioned as possible raiders.

Sure enough, the next week, it was Diller who struck, topping Viacom's initial offer of $8.2 billion with a staggering $9.5 billion counteroffer. Diller, 51, was a tough, frequently rude, sometimes imperious executive with a legendary temper. A programming genius, he rose from ABC-TV to become chairman of moviemaker Paramount Pictures when he was just 32. But, following battles with Paramount boss Martin Davis, Diller went to work for Rupert Murdoch, masterminding the highly successful start-up of the Fox TV network. He shocked Hollywood in February 1992 by resigning from Fox; in December he took over QVC. The move, it turned out, was intended to give Diller a position from which to exploit the new interactive technology. The Paramount bid was his point of entry— and a tidy piece of revenge aimed at Paramount boss Davis.

With Diller's offer the battle was joined, and a prolonged tug-of-war ensued in which each side enlisted financial partners to increase its bid. Propelled by Diller's move and constant rumors of new suitors, Paramount stock rose sharply. Meanwhile Redstone filed an antitrust suit against QVC, claiming its offer would be "the latest step in a systematic and broad-ranging conspiracy to monopolize the American cable industry" by TCI's Malone, who controlled Liberty Media, one of Diller's principal partners in QVC.

On September 29 Redstone countered Diller's offer by enlisting Blockbuster Entertainment boss H. Wayne Huizenga, the video-rental king, to invest $600 million in Viacom and strengthen the bid. Huizenga (pronounced High-zenga), 55, started in business as a private trash hauler, collecting garbage from 2 a.m. until noon in Pompano Beach, Florida, then showering and changing clothes to spend the rest of the day hunting up new customers. The eventual result: Waste Management, now called WMX Technologies, the world's largest garbage company. Using the same grit, Huizenga parlayed 19 Blockbuster stores into a 3,200 store empire and amassed a personal fortune of some $600 million. With the future of video stores clouded by the coming of interactive TV, he was seeking a stake in the new technology.

Five days later, Redstone landed yet another partner, NYNEX, the Baby Bell for New York and New England, which weighed in with a $1.2 billion cash infusion. Diller responded by adding some $500 million to his war chest from cable company Cox Enterprises. Viacom thereupon raised its offer to $10 billion and gained an advantage over QVC by making its tender offer two days ahead of QVC's $10.1 billion offer.

The battle led the parties to Delaware's Chancery Court. On November 29, Judge Jack Jacobs blocked Paramount's friendly merger, saying that the combination was a sale, not a strategic alliance, and that Paramount must therefore give due consideration to QVC's bid. On December 9 the Delaware Supreme Court upheld the decision. In effect, the ruling placed Paramount on the

WAYNE HUIZENGA: Blockbuster's heavy hitter needed to diversify as pay-per-view threatened video rentals.

auction block. As the year ended, Paramount was still "in play," Redstone's Viacom and Huizenga's Blockbuster seemed headed for a possible merger, "Killer" Diller was scrambling, and most observers were hoping for a speedy end to an initially amusing sparring match that had turned into a grinding slugfest. ∎

Emerging from a brutal decade of lost stature and lost profits, U.S. carmakers were finally on a roll

QUIET, PLEASE. THE NEW GENERATION OF POWer in Detroit is at work.

When Alexander James Trotman was named chairman of the Ford Motor Co. in October, there was no flourish or fanfare, not even a prior announcement. He was handed the keys to one of the largest and most powerful corporate kingdoms on earth in a small, no-frills gathering at the company's plant in Dearborn, Michigan, almost as an afterthought to the introduction of Ford's new Mustang. At General Motors 11 months earlier, affable, unassuming Jack Smith had landed just as unceremoniously in that company's top job. Following the virulent boardroom coup that ousted his predecessor, chairman Robert Stempel, and most of Stempel's top executives, Smith ascended with no ritual at all and settled down to business at the world's largest industrial corporation so quietly that he has seldom been seen or heard from in public since.

At Chrysler, Bob Eaton owed his job to another noisy boardroom battle, this one to persuade Chrys-

ler's miracle worker Lee Iacocca that it was time for him to retire. After the dust settled early last year, Eaton, a 29-year veteran of GM, drove up alone at 7:30 a.m. to Chrysler's factory gates in Highland Park, Michigan, in a new Grand Cherokee sports van, introduced himself to a plant guard and rolled through to work. Since then, Eaton has adopted Chrysler's informal team structure as if it were his own, pushing it along with the enthusiasm of a jolly but bookish college preceptor.

Such a modest and self-effacing style has not always been characteristic of a town that is better known for the flash and brassiness of its bosses, with cuff links the size of silver dollars and stogies the length of private yachts. Although few people outside the industry know their names, the three men who ascended to power at GM, Ford and Chrysler since the beginning of 1992 had been working hard to accomplish what many said Detroit could never do: reinvent the industry and profitably build cars that could stand bumper to bumper with the best the Europeans and Japanese had to offer. After two

■ INDUSTRY

Detroit
Turns the Corner

decades of spectacular management blunders that resulted in job loss on a Homeric scale, their success or failure was a legitimate test of the ability of American manufacturing to compete against the rest of the world.

A revolution in engineering, manufacturing and management had been proceeding in fits and starts since the mid-1980s at all three companies. It was finally starting to work. The evidence was found in a fresh generation of products: Chrysler's white-hot LH sedans and Ram pickups, Ford's Taurus, Explorer and Lincoln Mark VIII, GM's Cadillac STS, the new Chevy Camaro and the Honda- and Toyota-killer Saturn.

For a change, Detroit had a good year in 1993, enjoying it largely at the expense of the once indomitable Japanese competition. The Big Three's sales rose against Japanese automakers for the first time in a decade: U.S. cars posted sales increases of 10.7%, twice those of the Japanese carmakers, and sales in 1994 might break through the 15 million-unit barrier. Fully 76% of Americans said they were more likely to shop for an American car than they were five years earlier, according to a TIME/Yankelovich poll taken in December 1993.

Contrary to all expectations, the U.S. had become one of the world's lowest-cost pro-

ducers of cars, thanks mainly to a decade of ruthless job cuts, large investments in technology and the ever widening gap between dollars and yen. One result: profits were returning. All three companies posted gains for the first time since 1984. All told, GM's Smith estimated, the recovering industry was strong enough to add 1.5%—$20 billion—to the nation's gross domestic product in the last quarter of 1993. "It's been a long time, but you always thought of the U.S. auto industry as the engine of economic recoveries in the 1950s and '60s," said Smith. "I think we could be that kind of locomotive again."

That was an inspiring thought, barely imaginable in the early 1990s, when Detroit was mired in the worst economic crisis in the history of the auto industry. Collectively, the Big Three carmakers share the unholy distinction of having lost more money from 1990 through 1993 in the core North American market than they made there throughout the entire 1980s. By the end of 1993, their losses had reached $51 billion—more than $38 billion at General Motors alone.

GM had been so badly gutted by those losses that its U.S. business in 1992 actually had a negative net worth of $5.7 billion. Chrysler nearly went bankrupt twice: once with great fanfare and publicity in the early 1980s, and once quietly and painfully in the early 1990s. The

The future takes shape in Detroit: GM's luxurious Cadillac Concours, Ford's fresh take on the classic Mustang and Chrysler's affordable Neon.

K cars and minivans (and a government bailout) saved Chrysler the first time, and its new LH line of cars the second. Ford survived the near collapse of its automotive business in the 1980s and saw its market share steadily recover after 1990. But even Ford's financial resources could not protect the No. 2 automaker from a $9.3 billion loss over the past three years.

The critical state of the industry's finances may not have been the worst of its problems. Detroit's real enemy was its past, in an old and dying industrial culture of family intrigues, power struggles and near feudal domains. In the auto industry's narrow view, the Big Three did not lose momentum and market share; the hypercompetitive Japanese carmakers stole them. This form of corporate denial persisted in much of Detroit right through the 1980s. While its management dithered, the market share of the U.S. car industry slid from a pre-eminent 80% in the late '70s to a low of 63% in 1992. The industry continued to find ingenious ways to blame almost anyone else—government regulators, environmental fanatics, unfair trading practices and even fickle customers—for its own failings. Had defects in its products helped drive buyers away? Detroit didn't want to hear about it.

To be sure, the turnaround did not start yesterday. Its roots lay in the extraordinary hard times of the 1980s, which forced U.S. automakers to change. Through remorseless cost cutting, improvements in manufacturing technology and astute plant management, Ford by the late '80s had turned itself into a lean, global competitor with innovations like the aerodynamically styled Taurus family of sedans. GM started Saturn as an experiment to see if America could build a competitive small car. The

fully unionized plant in Spring Hill, Tennessee, which began producing cars in 1990, succeeded in turning out exciting, loaded-with-options vehicles at less-than-shocking sticker prices. In 1993 Saturn sales were up 19%.

None of the industry's other fledgling efforts could match Chrysler's. Under Iacocca, Chrysler jettisoned virtually every shred of its old management system. In its place the company assembled the best young designers, engineers and builders, put them together in platform teams and, heresy of heresies, trusted them to make most of their own decisions in creating the cars. "It's just the way we started building cars at the turn of the century," says Chrysler's chief engineer, Francois Castaing. "Maybe 600 or 750 technical people in small teams in a hangar, building five or six models at a time. You wouldn't believe how happy that makes people."

THE FIRSTBORN OF THE NEW SYSTEM—CHRYSLER Concordes, Dodge Intrepids and Eagle Visions—made their debuts in October 1992. These so-called LH cars, Chrysler's first all-new vehicles in more than a decade, drove the corporation away from its dated, budget-price lines and into the élite automotive company of some of the best nameplates in the world: Ford's Taurus, Toyota's Camry and Honda's Accord. The radical cab-forward design and high quality ratings of the LH cars made them instant hits; 138,723 units were sold through the end of their first model year.

Eaton, 53, Trotman, 60, and Smith, 55, each had spent his entire career within the auto industry. Still, they were unconventional choices for its top jobs. None of them fitted the mold of the clubby headquarters men who had

filled the executive suites before them. Modesty, humor (especially of the self-deflating variety), open discussion, candor and team play suddenly were in. Pomp, protocol, pretension and paperwork were distinctly out.

Ford's Trotman had forged his career by going against the patrician grain at every opportunity. As a product manager at British Ford in the late 1950s, he made his first mark by spurring the development of the Cortina, which became one of the company's most successful product introductions ever. After being formally named Ford's chairman and moving into the paneled corner suite on the 12th executive floor of the company's Dearborn headquarters building known as "the Glass House," Trotman turned to his secretary and asked his first question: "Is there a reason why I should ever have lunch in this building?"

Few in Detroit gave Eaton's succession at Chrysler much chance at all. A career GM man, he had spent his recent years in Europe, well away from the turmoil and strife that had gripped his industry's hometown. Chosen as something of a shotgun compromise in Chrysler's boardroom showdown between Iacocca and president Bob Lutz, Eaton could easily have become the short-term resident that many expected. But he stayed on, and not incidentally, so did Lutz, becoming a team that healed the rift and continued to build on the company's momentum.

No one personified Detroit's revamped culture more engagingly than GM's Jack Smith, who dispensed with nearly all the trappings of solemn power collected by his predecessors, including the corporate dining room. Instead of closeting himself in his corner 14th-floor suite at Detroit headquarters, Smith spent most of his 12- and 14-hour days in his modest office at GM's technical center in Warren, 15 miles away. And he slashed the number of bureaucrats at GM's Pentagonian main office from 13,000 to fewer than 2,000.

The three chief auto executives introduced another major innovation: they began meeting at private dinners once a month, covering mostly trade and political issues (almost anything, in fact, but pricing). Such collegiality would have been unthinkable in the past. The new spirit included meetings with President Clinton, Vice President Gore and other officials of a surprisingly friendly Administration. No other project was more ambitious than the agreement, announced in October, to share with the U.S. government the 10-year, $1 billion costs of developing ultralight, low-pollution vehicles. "The three of us have had more direct contact with this Administration in the past nine months than existed for the past 12 years," said Eaton.

The newly crowned three kings of the American road intended to continue steering Detroit in the right direction. "For guys who love cars," said Glenn Gardner, the engineer who launched Chrysler's first platform team, "there's nothing greater than seeing the first cars come off the line, chunk, chunk, chunk, and be letter-perfect." Gardner blew a little victory kiss in the air. Chunk. ∎

The men behind the revolution. Ford's Alex Trotman, left, gave free reign to a skunk-works operation that produced the new Mustang. GM's Jack Smith, center, brought "creativity teams" to the largest automaker. Chrysler's Bob Eaton, right, arrived without fanfare, deputies or attitude.

Baby Jessica: Whose Little Girl?

After a legal battle that dragged on for almost the entire life of 2½-year-old Baby Jessica, the Michigan Supreme Court ruled that Jan and

Baby Jessica says goodbye to the DeBoers and hello to the Schmidts.

Roberta DeBoer, a printer and a homemaker, had no right to keep their adopted daughter. Instead, the DeBoers were ordered to turn her over to her biological parents in Iowa, Dan and Cara Schmidt. Birth mother Cara had signed the infant over to the DeBoers in a private transaction days after her birth; changing her mind a month later, she filed a motion to get the child back. The DeBoers fought to keep Jessica, and two years of courtroom battles followed.

The Michigan court's decision sparked an uproar and challenged notions of adoption, the rights of children and common sense. As one of the most publicized cases concerning the rights of biological versus adoption parents, the saga of Baby Jessica fueled the movement to change the laws favoring biological parents— a point that offered small consolation to the DeBoers and the former Baby Jessica, now renamed Anna Lee Schmidt.

Return of a '60s Fugitive

Alice Metzinger lived a quiet, exemplary life in Oregon as a mother, teacher and restaurant consultant. Except that her name wasn't Alice Metzinger. It was Katherine Ann Power, and for 14 years she had been on the 10-most-wanted list of the FBI. Power was a '60s outlaw, a Brandeis University student who was radicalized by the war in Vietnam. With other student revolutionaries, she plotted a 1970 Brighton, Massachusetts, bank robbery in which police officer Walter Schroeder was killed. She was also accused of having fire-bombed a National Guard armory days before the bank robbery.

Power had escaped and lived for nine years in women's communes before settling in Oregon, but as she became increasingly depressed and haunted by her past, she resolved to turn herself in. On September 15 she surrendered to authorities in Boston, after reuniting with her parents, whom she had not seen for 23 years. She was sentenced to 8 to 12 years in prison and 20 years' probation.

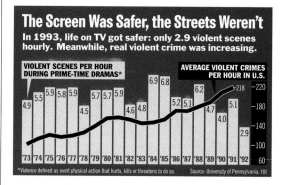

The Screen Was Safer, the Streets Weren't

In 1993, life on TV got safer: only 2.9 violent scenes hourly. Meanwhile, real violent crime was increasing.

VIOLENT SCENES PER HOUR DURING PRIME-TIME DRAMAS*

AVERAGE VIOLENT CRIMES PER HOUR IN U.S.

*Violence defined as overt physical action that hurts, kills or threatens to do so.   Source: University of Pennsylvania, FBI

Turnaround for the Homeless

The bad news: as homeless people continued to haunt the streets of American cities, toleration turned to distrust. The sympathy of the 1980s, which gave way to compassion fatigue by the turn of the decade, was now an open expression of loathing for the homeless. Once romanticized as impoverished casualties of an uncaring

society, America's homeless, who numbered anywhere from 600,000 to 3 million, were more likely to be demonized as pathological predators who spoiled neighborhoods and threatened the commonweal. The good news: cities like San Francisco and Orlando developed innovative programs that produced measurable benefits for both the homeless and their neighbors. And in Los Angeles an action committee with funding from industry built a prototype cluster of prefabricated domes that offered the homeless low-cost shelter from the elements.

"Blunts" were joints in disguise.

The Comeback of Pot
Flashback of the year? Marijuana, having finally shed its '60s image, made a comeback disguised inside a hollowed-out cigar, the Phillies Blunt, whose emblem suddenly was top street fashion everywhere. Rap groups like Cypress Hill openly expressed their love for the weed, and a University of Michigan survey showed that, after a decade of decline, use of both marijuana and LSD was increasing. Heroin was becoming more popular than crack, and the newest drug was gamma hydroxy butyrate, known as GHB, which offered a trancelike state. In December outspoken Surgeon General Joycelyn Elders remarked that legalizing drugs would reduce violent crime and suggested that the consequences of drug legalization should be studied. The White House forcefully repudiated Elders' comments, and G.O.P. lawmakers called for her resignation.

Monkey See, Monkey Do
Hollywood entertainment once again was castigated for encouraging copycat crimes. A five-year-old was alleged to be under the influence of MTV's cartoon adolescents *Beavis and Butt-head*, who liked to play with matches, when he started a fatal blaze in a trailer park. An even more clear-cut case of cause and effect took the life of Michael Shingledecker, 18, of Pennsylvania. Encouraged by a scene from *The Program*, a movie about a daredevil college quarterback, Shingledecker lay down on the double yellow line in the middle of Pennsylvania Route 62—and was hit by a truck.

Scorched, MTV moved Beavis and Butt-head to a later air time.

On Capitol Hill, his death haunted a long-scheduled Commerce Committee hearing on screen violence, where Attorney General Janet Reno threatened entertainment executives with government regulation if they did not enforce stricter standards in their offerings. Though Reno's threat was widely derided as at odds with the First Amendment guarantee of freedom of speech, the Walt Disney Company's Touchstone Pictures announced it was shipping new prints of *The Program* without the offending scene.

These prefabricated domes in L.A. offered an affordable solution to America's homeless problem.

America THE VIOLENT

Clinton and Congress get tough, as mayhem on Main Street turns small-town U.S.A. into Fortress America

PRESIDENT CLINTON COULD NOT HAVE known, of course, that the week in August he picked to talk about crime would be the week that crime was what everyone was talking about. On Tuesday, there was the man in fatigues who shot up a McDonald's in Kenosha, Wisconsin. The same day in Kansas City, Missouri, a 15-year-old went to the movies with his mother—and shot her as they watched the film. "I don't know why I did it," he said. On that Thursday in Burlingame, California, a man walked into a real estate office, shot one broker and wounded another before trying to kill himself. He had just been evicted from his home. And then Friday brought yet more troubling news: police announced that they had identified the body of James Jordan, father of superjock Michael Jordan, shot to death and floating in a creek in South Carolina. That was the kind of crime people would be talking about for a long time.

It was a fitting week, then, for Clinton to stand in the Rose Garden, ringed by a police contingent of rigid men and women in blue, and declare his support for a major crime bill based on the premise that "the first duty of any government is to try to keep its citizens safe, but clearly too many Americans are not safe today." Both the mood of the country and the climate of his presidency called for the flashing of a sword.

Bingeing on a diet of local news stories that graphically depicted crime invading once safe ports—schools, restaurants, courtrooms, homes, libraries—Americans came to regard the summer of 1993 as a season in hell. An epidemic of shooting sprees in malls fostered the perception that almost no place was safe anymore. Fear led to a boom in the security industry and the transformation of homes and public places into fortresses. "People are worried more. They're worried sick," said Amital Etzioni, a sociologist at George Washington University. "There is a new level of fright, one that is both overdone and realistic at the same time."

A TIME/CNN poll taken in the summer revealed the extent of the nation's concern. Of those surveyed, 61% claimed the amount of crime in their community had increased in the previous five years; only 5% said it had decreased. Thirty per cent thought that suburban crime was at least as serious as urban crime—double the number who said that was true five years before. FBI statistics tally with those perceptions, showing two different trends in crime rates: occurrences of violence in cities and towns with populations under 1 million were nudging upwards, while such incidents were declining in the densest urban enclaves.

The broadening of targets to include suburban and rural preserves—and the savageness of the crimes that filled the news—left far more Americans feeling vulnerable. "The fear is getting worse because there is no pattern to the crime," said James Marquart, a criminal-justice professor at Sam Houston State University. "It is random, spontaneous and episodic." According to the National Victim Center, victim-advocacy groups multiplied nearly eightfold from 1985 to 1993.

While experts agreed that the rash of too-close-to-home crimes had deepened Americans' anxiety, they disagreed on what had touched off the violence. Some

believed that crime waves are cyclical. Many faulted Hollywood, which rushes sordid re-creations to TV and cinema screens before the corpses are even cold. "We have created a culture that increasingly accepts and glamourizes violence," said Dewey Cornell, a clinical psychologist at the University of Virginia. "I don't care what the network executives say. It does desensitize you." Others pointed accusingly at the news media. "Every crackpot out there knows that if he can take an automatic weapon into a fast-food restaurant, the more people he can shoot, the more attention he's going to get," said Houston homicide sergeant Billy Belk. "So it encourages these weirdos."

Many experts dug deeper, but the roots they pulled up were a tangled mess of societal ills. "We have a whole generation of kids suffering from neglect," said sociologist Stephen Klineberg of Houston's Rice University. "There is no one at home when they return from school, and this neglect in socialization results in increased violence." Others cited neglect's twin evil, child abuse, or that distant relative, school truancy. Liberals decried poverty; conservatives faulted the decline of family values.

As the experts argued, many Americans were taking safety matters into their own hands. "When people are besieged with new reports of crime every day, the perception grows that, by golly, maybe the cops are ineffective," said crime expert Marquart. "It reinforces the perception of the criminal-justice system not working, and the next thing you know, people are mobilizing to protect themselves."

In the past five years security precautions have increased at hospitals, schools, shopping malls, offices, court-houses and even libraries. And for good reason. Within the past year, librarians have been killed behind their desks in Sacramento, California, and Buckeye, Arizona. Incidents of violence against health-care workers have increased 400% since 1982, said Ira A. Lipman, chairman of the National Council on Crime and Delinquency and head of Guardsmark, Inc., the nation's fifth-largest security company. "Companies are very concerned because one incident in a shopping mall can destroy business."

Across the U.S., companies that offer security devices reported booming sales in both low-tech paraphernalia (Mace, burglar bars, door alarms) and high-tech apparatus (video doorbells, motion-detection devices). Drivers fearful of carjackings bought cellular phones. In 1992 an estimated 16% of all U.S. homes installed electronic systems. Video surveillance was becoming more popular. Steve Gribbon of the Alert Centre Protective Services, a Colorado-based security company with 200,000 customers in 48 states, noted: "Five or six years ago, only estates in the $700,000-to-$1 million range used them. We're now seeing them in $200,000 homes." Many were also thinking of gun ownership. Says Anthony Potter, a private security counsel in Atlanta: "I know a lot of people who five years ago would not have thought about asking me about guns. Now they're asking me what kind they should buy."

From coast to coast, people were sealing off their homes and neighborhoods with iron gates, razor-ribbon wire and iron spikes. The home of Billy Davis in Pico Rivera, southeast of Los Angeles, offered a glimpse of the paranoia that was fast turning homes into fortresses. His two-story frame house was outfitted with motion-sensitive floodlights, video monitors, infrared alarms and a spiked fence topped with razor wire. A metal cage surrounded the patio. Bars adorned every window. A Doberman pinscher guarded the yard; a security guard patroled the driveway. "The wrong people are behind bars," said Anne Seymour of the National Victim Center. "People are putting themselves behind bars because we as a nation have failed to put the right people behind bars."

While such precautions made some people feel safer, others worried about the "Balkanization" of America. "All of this leads to a breakdown of any sense of community," says Camillo José Vergara, who has been photographing the gradual fortressing of urban areas over the past 20 years. "Each family tries to make a living within its own fort and is unconcerned about what goes on outside." Moreover, homegrown solutions often breed new problems. When neighborhoods barricade themselves in, they often cut the access of police, ambulance drivers and fire fighters. When public institutions like courts and libraries erect barriers, the concept of access in a democratic society is threatened.

In the end, gates, gadgetry and gizmos might not be enough. "I don't think you can build gates high enough to eradicate the fear," said Los Angeles city councilwoman Rita Walters. "You've got to eliminate the source of the fear." Until such time, the public arena could become a coliseum of blood sport, where no place is sacred and all sanctuaries suspect. ∎

To Stop the Slaughter

BILL CLINTON'S CRIME BILL, WHICH WAS ANNOUNCED in August, had the distinct ring of traditional Republican law-and-order rhetoric, though it included provisions designed to assuage liberal Democrats. The bill provided for spending $3.4 billion for 50,000 new police officers, a "major down payment," Clinton said, on his campaign promise of 100,000 new cops. Other provisions would send young offenders to military-style boot camps instead of prison, would limit the ability of those convicted of capital crimes to file endless "habeas corpus" appeals, and would expand to 47 the number of crimes subject to the death penalty.

A buyback program in Omaha netted 1,124 guns from local young people.

The President won a victory for a keystone of his plan with the November passage of the Brady Bill, which mandates a five-working-day waiting period for gun buyers while their backgrounds are checked. The measure was approved by the House and passed in the Senate by a voice vote the day before Thanksgiving, after Republican opposition to it collapsed under the weight of public opinion and Democratic attacks. Clinton hailed the bill's passage as "a wonderful Thanksgiving present."

Two weeks later the nation recoiled from yet another violent attack, as gunman Colin Ferguson shot and killed six passengers on a Long Island Rail Road commuter train outside New York City. His weapon: a 9-mm semiautomatic Ruger pistol. Following the attack, the President called for tougher laws and licensing and a ban on assault weapons. But the frightened public had the last word: in the wake of the mass murder and the passage of the Brady Bill, gun sales soared around the country as citizens raced to buy firearms before the new waiting limit took effect.

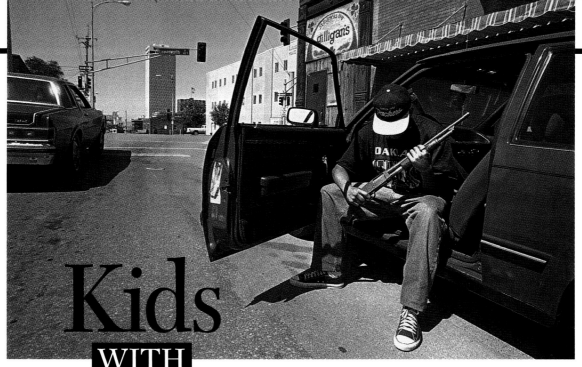

Kids
WITH
GUNS

DOUG WASN'T THAT NERVOUS WHEN HE finally got his gun. Just awfully self-conscious and kind of giddy. In the parking lot of a McDonald's in Omaha, Nebraska, Doug paid $25 for a used semiautomatic 12-gauge shotgun. That night he cut down the barrel, transforming it into the weapon of choice among many teenage toughs: a pistol-grip, sawed-off shotgun. At 16, Doug was finally a force to be reckoned with at Father Flanagan High School in his white, working-class neighborhood. "If you have a gun, you have power," he says. "Guns are just a part of growing up these days."

Doug's case reflects a growing national tragedy: Gunshots now cause 1 of every 4 deaths among American teenagers, according to the National Center for Health Statistics. Bullets killed nearly 4,220 teenagers in 1990, the most recent year for which figures are available, up from 2,500 in 1985. An estimated 100,000 students carry a gun to school, according to the National Education Association.

Not long ago, many Americans dismissed the slaughter as an inner-city problem. But now the crackle of gunfire echoes from the poor, urban neighborhoods to the suburbs of the heartland. Omaha, with a population of 340,000, is just an average Midwestern city, which is why the story of its armed youth shows how treacherous the problem has become. The tidy suburban neighborhood of Benson has been taken by surprise. Three dozen

Gunshots now cause 1 of every 4 deaths among American teenagers

shaken parents and troubled teenagers gathered on a rainy Tuesday night at the Benson Community Center, bracing

Gotta getta gun: Bullets killed more than 4,200 U.S. teens in 1992.

for summer's onslaught and groping for solid ground in a world where a semiautomatic handgun can be the most exciting thing in a boy's life, the 1990s equivalent of a shiny new bicycle. "My son was shot last summer," announces Chris Messick, a mother of three. "They almost shot his head off."

Mike Spencer, a divorced father of two, rises slowly to speak but the tears flow before the words. He stammers, "What in God's name are you kids doing with your lives?" In the corner, seven young men sink lower and lower in their chairs. Joseph Henry, a father of six, stands up. "I've been to four funerals in North Omaha, all kids," he says. "Can't young people get together without slaughtering each other?"

The mayhem has spawned another group, MAD DADS, which stands for Men Against Destruction—Defending Against Drugs and Social Disorder. Members start praying about 10 o'clock every Friday night, just before they hit the streets armed with two-way radios, police scanners, video cameras and a gutsy determination to stop kids from shooting one another. MAD DADS sponsored two gun-buyback programs in the winter of 1992-93, offering up to $50 for a working weapon, with no questions asked. Total haul: 558 guns. In May 1993 they staged another buyback. The take: 1,124 guns, which will be welded into a monument by a local artist. Among them was Doug's shotgun. "I did a lot of crazy things with that gun, and I didn't want to get caught with it," Doug says. He plans on getting a handgun next. ■

Born Gay in the

Two new studies provoke a re-examination of what it means to be gay

ARE SOME PEOPLE BORN GAY, GENETICALLY PRE-determined to grow into homosexual adults? How many American men consider themselves gay? Should gay men and lesbian women be allowed to adopt and raise children? In 1993, as Americans continued to question the role of homosexuals in a free society, the tired terms of the debate were refreshed by new findings from sociology and genetics. A controversial survey of sexual practices claimed that the number of gay men in America may have been drastically overstated, while a team of scientists at the National Cancer Institute claimed to have found evidence that gay tendencies in men were genetic in origin. Through it all, gays continued to demand equal rights for themselves, including the right to be parents.

Gay men loom large in the nation's consciousness, even by American standards of interest-group celebrity. They appear at Roseanne's side on prime-time television, star as superheroes in comic books and even surface on Capitol Hill, where lawmakers fuss over showering habits in military barracks. But in April, as they prepared for the largest march on Washington in six years, gay men became the first put-upon minority in the country to have struggled toward a moment of national definition only to find themselves abruptly redefined: a major national survey shrank their population to a tenth of what it had once been touted to be.

The study, one of the most thorough reports on male sexual behavior ever, found that only 1% of the 3,321 men surveyed said they considered themselves exclusively homosexual. Carried out by researchers at the Battelle Human Affairs Research Centers in Seattle, the survey was designed to study how many men engage in

LOSING NUMBERS?
As gays marched in the capital, scientists questioned their prevalence in the U.S.

the kinds of sexual behavior that put them at greater risk of developing AIDS. But its scientific verdict (men are still having too much unprotected sex) was overwhelmed by a political one. "Bill Clinton and Jesse Helms worry about 10% of the population," said ACT UP co-founder Larry Kramer. "They don't worry about 1%."

In seeking to win political clout and public acceptance, gays and their leaders have long sought refuge in numbers—specifically in the 10% figure for homosexuality that Alfred Kinsey turned up in his 1948 study of human sexuality. Since then, the famous 10% had slipped into treatises and talk shows, and not just because there were few other studies to refute it. It was also good propaganda for gays. "It became part of our vocabulary," says Kramer. "Democracy is all about proving you have the numbers." Some gays refused to give up the statistic. The San Francisco-based magazine *10 Percent*, a national quarterly devoted to gay culture, made it clear that it had no intention of changing its name. Many gay leaders rushed to discredit the 1% figure, pointing out that people are reluctant to discuss their most intimate sexual habits with a clipboard-bearing stranger. Moreover, they claimed, the age period to which the survey was limited—men between 20 and 39—is one in which many adults have still not come to terms with their sexual orientation. And some gay leaders argued that the survey coldly compiled sexual acts without dwelling on the more complex and elusive question of sexual identity.

Recent surveys from France, Britain, Canada, Norway and Denmark all point to total numbers lower than 10% for gays and tend to come out in the 1%-to-4% range. One of the most comprehensive surveys of sex in America ever done will be released in 1994 by University of Chicago researchers. So far, it shows that of the

USA

FINDING GAY GENES?
Participants Rick and Randy Gordon said the study confirmed their belief in a gay destiny.

1,500 men surveyed, only 2% had engaged in sex with another man in the previous 12 months.

The one point of agreement was that both the scientists and the politicians still know very little about Americans' private predilections. Part of the reason so much fiction has persisted is that scientists have not succeeded in securing federal funding to do much research. In the late 1980s, Congress approved two national surveys of sexual behavior, one for adults and the other for teens. But conservatives, led by Senator Jesse Helms and Representative William Dannemeyer, killed the measures. They argued that studies would give homosexuality more standing than it deserved.

What makes people gay? In July scientists brought welcome light to an area too often dominated by searing heat, when they released studies that made the most compelling case yet that homosexual orientation is at least partly genetic. A team at the National Cancer Institute's Laboratory of Biochemistry reported in the journal *Science* that families of 76 gay men included a much higher proportion of homosexual male relatives than are found in the general population. Intriguingly, almost all the disproportion was on the mother's side of the family. That prompted the researchers to look at the chromosomes that determine gender, known as X and Y. Men get an X from their mother and a Y from their father; women get two X's, one from each parent. Inasmuch as the family trees suggested that male homosexuality may be inherited from others, the scientists zeroed in on the X chromosome.

Sure enough, a separate study of the DNA from 40 pairs of homosexual brothers found that 33 pairs shared

119

"Unfit Parents"?

In early September, Judge Buford Parsons Jr. of the Henrico County Circuit Court in Virginia declared that Sharon Bottoms was "an unfit parent" to her two-year old son Tyler. His one reason: she was a lesbian. That judgment, based on Virginia legal precedent and accompanied by the judge's personal reproof, turned Sharon Bottoms and her lover April Wade into national symbols in the growing controversy over whether gays should be allowed to raise children in a family setting.

It is impossible to say how many children have gay parents, in part because there are no solid numbers on gay adults. Moreover, the vast majority of such families live quietly, unobtrusively, far from the evening news. What seems certain is that the number of children who are aware they have gay parents is growing. Children of gays are often born to parents in heterosexual marriages who subsequently come out. That has always been true, except for the coming-out part. Today's gay father or mother is much more apt to be candid than those of a generation ago, so that a much larger percentage of today's children are aware of their parents' orientation. Most of the rest of the children with gay parents are born to lesbians via artificial insemination; estimates of how many such babies have been born range from a thousand or so to tens of thousands. There are only a few hundred documented cases of adoption or foster parenting by open gays. But many prospective parents conceal their orientation, so the actual number is surely larger.

When gay parents do face adoption, custody or visitation battles in court, the outcome is apt to vary from state to state—indeed from judge to judge. New Hampshire and Florida categorically bar gays as adoptive parents. Eight states permit a lesbian to adopt her lover's child and become a second parent. Virginia is one of just four states where legal precedent deems gay parents unfit, but Judge Parsons nonetheless granted Sharon Bottoms a weekly visit, ensuring that she would remain a presence in Tyler's life. ∎

EMPTY NEST
Sharon Bottoms, left, and April Wade: overruled in Virginia.

five different patches of genetic material grouped around a particular area on the X chromosome. Why is that unusual? Because the genes on a son's X chromosome are a highly variable combination of the genes in the mother's two X's, and thus the sequence of genes varies greatly from one brother to another. Statistically, so much overlap between brothers who also share a sexual orientation is unlikely to be just coincidence.

The fact that 33 out of 40 pairs of gay brothers were found to share the same sequences of DNA in a particular part of the chromosome suggest that at least one gene related to homosexuality is located in that region. Homosexuality was the only trait that all 33 pairs shared; the brothers did not all share the same eye color or shoe size or any other obvious characteristics. Nor, according to the study's principal author, Dr. Dan Hamer, were they all identifiably effeminate or, for that matter, all macho. They were diverse except for sexual orientation. Says Hamer: "This is by far the strongest evidence to date that there is a genetic component to sexual orientation. We've identified a portion of the genome associated with it."

The link to mothers may help explain a conundrum: If homosexuality is hereditary, why doesn't the trait gradually disappear, as gays and lesbians are probably less likely than others to have children? The answer suggested by the new research is that genes for male homosexuality can be carried and passed to children by their mothers, while not causing the women themselves to be homosexual. A similar study of lesbians by Hamer's team is taking longer to complete because the existence and chromosomal location of responsible genes is not as obvious as it is in men. But preliminary results from the lesbian study do suggest that female sexual orientation is also genetically influenced.

Whatever its ultimate scientific significance, however, the study's social and political impact is potentially even greater. If homosexuals are deemed to have a foreordained nature, many of the arguments now used to block equal rights would lose force. Opponents of such changes as ending the ban on gays in uniform argue that homosexuality is voluntary behavior, legitimately subject to regulation. Gays counter that they are acting as God or nature—in other words, their genes—intended. Though some gay leaders felt the study might be used to imply that homosexuality is wrong and defective, others agreed with Randy Gordon, who with his twin brother Rick took part in the survey. Said Gordon: "If homosexuality is genetic, there is nothing you can do about it. If there is more research like this in years to come, hopefully homosexuality will be accepted rather than treated as an abnormality." ∎

Sex and the Single Priest

Clerical misconduct, both admitted and alleged, haunts the Church

THE MESSAGE THUNDERED OUT OF THE VATICAN with the force of the Gospel from which it was taken: "For him who gives scandal, it would be better to have a great millstone hung around his neck and to be drowned in the depths of the sea." After years in which its leaders downplayed the sex scandals that have plagued the Roman Catholic Church in the U.S., Pope John Paul II thus publicly acknowledged the enormity of the problem. Indeed, the American bishops, who had long petitioned Rome for special disciplinary powers to deal with the crisis, were deeply aware of its dimensions.

For starters, the hierarchy in June suffered the embarrassment of having to elect a new national secretary to replace Archbishop Robert Sanchez of Santa Fe, who resigned from his see amid revelations that he had conducted affairs with three young women. And Sanchez's resignation was only one of a series of scandals and accusations that troubled the American church in 1993, especially concerning child molestation. In Wisconsin a lengthy investigation commissioned by the Capuchin branch of the Franciscans reported that nine friars stood accused of sexual misconduct at a rural boys' boarding school run by the venerable order. The report disclosed that at least 21 students of the school, St. Lawrence Seminary in Mount Calvary, Wisconsin, said they had been accosted by members of the order. In November, the California Franciscans revealed that sexual abuse had taken place at St. Anthony's Seminary in Santa Barbara for more than 20 years. A yearlong investigation commissioned by the order uncovered proof that at least 34 boys were molested by 11 friars from 1964 to 1987. Prosecutions were not expected, however, since the six-year statute of limitations on sex crimes had run out.

Earlier in the year, New York's John Cardinal O'Connor had summoned all his 1,200 priests to closed-door meetings to discuss how to handle child-molestation cases. The archdiocese faced two civil suits over misdeeds of clerics, and O'Connor warned that "a grenade could explode at any time, and another and another." Before the year was out, just such a grenade rocked Chicago. John Cardinal Bernardin, one of U.S. Catholicism's most influential leaders and a pioneer in efforts to root out sexual abuse by the clergy, was himself accused of having molested a teenager in the mid-1970s. The accuser, now a 34-year-old man who said he began recalling the incident after therapy, filed a $10 million lawsuit against Bernardin and the church. The Cardinal immediately denied the charges and referred the matter to a church review board, but the questionable allegation drew further unwanted attention to the embarrassing problem.

After Archbishop Sanchez resigned from his see, parishioners were asked to contribute to his defense.

The scandals forced the American clergy—and, ever so reluctantly, the Vatican—to reexamine the nature and traditions of the priesthood. For some advocates of change, the key to reform was dropping the 870-year-old tradition of priestly celibacy. In June the National Office of Black Catholics, a Washington-based advocacy group, issued a plea to the Pope to make celibacy optional, thus helping to alleviate the shortage of priests and discourage further scandals.

The Pope remained committed to a celibate clergy. He urged the American bishops "not to lose heart," but they faced suits for many millions of dollars filed by victims who felt that the church did not act as quickly as it should have in the face of its errant clergymen. As for the sinners among the ranks who gave scandal, many church officials felt that they should not be denied forgiveness. The men, women and children who suffered from their transgressions, however, believed that any forgiveness must be preceded by some healing penance—on the part of the church as well as the transgressors. ■

Turning a Page on The Past

When Sears dropped its famous catalog, it closed the books on an era of innocence and optimism

1918 HOUSE KIT, $1,465 WITH FREE BUILDING PLANS

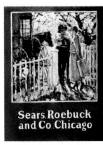

1925 SPRING AND SUMMER CATALOG

IT WAS AN ANNUAL AND UNFAILINGly upbeat report on the American horn of plenty. All this *stuff* for sale, more in heaven and earth than was dreamed of in even the maddest consumer's philosophy: buggy whips and barbering aids, covered wagons and canaries, tires and trousseaux, Mickey Mouse beanbag chairs and models of B-17s, countless doodads that seemed unnecessary until they popped up on the page. From the Sears catalog, known affectionately as the "big book," customers could order everything necessary to equip a house: furniture, appliances, rugs, cooking and eating utensils and paint. Between 1908 and 1937, they could also order the house itself. All told, Sears sold 100,000 prefabricated models, and most of them are still standing and occupied today.

Some of the items advertised in the early years seem, well, unseemly now. Before the Food and Drugs Act of 1906, the catalog listed a number of dubious medicinal aids, including laudanum, a notoriously addictive, opium-based headache remedy and sedative. Pistols and rifles were aggressively marketed for years. The big book luxuriated in excess. Who had ever thought of buying a car by mail? The 1910 catalog offered an automobile called a motor buggy—manufactured by Sears—for $395.

By current standards, the big book ranked low in user-friendliness. For more than 80 of its 97 years, it did not offer home-delivery service. People who wanted to buy something listed could mail in their order but then had to journey to a place populous enough to sustain a Sears

1927 BASEBALL GLOVES, $1.15-$3.39

store or catalog center to pick it up. No use making a call; the big book, after all, was born when customers had no telephones. Only in 1988 did 800-number operators start standing by, ready to take orders day and night. And such updated procedures, for all their added charms to the busy users, robbed the catalog of a certain *gravitas*. At its bulky, clunky, inconvenient best, the big book was both a commercial bonanza for its parent company and a moral force in American life. While it filled countless heads with new sorts of cravings, it officially lectured against impulse buying and it always took care to promote the educational benefits of travel.

Sears' announcement early in the year that its 1993 catalog, all 1,556 pages of it, would be the last probably didn't mean much to couch potatoes cradling their Touch-Tone phones while watching the Home Shopping Network on cable. But for most people over a certain age—say 35, maybe 40—the news was slightly unnerving. Even those who hadn't seen the big book since their childhood recognized a loss, not neces-

1993 24-LAMP TANNING BED, $2,999.99

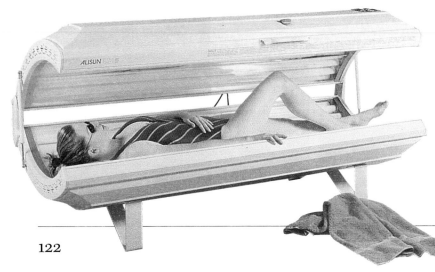

sarily of a shopping aid but of an innocence and optimism and simplicity of desire that the catalog both thrived on and fed.

For willing buyers were not the only ones stirred by the yearly arrival of the book. Founder Richard Warren Sears' best marketing insight was to aim the catalog at rural America, where, throughout much of the 19th century, roughly 70% of the people lived. Never mind being unable to window-shop like their city cousins; many of these potential customers were looking for a place to buy inexpensive windows.

1897 LAUDANUM (OPIUM), 40-OZ. BOTTLE, 29¢

So the big book regularly found its way into pockets of isolation—geographic or social—where it provided a view of the world beyond the village green, the town intersection, the empty horizon. Its reach and destinations made it an early form of mass entertainment, unencumbered by competition of any sort. It was thus a book of revelations. So *this* is what people who work in offices are wearing. *That* is what an up-to-date kitchen is supposed to contain. And *this* is what ladies look like in their underwear. It mattered little that the line-drawn lingerie ads stressed upholstery rather than allure. They were the closest thing to printed erotica that many households ever saw; they taught boys—and girls too, for that matter— a little about what adulthood had in store.

1944 MODEL OF B-17 BOEING FLYING FORTRESS, 43¢

The catalog appealed directly to people eager for genteel refinements— bathtubs, butter knives—but wary of sophistication. The big book once ran verse about itself on its cover. Typically, the commission had gone to Edgar A. Guest, America's most easily understood poet. Guest began, "I know the markets of the earth and wondrous

1931 ULTRASMART SILHOUETTE FOUNDATION, $2.98

tales I tell/ Of all the new and pretty things the whole world has to sell." The Sears catalog was not the place to go in search of the avant-garde.

This resolute, unswerving squareness constituted the big book's greatest charm and its lasting value as a record of middle-class American life. The Sears catalog assumed, correctly for nearly a century, that there were millions and millions of people out there who all wanted roughly the same sort of things, who all aspired to lead similar kinds of lives. Such conformism has received a thorough drubbing from writers and intellectuals, but the Sears catalog and the masses who used it provided a core, a cohesiveness to a new, developing, expanding society. The values it espoused were material, to be sure. An important side

1897 DOUBLE-ACTION POLICE REVOLVER, $1.68

effect was stability: roots planted, fence posts dug in, major appliances bought, were heavy investments in the present and future.

The catalog may have been undone by economics, but changing tastes played a role as well. Hardly anyone admits to being a rube anymore. The United States is well on its way to becoming a nation of hipsters, looking for designer labels rather than inexpensive, durable goods. The American marketplace has splintered into specialty shops and glossy mini-catalogs hawking their wares. The *faux* outdoorsy types consult L.L. Bean; those interested in bedroom costumes turn to Victoria's Secret. The big book's children finally devoured their parent.

Still, as serials go, it had a terrific run: nearly a century. The catalog was never long on plot. But it was generous, even munificent, in its details. ∎

1953 SILVERTONE ALL-NEW 21" TV, $339.95

Big Mouths

Radio's reigning ravers dominate the dial—but are **Howard Stern** and **Rush Limbaugh** secretly dittoheads in denial?

ONE IS A FAT, BALDISH, OLD-fashioned middle American guy with a delivery like Robert Preston in *The Music Man*, a conservative ideologue who has never owned a pair of jeans, gorges on $250 meals of caviar and steak, revels in drinking "adult beverages" and gets embarrassed when a friend makes a bawdy crack about a female reporter interviewing him. The other is a skinny, 6-ft. 5-in. longhair who wears jeans, dark glasses and five earrings, a teetotaler who eats no red meat and whose radio shows inevitably include stretches of Butt-head, uncensored sex raps. One is a cracker-barrel commentator descended from the Great Gildersleeve, Paul Harvey and Ronald Reagan, whose often arch, sometimes tiresome rants about "commie libs" have the propulsive fluency of parliamentary debate; the other, a radio vérité comedian who is an odd fin-de-siècle hybrid of Joe Pyne, Woody Allen and Lenny Bruce, whose rambles about himself, show business and the world in general are at once appalling and exhilarating. They seem antithetical generational caricatures—even though the commentator, Rush Limbaugh, 42, is a baby boomer only three years older than the foul-mouthed comic, Howard Stern.

At first glance—and to hear both the Limbaugh camp and Stern tell it—they are utterly dissimilar. "He hates to be compared to Stern," says Limbaugh's TV producer, Roger Ailes. "Stern is a pure entertainer. Rush was invited to have dinner with Anthony Kennedy and Margaret Thatcher last month." Says Stern: "My biggest fear is being lumped in [with Limbaugh]."

Limbaugh is a more or less conventional pundit whose agenda is the standard public agenda: government programs vs. free-market solutions, self-reliance vs. entitlements. He has real influence—"the power," says Clinton White House consultant Paul Begala, "to put something like Zoë Baird on the radar screen." Stern doesn't seek power or influence, and doesn't have any. He is smart and often sensible but intellectually lazy. He will never appear on a Washington round-table program, but his wildly, unwholesomely eclectic agenda is actually very much like that of an average Joe who doesn't tidily segregate his thoughts on sex from his thoughts on health-care reform, and who doesn't see politics as the primary vehicle for his hopes and fears.

Sure, one's a prurient, free-associating rocker manqué and one's a tub-thumping right-winger, but how much more illuminating to see Limbaugh and Stern as flip sides of a single brassy, very American coin. They are not just analogous but kindred phenomena, each man rising on adjacent zeitgeist updrafts. "They're both ambassadors in the culture of resentment," says *Newsday* media critic Paul Colford. Their core audience is drawn from the broad American middle class: small-businessmen, taxi drivers, working stiffs who unapologetically enjoy action movies, who feel besieged by (and may secretly enjoy feeling besieged by) the nuttier extremes of political correctness.

These days, in fact, America can pretty much be divided in two: on one side are Rush's people and Howard's people, and on the other the decorous and civilized who tend to be uncomfortable with strong broadcast opinion unless it comes from Bill Moyers, Bill Buckley or, if pressed, Andy Rooney. The Rush and Howard people—who, like their avatars, have more in common than they know—seem to be winning, or certainly proliferating.

The array of forces can be reckoned roughly. Limbaugh now claims 20 million listeners on radio, of whom, his TV producer Roger Ailes figures, two-thirds largely agree with his ideological conservatism—the "dittoheads," as Limbaugh calls his fans. More than 3 million dittoheads bought his first book in 1993, and his second, *See, I Told You So*, had a first printing of 2 million, the largest in U.S. history. On his syndicated TV show, which is broadcast mainly late at night, he draws a bigger audience than Conan O'Brien or Arsenio Hall.

As for Stern, somewhere between 4 million (according to the rating company Arbitron) and 16 million (according to Stern) listen to him on the radio, where, like Limbaugh, he broadcasts live for several hours every weekday. Two weeks after Stern's book *Private Parts* came out, there were 1 million copies in bookstores. His interview show on cable's E! is often the highest-rated program on that (smallish) entertainment-news channel.

Limbaugh and Stern are popular because their audiences consider them uniquely honest, commonsensical, funny and a bit reckless (more than a bit in Stern's case) at a time when most people on radio and TV seem phony, impersonal, dull, dissembling, hedging. Both are irreverent, acute, bombastic, iconoclastic, and outland-

ishly populist rabble-rousers. They are national ids, gleeful and unfettered. Howard is Rush's evil twin, Goofus to his Gallant.

Yet both Limbaugh and Stern are closer to the rough center, and closer to each other, than almost anyone customarily imagines. They were both born on Jan. 12, Limbaugh in Cape Girardeau, Missouri, Stern on Long Island, New York. Limbaugh's father owned a piece of a local radio station where Rush III got his start, and Stern's father was a Manhattan radio engineer. Limbaugh tried strenuously to please his father, and, according to his brother David, "echoes of my dad reverberate through everything my brother says." Stern says his father continually screamed that he was a "moron." Neither dated much in high school. Both work very conscientiously and don't pursue hobbies or very active social lives. Both are shy and charming in real life. On the air, Limbaugh half-jokingly boasts he is "the epitome of morality and virtue" and Stern half-jokingly calls himself "King of All Media."

Both complain about being misrepresented. Both sometimes make ugly cracks about blacks, and both could be considered pigs, happily unenlightened. "I love the women's movement," Limbaugh has written, "especially when I'm walking behind it." Both interlard their radio talk with bits of hard rock. Each believes, with some justice, that he is being made a special target by the Federal Government. Limbaugh says he feels persecuted by Democratic Congressmen who want to re-establish broadcasting's Fairness Doctrine in order to pressure TV and radio stations to cancel his shows. And the FCC is going after Stern vigorously, during the past year fining Stern's employer $1.1 million for his unremitting vulgarity.

Stern is at heart a deeply perverse jester, and looks and sounds like the pedal-to-the-metal performance artist one expects. His unedited riffing can often be, as charged, disgusting: his jokes several years ago about his wife's miscarriage were inexcusable, his now defunct TV show's low-rent T&A spectacle a depressing glimpse into a New Jersey heart of darkness. Limbaugh the humorist, on the other hand, is a curious new species. "The political turf of satirists has almost always been left," ABC News analyst Jeff Greenfield says. "It's one thing to attack liberals. But to be laughing at them—that's when

Limbaugh on Stern:
❝I do not want the government fining stations … [but] I didn't say what he's doing is right or good.❞

Stern on Limbaugh:
❝He heard my show and figured out what to do. Rush owes me a lot. I feed that big fat head of his.❞

some people get crazy." Limbaugh calls the grandly elegant Secretary of the Treasury "Lord Bentsen."

Stern graduated with good grades from prestigious Boston University; Limbaugh dropped out of Southeast Missouri State after a year and had a nondescript disk-jockey and p.r. career, getting fired from five jobs during his 20s and 30s. Howard met his wife in college in 1974, married her four years later and proudly says he has been faithful to her. Alison Stern, the very picture of the cheerful, wholesome middle-American housewife, raises their three daughters, ages 9 months to 10 years, at the family home in a conservative well-to-do Long Island suburb. Limbaugh has been married twice, the first time for 18 months, the second time to a Kansas City Royals usherette; he is childless and lives alone in a small apartment on Manhattan's ultra-liberal Upper West Side.

Which is not to suggest that Limbaugh's ideological sincerity and coherence are anything less than total. He plainly believes what he says and mostly argues his cases lucidly, particularly by radio standards. He harps on liberal straw men in a way that seems more properly circa-1973 ("long-haired, maggot-infested, dope-smoking peace pansies"), and his logic can be unforgivably specious (against the pro-choice argument for abortion: "Can a woman choose to steal, using her own body?"). But in fact his views on abortion are relatively nuanced. Nor is it kooky or even wrong to assert, as Limbaugh has, that increased school expenditures don't necessarily produce better education, that means testing for Social Security would be a fine idea, that taking responsibility for one's own life is all-important.

Limbaugh and Stern exist in parallel universes, but in symbiosis. Stern was successfully raising the threshold of provocative radio performance for years before Limbaugh came along. And certainly Limbaugh's unbudging commitment to free speech helps make Stern possible. "Stern and Limbaugh make radio a more interactive, more vibrant medium," says Everette Dennis of Columbia University, the executive director of the Freedom Forum Media Studies Center. "It's the triumph of the individual." Love 'em or hate 'em—and there's no middle ground—radio's reigning ravers make the circus-cum-marketplace of ideas quirkier, livelier, more bracing, more free, more American. ∎

Barbara Ehrenreich

Won't Somebody Do Something Silly?

MORE THAN ONCE IN THE PAST COUPLE OF years we seemed to be on the verge of a major new trend, the theme of which was angels. People were snapping up angel pins and wearing them on their shoulders, where normally the chip is carried. Soon there would be a rage for choir music, angel food cake and Marshmallow Fluff. Huge feathery wings would sprout from trench coats and parkas. But alas, even with a boost from a TIME cover story, angels sputtered and stalled and never quite got off the ground.

Possibly related is the failure of the great altruism trend to appear on schedule. As predicted by Arthur Schlesinger Jr. and other seers, the '80s were supposed to be followed by something closely resembling the '60s: concern for the underdog, lower standards of personal hygiene, giving all for the cause. Perhaps it just seemed too overwhelming—considering that to balance the greed of the '80s, commuters would have had to strip the very coats from their backs and donate them to unwashed vagrants, along with the keys to their country homes. So the altruism trend, along with the angels, remains a gleam in a trend watcher's eye.

Once America was the great exporter of trends—not just fads, like multiple earrings and cholesterol anxiety, but whole new life-styles involving characteristic garments and substances of choice. In 1967, for example, the first hippies were detected in San Francisco, and within a year the historic fountains of Europe were crowded with pot-smoking young people clad only in feathers. In 1984 America produced the first yuppies, who have since moved on to infest London and Frankfurt. Why, the very concept of life-style is an American invention, implying that there is more than one choice.

But there hasn't been a serious life-style trend since the couch potato was sighted, in about 1986, on one of its rare forays to the video store. Cocooning remains a significant mass enterprise, encouraged by the availability of 500 new cable channels and microwavable popcorn. But if you want an outdoor trend, one that demands emulation and is inspired by zest rather than a fear of human interaction and bizarre weather events, then there is nothing at all. The only trend worth mentioning is trendlessness.

This is hard on journalists, who are trained to spot trendlets in their infancy and hype them into vast cultural sea changes. A TIME cover story in 1991, for instance, announced a "new simplicity" trend involving antimaterialism and wood-burning stoves—and then the new simplicity turned out to be only the old recession. Or there was CBS News's pitiful attempt to claim alternative healing as a newsworthy trend. Healing with crystals and chamomile may have been trendy and exciting in 1974. Today, among the 37 million uninsured, chamomile has long since replaced penicillin.

All right, there have been a number of certifiable trendlets in recent years, but most were too sickly and feeble to grow. Menopause mania proved to be a flash, so to speak, in the pan, and "smart drugs" couldn't compete with the far more numerous dumb ones. As a result, we've been forced to import trends like karaoke or revive fossil trends like troll dolls, which first showed their wizened little rubber faces 30-odd years ago. Even our gossip has to be imported, since we lack homegrown equivalents of the topless, toe-sucking, dysfunctional royals.

Perhaps we should welcome the posttrend era. We no longer rush off, herdlike, to become Jesus freaks or Valley Girls at the first hint from the national media. It takes maturity to see a fetching new image—say, Madonna in gold tooth and riding crop—without thinking, "Hey, wow, that could be me!"

But there's something sad too about the decline of the American trend industry. Trend setting requires innovation, ebullience and a level of defiant frivolity such as has not been seen in these parts for years. Maybe we've had too many Presidents with programs distilled from focus groups. Or perhaps cocooning was by its nature the ultimate and final trend, after which no more are biologically possible: like the dodo snuggling into its nest, we have found our evolutionary niche, which turns out to be the couch in the den.

Patriotism demands at least one more world-shaking, American-made trend. Surely the nation that invented goldfish swallowing and the leisure suit is not willing to exit the millennium watching reruns on Nick at Nite. Arise, ye pallid twentysomethings, and do something deeply silly! ■

Science

A Super Hole in the Ground

The project was 20% complete. The government had already spent $2 billion, and 45,000 contracts worth $850 million had been drawn up in 48 states. Already 15,000 workers were on the job. The goal: to create the most powerful tool ever designed to study the nature of matter, the superconducting supercollider. Then, in late October, the House of Representatives canceled the project by a vote of 282 to 143. The result was a superfluous, 14.7-mile-long supertunnel that had been laboriously excavated under the Texas prairie. Its value: zilch.

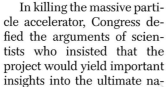

Gene maps: Eureka!

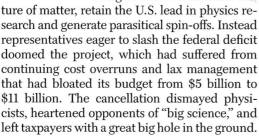

For sale: a big tunnel.

In killing the massive particle accelerator, Congress defied the arguments of scientists who insisted that the project would yield important insights into the ultimate nature of matter, retain the U.S. lead in physics research and generate parasitical spin-offs. Instead representatives eager to slash the federal deficit doomed the project, which had suffered from continuing cost overruns and lax management that had bloated its budget from $5 billion to $11 billion. The cancellation dismayed physicists, heartened opponents of "big science," and left taxpayers with a great big hole in the ground.

The Great Gene Hunt

1993 was an extraordinarily productive year for the genetic engineers racing to unravel the secrets of human DNA. Scientists pinpointed genes linked to more than half a dozen major ailments, including Lou Gehrig's disease, Huntington's disease, colon cancer, hyperactivity and a type of diabetes. American and French teams also sketched out the first rough map of the entire human genome, all the information contained on the 23 pairs of human chromosomes. Other researchers explored ways to use this information to replace damaged genes. The first beneficiaries of "gene therapy," two Ohio girls who had an immune-deficiency disease, made their public debut after three years of successful treatment. More than 50 similar experiments were under way as the year ended.

Hot Spot at Princeton

For four seconds or so on December 9, the hottest spot in the solar system by a sizable margin was in Plainsboro, New Jersey, where scientists at the Princeton Plasma Physics Laboratory successfully ignited the largest-ever nuclear-fusion reaction, generating more than 3 million watts of energy from the superheated gas inside the doughnut-shaped Tokamak Fusion Test Reactor. Yet, though the achievement was a milestone, the $1.6 billion machine produced only one-eighth as much power as it consumed. The next day the reactor raised its output to 5 million watts, and scientists hailed the results as an important step toward the eventual harnessing of fusion energy, which promises someday to provide a safe, clean power source that uses fuels extracted from ordinary water.

WRONG STUFF

❝It's not a failure. What we're doing is just delaying another success.❞

—ASTRONAUT FRANK CULBERTSON JR., COMMANDER OF THE SHUTTLE *DISCOVERY*, ON ITS FOURTH LAUNCH DELAY

Fermat Solved! (Maybe)

Fermat's Theorem, the puzzler that stumped the world's greatest mathematical minds for more than 350

years, was finally solved by a Briton, Andrew Wiles of Princeton—or was it? Fermat's theorem states that the equation $x^n + y^n = z^n$ has a positive,

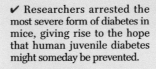

whole number solution only if the exponent n is 2. In the familiar formula for finding the hypotenuse of a right triangle, for example, $3^2 + 4^2$ equals 5^2. But if the exponent is an integer (non-fraction) greater than 2, there is no combination of x, y and z that

Wiles, all smiles. But did he have the answer to Fermat?

will work. In 1637 Pierre de Fermat, the French mathematician, maintained he had found a "marvelous proof" of the theorem, but didn't have room to write it in the margin of his notebook; hence the search. Wiles rocked the math world when he announced his solution in a lecture at Cambridge University in England in June, but by the end of the year a flaw had been found. Wiles claimed he could resolve it.

The Puzzle of the Maya

A series of dramatic discoveries, including four lost cities in the jungles of southern Belize, shed new light on the ancient civilization of the Maya. The cities were uncovered in rough terrain that experts assumed the Maya would have shunned. Two of the sites had never been looted, promising to provide researchers with a wealth of clues to the still largely unsolved puzzle of who the Maya were, and why their civilization, which flourished in Central America between the years 250 and 900 A.D., suddenly collapsed. The Maya perfected the most complex writing system in the hemi-

The Mayan pyramid at Chichén Itzá is aligned to the solar equinox.

sphere, mastered mathematics, and built massive pyramids all over central America. New theories suggest that uncontrolled warfare, water shortages and overpopulation led to the demise of the ancient culture.

No Rest for the Whales

Cries of "Save the whales" once again resounded around the globe as Norway announced it would defy the International Whaling Commission and resume hunting. With Oslo's approval, Norwegian vessels hauled in 160 whales for commercial sale, generating an uproar of protest. Norway insisted it would continue the policy; Iceland, which quit the IWC last year over the issue, said it would resume whaling in 1994, and Japan lobbied the IWC to allow limited whaling. The three nations supported the ban on hunting some larger species, like the blue, sperm and right whales and claimed their hunting of smaller minke whales would not threaten that plentiful species.

Norway and Japan sharpen harpoons.

CLONING:
Where Do We Draw The Line?

Researchers duplicate a human embryo, provoking cries that technology has gone too far

WHEN IT HAPPENED—AFTER years of ethical hand wringing and science-fiction fantasy—it was done in such a low-key way by researchers so quiet and self-effacing that the world nearly missed it. The landmark experiment was reported by research scientist Dr. Jerry Hall at a meeting of the American Fertility Society in Montreal in October. Afterward, colleagues came up to congratulate Hall and say "nice job." Others voted to give his paper, written with his supervisor, Dr. Robert Stillman, the conference's first prize. But nobody seemed to want to pursue the one fact that made his little experiment—in which he started with 17 microscopic embryos and multiplied them like the Bible's loaves and fishes into 48—different from anything that had preceded it. Hall flew back to George Washington University, where he is director of the in-vitro lab and where Stillman heads the entire in-vitro fertilization program, reassured that people would view his work as a modest scientific advance that might someday prove useful for treating infertility.

How wrong he was. When the story broke two weeks later—on the front page of the New York *Times* under the headline SCIENTIST CLONES HUMAN EMBRYOS, AND CREATES AN ETHICAL CHALLENGE—everybody focused on the one thing that the scientists seemed willing to overlook: the cells Hall had manipulated came not from plants or pigs or rabbits or cows, as in the past, but from human beings.

Once it was out, the news that human embryos had been cloned flew around the world. That afternoon the switchboard at George Washington logged 250 calls from the press. By the next day more calls and faxes were flooding in. French President François Mitterrand pronounced himself "horrified." The Vatican's *L'Osservatore Romano* warned in a front-page editorial that such procedures could lead humanity down "a tunnel of madness."

It was the start of the fiercest scientific debate about medical ethics since the birth of the first test-tube baby 15 years ago. A line had been crossed. A taboo broken. A Brave New World of cookie-cutter humans, baked and bred to order, seemed, if not just around the corner, then just over the horizon. Ethicists called up nightmare visions of baby farming, of clones cannibalized for spare parts. Critics decried the commercialization of fertility technology, and protesters took to the streets, calling for an immediate ban on human-embryo cloning. Scientists steeled themselves against a backlash they feared would obstruct a promising field of research and close off options to the infertile couples whom the original experiment had intended to serve.

The experiment at the center of the controversy seems, in many ways, unworthy of the hoopla. It is not the *Jurassic Park*–type cloning most people think of, in which genetic material from a mature individual—or DNA from an extinct dinosaur—is nurtured and grown into a living replica of the original. This is far beyond the reach of today's science. There is a vast difference between cloning an embryo that is made up of immature, undifferentiated cells, as the George Washington researchers did, and cloning adult cells that have already committed themselves to becoming skin or bone or blood. In the new procedure, the cells were just copied with their genes intact, a process that agricultur-

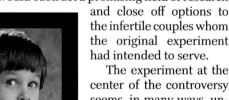

Do you think human cloning should be completely legal?

Completely legal	3%
Legal but regulated	46%
Illegal	46%

From a telephone poll of 500 adult Americans taken for TIME/CNN on Oct. 28 by Yankelovich Partners Inc. Sampling error is ±4.5%.

Do you think human cloning is morally wrong?

Yes	58%
No	31%

Do you think it is against God's will?

Yes	63%
No	26%

al researchers have used to clone embryos from cattle and pigs for more than a decade.

What brought the research into the human arena was the rapidly developing field of in-vitro fertilization. In clinics popping up around the world, couples who have trouble conceiving can have their sperm and eggs mixed in a Petri dish and the resulting embryos transferred to the mother's womb. The process is distressingly hit-or-miss, though, and the odds of a successful pregnancy go up with the number of embryos used.

A woman with only one embryo has about a 10% to 20% chance of getting pregnant through in-vitro fertilization. If that embryo could be cloned and turned into three or four, the chances of a successful pregnancy would increase significantly. This is the reason Hall and Stillman began experimenting with cloning. But they were not trying, in their initial effort, to produce clones that would actually be implanted in their mothers and later born. The scientists said they just wanted to take the first step toward determining if cloning is as feasible in humans as it is in cattle. Working in George Washington's in-vitro fertilization clinic, they selected embryos that were abnormal because they came from eggs that had been fertilized by more than one sperm; these flawed embryos were destined for an early death whether or not they were implanted. Thus Hall and Stillman saw nothing unethical about experimenting with them, and they got permission to do so from the university.

When one of the single-celled embryos divided

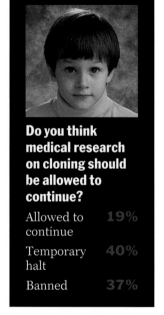

Do you think medical research on cloning should be allowed to continue?

Allowed to continue	19%
Temporary halt	40%
Banned	37%

into two cells, the first step in development, the scientists quickly separated the cells, creating two different embryos with the same genetic information. (This sometimes happens naturally inside a mother, and the result is identical twins.) In the process, though, the researchers had to strip away an outer coating, called the zona pellucida, without which an embryo cannot develop. Over the years, Hall had been working with a gel derived from seaweed that could serve as a substitute for the zona pellucida. In the trickiest part of the development, Hall then put the artificial coating around the cloned embryos—and they began to grow and develop. The experiment was a success.

The scientists replicated their procedure many times, producing 48 clones in all. That was the entire experiment. None of the clones grew for more than six days. The scientists had no intention of starting an embryo factory, selling babies or doing anything else that

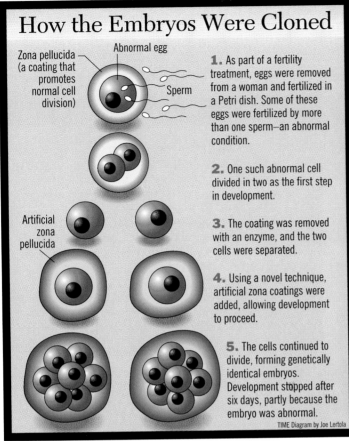

How the Embryos Were Cloned

Zona pellucida (a coating that promotes normal cell division)

Abnormal egg

Sperm

Artificial zona pellucida

1. As part of a fertility treatment, eggs were removed from a woman and fertilized in a Petri dish. Some of these eggs were fertilized by more than one sperm—an abnormal condition.

2. One such abnormal cell divided in two as the first step in development.

3. The coating was removed with an enzyme, and the two cells were separated.

4. Using a novel technique, artificial zona coatings were added, allowing development to proceed.

5. The cells continued to divide, forming genetically identical embryos. Development stopped after six days, partly because the embryo was abnormal.

TIME Diagram by Joe Lertola

of producing clones for spare parts, called it "a modern form of slavery."

Hall and Stillman were totally taken aback by the furor they had created. "I revere human life," said Hall, his voice choking with emotion. "But we have not created human life or destroyed human life in this experiment." To Hall and Stillman, human cloning is simply the next step in the logical progression that started with in-vitro fertilization and is driven by a desire to relieve human suffering—in this case, the suffering of infertile couples. That is certainly the least controversial of the technology's potential applications. In a TIME/CNN poll whose results are shown in this story, Americans were evenly split on whether they approved or disapproved of cloning for this purpose.

More than 25 countries have commissions that set policy on reproductive technology. Should the U.S. adopt similar restrictions? That may be difficult at this point. There is no federal funding for embryo research; experiments are financed largely by private money, much of it derived from the booming business of in-vitro fertilization. Making matters even more complicated, there is no federal body charged with setting artificial-fertilization policy in the U.S. Instead, policy is set by a patchwork of state laws, professional societies and local review boards, like the one at George Washington that gave the go-ahead to Hall and Stillman.

Having set the terms of the debate—which focused not on what had actually happened but on the frightening scenarios that could arise sometime in the future—the ethicists clearly carried the day. Hall and Stillman retreated to the last refuge of the research scientist. "We have set out to provide some basic information," said an exasperated Hall on *Larry King Live.* "It's up to the ethicists and the medical community, with input from the general public, to decide what kind of guidelines will lead us."

But that stance may not be adequate in the years to come, as genetic engineering and cloning begin to converge. It is becoming increasingly apparent to the researchers exploring these frontiers that they have to become ethicists as well as scientists. Technology tends to develop a momentum of its own. The time to discuss whether it is right or wrong is before it has been put to use, not after. ∎

ethicists worry about. The experiment was first described to the world, however, not by the scientists but by medical ethicists led by Arthur Caplan, director of the Center for Bioethics at the University of Minnesota. As soon as Caplan heard the news from the American Fertility Society meeting, he phoned Gina Kolata, a reporter at the New York *Times,* who broke the story.

As a result, Caplan helped shape the discussion that followed. For example, although Hall's technique cannot produce more than two or three clones of any embryo, several stories written about his experiment included the scenario, put forward by Caplan and other ethicists, in which an infertility clinic offers prospective parents a catalog filled with children's photographs. Below each picture is a report on the child's academic and social achievement. Couples could choose a picture, receive a frozen embryo, and then raise that child—not a sibling or near relative, but an exact genetic duplicate.

"This is the dawn of the eugenics era," declared Jeremy Rifkin, founder of the Foundation on Economic Trends, a biotechnology-watchdog group in Washington. Painting a dark picture of "standardized human beings produced in whatever quantity you want, in an assembly-line procedure," Rifkin organized protests outside George Washington University and other reproductive-research institutions. The reaction from around the world was even more heated. In Germany, Professor Hans-Bernhard Wuermeling, a medical ethicist at the University of Erlangen, repelled by the notion

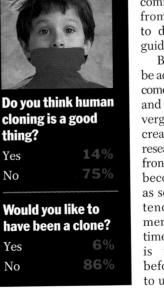

Do you think human cloning is a good thing?

Yes 14%

No 75%

Would you like to have been a clone?

Yes 6%

No 86%

■ SPACE

NASA Clears Its Image

The beleaguered agency saves the Hubble. But can it save itself?

AS THE EARLY DECEMBER LAUNCH DATE LOOMED for the Hubble Space Telescope repair mission, NASA's veteran spin controllers did their best to lower public expectations. The seven astronauts who would ride into orbit aboard *Endeavour* faced the toughest assignment ever handed to a shuttle crew and the most complicated mission since the moon shots of two decades earlier. Their mandate was to sharpen the telescope's marred eyesight, the result of an improperly manufactured mirror, by fitting the instrument with corrective lenses. They were also to revamp some faulty electronic systems, put in new gyroscopes and replace two unstable solar-energy panels. Getting the job done would require wrestling huge pieces of machinery into tight spaces, disconnecting and connecting fragile electronic equipment and making sure no loose screws damaged the delicate telescope—all while wearing puffy pressure suits and bulky gloves in a vacuum at zero gravity and at -300° F. In theory, NASA said, the crew could complete this orbital overhaul in five

six-hour space walks; in practice, there would almost certainly be a few major flubs.

As it turned out, the spin cycle was unnecessary. *Endeavour's* exquisitely trained crew breezed through every job on their work order and even managed to make their tasks look like fun. "Piece of cake!" shouted Kathryn Thornton, perched atop the shuttle's 50-foot robot arm as she sent a mangled solar-energy panel off into space.

Although the final verdict on the repair job would not be rendered until January 1994, after many weeks of tests, NASA and the crew were confident and euphoric. The spacefarers had done more than salvage a telescope: they had also created a kind of time warp. For a few days, America was back in the 1960s, an era when space was a grand frontier to be tamed, and when NASA's technical brilliance and right-stuff bravado made the agency seem virtually unstoppable.

In recent years the space agency's reputation had plummeted. Ever since the *Challenger* blew up less than two minutes after lift-off in January 1986, killing all seven astronauts aboard, the agency had seemed lost in space. More often than not, shuttle launches had been delayed by glitches. Satellites had mysteriously stopped transmitting while in orbit. Space probes had broken down en route to Jupiter and Mars. Along with the setbacks came a crisis in the spirit of space adventure—a loss of vision and will to probe the unknown.

The Hubble repair mission proved that astronauts could handle construction and repair work in orbit, the skills essential to NASA's plan to build and operate a space station by the end of the decade. Yet space extravaganzas no longer seemed enough to keep the public and Congress behind the space program. The questions that haunted NASA before the Hubble mission would not go away. Why did the U.S. need a space program? And should NASA, with its badly checkered history, be in charge?

While NASA was once an aggressive, creative engineering shop, it had grown into a bloated bureaucracy. A White House committee appointed by President Clinton to investigate NASA's projected space station concluded its work in June by recommending that both the station and NASA itself be redesigned.

The revamping fell to NASA Administrator Daniel Goldin, the ex-chief of the space division at TRW and one of only two Bush appointees to survive the change of presidential administrations. Realizing that NASA could justify itself only if it became more cost-effective and relevant to the economic needs of society, Goldin trimmed its annual expenditures, slashed the number of U.S. managers and laid plans to reduce shuttle operating costs. He also reconfigured the space station project by inviting Russia to join the program, which also included Japan, Canada, Italy and the European Space Agency. On the eve of *Endeavour's* launch, Goldin claimed, "You can't make progress unless you take risks." In fixing the Hubble, NASA took the risk and got the job done. ■

Meet *Mononychus*, a new link between dinosaurs and birds.

A COOL AND MISTY DAWN, CIRCA 78 MILLION B.C. A LONE TRIceratops interrupts a leisurely meal of ferns and twigs to glance around uneasily. Though the 11-ton creature is an intellectual lightweight, it senses danger lurking in the surrounding forest. Suddenly, out from behind a tree lumbers one of the largest and fiercest carnivores that have ever lived: *Tyrannosaurus rex.* Although this beast is a mere adolescent, it is 15 ft. tall and armed with dagger-sharp teeth. The cold-blooded triceratops attempts a retreat, but it can only move slowly. It is too soon after sunrise, and the triceratops hasn't had time to absorb the heat it needs to rouse its sluggish metabolism. The T. rex has the same cold-blooded problem, but its longer legs enable it to catch the docile, plant-eating triceratops. And then . . .

Wait! Time out! There is something wrong with this picture. Nearly everything, in fact. Two decades ago, paleontologists might have signed off on such a scenario, but not today. An avalanche of new evidence—from fossilized bones and even footprints—has completely transformed scientific thinking about dinosaurs. *Triceratops* and other herbivores were not necessarily dull witted, nor did they wander around alone; they probably traveled in vast herds and went on annual migrations. Predators, too, were social. All but the oldest and biggest tyrannosaurs traveled in packs like prowling wolves. Dinosaurs probably were not cold-blooded either. They could move along briskly, even in cool weather; some lived above the Arctic Circle, where the sun never rises in winter. Even the idea that all the dinosaurs died out 65 million years ago is now passé. Many experts believe that one resilient line is still flourishing today. The common name for these modern dinosaurs: birds. Observes Mark Norell, a paleontologist at the American Museum of Natural History in New York City: "Birds are more closely related to *Tyrannosaurus rex* than

New Visions Of DINOSAURS

T. rex is to almost any dinosaur you've ever heard of."

This rewriting of conventional wisdom has accelerated in the past 10 years. New fossil beds have been found and old ones rediscovered in the Gobi Desert, along the ancient Silk Road in China, on the margin of the Andes and in the jungles of Laos and Thailand. Despite the remarkably small number of scientists working in the field—only about 100 worldwide—a new dinosaur species is found on average every seven weeks. One of the latest: a new species from Mongolia, announced in April by Norell and several U.S. and Mongolian scientists. Known as *Mononychus* (meaning one claw), the turkey-size animal looked like a modern, flightless bird, complete with feathers, but had bone structures char-

acteristic of both birds and dinosaurs. Its discovery cements the bird-dinosaur link even more firmly.

Thanks largely to the explosion of information, dinosaurs are more popular than ever. In light of the new insights, museums around the world are rearranging the old stilted skeletons on display into new dynamic poses and adding robotic dinos and interactive computer games. Dinosaur theme parks are booming, while toy stores overflow with dinosaur puzzles and models, not to mention the omnipresent videosaurus Barney. Early in June, dino-mania reached fever pitch with the premiere of Steven Spielberg's movie version of the Michael Crichton thriller *Jurassic Park*.

Yet despite all the hoopla and the significant recent

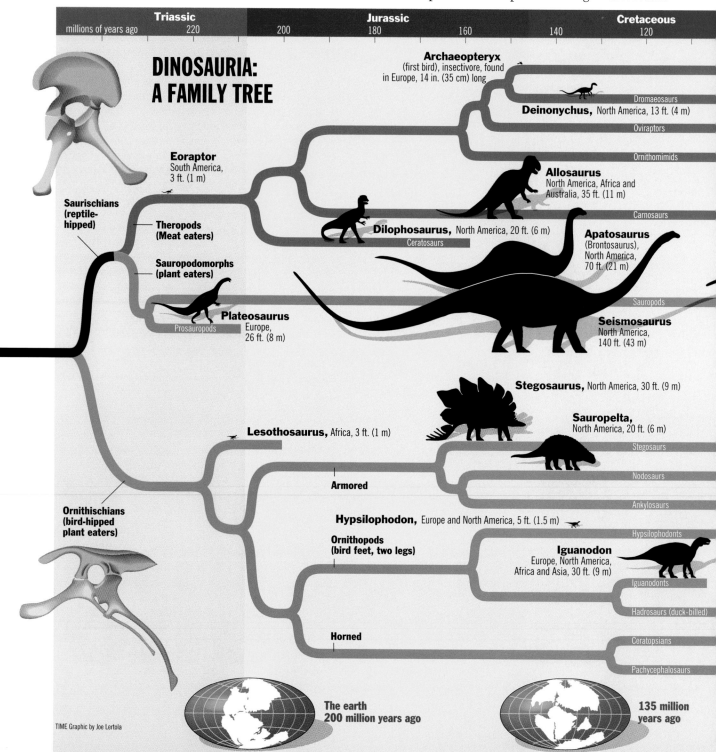

DINOSAURIA: A FAMILY TREE

| Triassic | | Jurassic | | | Cretaceous | |

millions of years ago | 220 | 200 | 180 | 160 | 140 | 120

Archaeopteryx (first bird), insectivore, found in Europe, 14 in. (35 cm) long

Dromaeosaurs

Deinonychus, North America, 13 ft. (4 m)

Oviraptors

Ornithomimids

Eoraptor South America, 3 ft. (1 m)

Allosaurus North America, Africa and Australia, 35 ft. (11 m)

Carnosaurs

Saurischians (reptile-hipped)

Theropods (Meat eaters)

Dilophosaurus, North America, 20 ft. (6 m)

Ceratosaurs

Apatosaurus (Brontosaurus), North America, 70 ft. (21 m)

Sauropodomorphs (plant eaters)

Plateosaurus Europe, 26 ft. (8 m)

Prosauropods

Sauropods

Seismosaurus North America, 140 ft. (43 m)

Stegosaurus, North America, 30 ft. (9 m)

Sauropelta, North America, 20 ft. (6 m)

Stegosaurs

Lesothosaurus, Africa, 3 ft. (1 m)

Armored

Nodosaurs

Ankylosaurs

Hypsilophodon, Europe and North America, 5 ft. (1.5 m)

Hypsilophodonts

Ornithopods (bird feet, two legs)

Iguanodon Europe, North America, Africa and Asia, 30 ft. (9 m)

Ornithischians (bird-hipped plant eaters)

Iguanodonts

Hadrosaurs (duck-billed)

Horned

Ceratopsians

Pachycephalosaurs

The earth 200 million years ago

135 million years ago

TIME Graphic by Joe Lertola

finds, the information about dinosaurs remains spotty. "We probably don't even know 1% of all the species," admits Jack Horner, curator of paleontology at the Museum of the Rockies in Bozeman, Montana. Even so, scientists have made tremendous progress in understanding how dinosaurs lived and behaved.

Were dinosaurs warm-blooded creatures? The assumption that dinosaurs were ectothermic—cold-blooded—was originally based on a simple argument. Reptiles are ectothermic—they can't regulate their body heat. If they get too hot, they die. If they get too cold, they get sluggish. Dinosaurs were closely related to reptiles. End of argument.

As early as the 1950s, though, some researchers claimed that the rich blood supplies within dinosaurs' bones, as evidenced by the channels left behind in fossils, were more like those of fast-growing (and warm-blooded, or endothermic) birds and mammals than like those of reptiles. Maybe dinosaurs were warm-blooded after all.

There are no maybes about it as far as Robert Bakker is concerned. Long-haired, bearded and strongly opinionated, freelance paleontologist Bakker has been the bad boy of the field for years, and does not suffer fools gladly. "There are still a few of my colleagues who think, 'If it walks like a duck, breathes like a duck and grows like a duck, it must be a turtle.'"

The fact that dinosaurs were warm-blooded should be obvious, says Bakker, because they had chest cavities large enough to hold huge hearts, like birds. Additional evidence is found in their migratory patterns. "There's no question that dinosaurs got as far north and as far south as there was land," says Bakker. "The ones you find in the far north are the same ones you find in the south, so they could live in a wide range of climates. Also, I don't see any way dinosaurs could have survived up there unless they migrated, and migration takes energy. They would have to have been warm-blooded."

Scientists now recognize that there are, in fact, five or six different kinds of warm- and cold-bloodedness, and that they are sometimes hard to distinguish, even in living animals. Moreover, making generalizations about the relationship between an animal's activity level and its metabolism can be misleading. "We tend to think that cold-blooded animals are sluggish, but that's not very accurate," says Yale paleontologist John Ostrom. "Some snakes, lizards and crocodiles can move faster than humans. At the same time, we tend to think that warm-blooded animals are very active, but the average house cat spends a lot of time snoozing."

The current consensus is that dinosaurs were not strictly cold-blooded, but fell short of being full-fledged endotherms, or hot-blooded creatures. "The problem," notes Michael Brett-Surman of the Smithsonian Institution, "is that there is no such thing as 'the dinosaur.' There were seven groups living 150 million years ago that started out as one thing and perhaps evolved into something else." Although *Velociraptor* and other small, meat-eating bipeds may have been warm-blooded, Brett-Surman believes that large predators like *T. rex*, which went through three vastly different growth stages, may have had a variable metabolism.

THIS YEAR'S MODEL
Business is booming at a Canadian factory that creates new dinosaur models for museums.

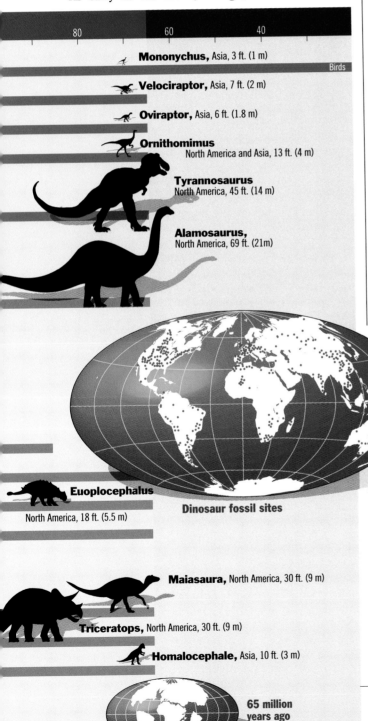

80　60　40

Mononychus, Asia, 3 ft. (1 m)

Birds

Velociraptor, Asia, 7 ft. (2 m)

Oviraptor, Asia, 6 ft. (1.8 m)

Ornithomimus
North America and Asia, 13 ft. (4 m)

Tyrannosaurus
North America, 45 ft. (14 m)

Alamosaurus,
North America, 69 ft. (21m)

Dinosaur fossil sites

Euoplocephalus
North America, 18 ft. (5.5 m)

Maiasaura, North America, 30 ft. (9 m)

Triceratops, North America, 30 ft. (9 m)

Homalocephale, Asia, 10 ft. (3 m)

65 million years ago

137

ON THE FRONTIER

Paleontologist Martin Lockley inspects fossilized tracks by Colorado's Purgatoire River.

A 7-ft.-tall juvenile *T. rex*, he speculates, was probably very active, capable of scampering like a ground-bird. By contrast, mid-size dinosaurs, averaging 12 ft. to 15 ft. in height, were probably somewhat less agile and may have traveled in packs. A full-grown, 40-ft.-long, eight-ton tyrannosaur must have slowed down even more, and may even have reverted to a solitary life-style.

Were dinosaurs social creatures? One argument that supports this idea is based on the vast trackways that have been uncovered in both North America and Asia. Hundreds of sauropods—*Apatosaurus* and its kin— would evidently travel in herds across the late Jurassic landscape, leaving footprints as they went; similar trackways have been discovered for *Triceratops* and *Maiasaura*. The tracks of the theropods, the aggressive predatory group that includes *T. rex*, are often found in multiple sets, a strong clue that they traveled, and presumably hunted, in packs.

Footprints can tell scientists more than that, though. Their depth and spacing also give testimony about dinosaurs' size, weight and speed. All the evidence suggests that dinosaurs in general were strong and efficient walkers, capable of maintaining a brisk pace. Theropods, in particular, observes paleontologist James Farlow of Indiana University–Purdue University at Fort Wayne, had a walking pace of 3 to 6 m.p.h. and a top running speed of between 22 and 25 m.p.h. "That's not as fast as an ostrich or a good racehorse," he says, "but it's faster than anything a human can do."

Were dinosaurs like birds? The notion that dinosaurs and birds are related dates back over a century. In 1861, quarry workers near Solnhofen, Germany, uncovered the fossil of a pigeon-size creature. Its bone structure and teeth were similar to those of dinosaurs. Yet along with the bones, the 150 million-year-old limestone in which it was trapped had also preserved the unmistakable impressions of feathers and wings. It was ultimately decided that *Archaeopteryx*, as it was named, was a transitional animal, related to dinosaurs but well along the evolutionary pathway to modern birds.

As happens so often in paleontology, though, the story has become much more muddled. The confusion began in 1964 with the discovery of a 13-ft.-long theropod called *Deinonychus* that was remarkably similar to *Archaeopteryx*, perhaps 50 million years more recent, but lacked wings and feathers. Apparently, the evolution from theropod to bird took many turns and detours.

Now comes *Mononychus*, one of the fruits of the first Western expeditions into the Mongolian Gobi in 60 years. "Central Asia probably has the greatest dinosaur-yielding potential of any area in the world," says Michael Novacek, dean of science at the American Museum of Natural History, who went to the Gobi in 1990 and has returned every year since. "There are areas the size of Montana that haven't even been prospected. You could spend a whole lifetime there."

Mononychus may be the discovery of a lifetime. The small predator, with its mouthful of sharp teeth and long tail, looked quite similar to the theropods. Even so, says paleontologist Mark Norell, it shares a number of features with modern birds. "In *Archaeopteryx*, for example," he explains, "the fibula (the thin bone in the leg) touches the ankle. In birds that doesn't happen, and the same is true of *Mononychus*. Birds have a keeled sternum (or breastbone), where the flight muscles attach. *Mononychus* also had a keeled sternum." Some of *Mononychus*' wristbones were fused together, which is another hallmark of adaptation for flight, suggesting that *Mononychus* may have evolved from a flying animal, just as ostriches and emus are descended from flying birds. That being the case, it was probably covered with feathers.

Some researchers are skeptical, of course, about how *Mononychus* is labeled and about the larger question of how dinosaurs are related to birds. But since scientists cannot really decide for sure whether *Mononychus* should be considered a primitive flightless bird or a dinosaur, it seems plausible that there is really no essential distinction: it was both. ∎

Who's Afraid of the Big Bad Bang?

SCIENTISTS, IT SEEMS, ARE BECOMING THE NEW villains of Western society. Once portrayed as heroes, they now appear in movies betraying Sigourney Weaver to bring home an alien for "the Company" or ignoring Susan Sarandon's desperate search for a cure for her son. We read about them in the newspapers faking data, and we see them in front of congressional committees defending billion-dollar research budgets. We hear them in sound bites trampling our sensibilities by comparing the Big Bang or some subatomic particle to God.

In 1992 a journalist named Bryan Appleyard rode this discontent to the top of Britain's best-seller lists with a neoconservative polemic called *Understanding the Present*, subtitled *Science and the Soul of Modern Man*. Science, he maintains, devalues questions it can't answer, such as the meaning of life or the existence of God. Its relentless advance has driven the magic out of the world, leaving us with nothing to believe in. With no standards, liberal democracies descend into moral anarchy and cultural relativism. Once Galileo first looked through that telescope, it seems, the Los Angeles riots

were only a matter of time. Science, he concludes ominously, must be "humbled."

Appleyard would lay the woes of the 20th century at Stephen Hawking's wheelchair. Commenting on Hawking's hope that physicists may soon construct a theory that would unite all the forces of nature into one equation suitable for a T shirt, a so-called theory of everything, he declaims that it could predict that "a particular snowflake would fall on a particular blade of grass." Never mind that such deterministic ambitions died long ago with the discovery of quantum uncertainty. Faced with such a bleakly predictable universe, who would not reach for the candles and tarot cards?

Scientists are partly to blame for this mess. They have silently acquiesced in the proposition that if we just keep writing checks and leaving them alone, science could solve the problems of the world. They have promoted the presentation of themselves as antiseptic drones, whose work is uncorrupted by influences like sex, greed or ambition, which muddy life for the rest of us. But science is done by real people who do not check

their humanity at the lab door. Lamentably but humanly, they *do* shoot their mouths off too much about God and the egregiously misnamed theory of everything. Young Turks for the past hundred years have proclaimed the imminent end of physics, but every advance has only opened new vistas of mysteries. There is no reason to think we even know the right questions yet, let alone the ultimate answers. The currency of science is not truth, but doubt.

And, paradoxically, faith. Science is nothing if not a spiritual undertaking. The idea that nature forms some sort of coherent whole, ruled by laws accessible to us, is a faith. The creation and end of the universe are theological notions, not astronomical ones.

We can only wonder whether some law of laws will stand revealed some day at the end of the grudging trial-and-error process of science. The theory of everything, even if it existed, however, could not pretend to tell us what we most want to know. It could not tell us *why* the universe exists—why there is something rather than nothing at all. And it could not tell us if our lives have meaning, if God loves us.

Written on a piece of paper or on a T shirt, the theory of everything would be just decorative trim around the grand mystery of why anything or any law exists. But by reminding us of our deep cosmic ignorance, science, far from dulling the mystery of existence, sharpens it the way garlic wafting on the evening breeze whets your appetite. It reminds us that we dwell in a mystery that is more to be savored than solved.

On God's love science is also silent, and that silence is the wind of liberation. Physicists can neither prove nor disprove that Jesus turned water into wine, only that such a transformation is improbable under the present admittedly provisional physical laws. Quantum theory and tensor equations are part of nature as much as trees and rains and sex are. We are, all of us, including Appleyard, free to make what we want of it. We are free to wake up every morning grateful for the feeling of sunshine on our face or grumpy at the prospect of tomorrow's rain. The fact that science cannot find any purpose to the universe does not mean there is not one. Cosmic ignorance does not diminish us; it ennobles us. ∎

A tower gallery shows Jewish life in a single Lithuanian town.

Never Forget

A fortress against forgetting, the United States Holocaust Museum was formally opened in April. Designed by architect James Freed and built along the edge of the Mall in Washington, the museum employs films, photographs and heartbreaking artifacts to tell the story of all the peoples the Nazis set out to annihilate. Freed's design mirrors the twisted spirit of its subject matter. The roof is a procession of camp watchtowers, the enormous Hall of Witness a sort of evil atrium with steel-braced brick walls reminiscent of crematoria. A staircase narrows unnaturally toward the top, crowding visitors into mobs. An immediate success, the museum drew far more visitors than anticipated.

Opening the Barnes Door

Albert Barnes, one of the greatest American patrons of art, amassed a renowned collection of modern French works in the first decades of the century: 180 Renoirs, 69 Cézannes, 60 Matisses, 44 Picassos, and more.

A difficult, eccentric man, Barnes built a museum to house his works, the Barnes Foundation, outside Philadelphia. Following his death in 1951, control of the museum eventually passed to Lincoln University, a small black institution, and access to it was restricted. But in the '90s a new advisory committee reinvigorated the collection, though not without controversy. Under president Richard Glanton, a lawyer, the foundation mounted a once-only worldwide tour of paintings from the collection, which opened in May at the National Gallery of Art in Washington. Eighty-two masterpieces were made openly available to the public for the first time. Some critics charged the new Barnes leadership with

The Barnes let its Van Goghs go.

betraying the spirit of its founder, but the average art lover rejoiced in the discovery of a rich trove of glorious paintings.

Breakthrough! Hollywood Reads

Turning to the printed page for inspiration, Hollywood produced a clutch of movies with more adult themes. Martin Scorsese adapted Edith Wharton's *The Age of Innocence*; the Merchant/Ivory team scored with a lavish version of

Crichton's big lizards made big-screen bucks.

Kazuo Ishiguro's *The Remains of the Day,* and Steven Spielberg's adaptation of Thomas Keneally's Holocaust novel *Schindler's List* won enthusiastic reviews at the end of the year. Meanwhile, Hollywood turned to thrillers for big-star vehicles: lawyer-novelist John Grisham's *The Firm* and *The Pelican Brief* were both huge hits, and the moderate success of Michael Crichton's *Rising Sun* was dwarfed by the monster grosses for the movie version of his *Jurassic Park,* the No. 1 box-office hit of all time.

Pei's Paris Palace of Art

About their own culture, all Frenchmen are hyperbolists. But in the case of the renovation of the Grand Louvre museum, launched in 1981, they might just have cause to boast. When President François Mitterrand opened the Louvre's newly rebuilt Richelieu wing in November, he greatly expanded the world's most famous museum and, for the first time in history, allowed the Louvre to be dedicated entirely to its extraordinary art collections. The project's hero: architect I.M. Pei, who was accused of æsthetic heresy when in 1989 he unveiled his modernistic glass pyramid in the museum's vast central courtyard.

Though Pei offended some observers this time around by combining museum space with an underground shopping gallery that included fast-food counters and boutiques, his elegant designs carried the day. Providing new windows, enclosing three interior courtyards with glass roofs, mixing natural and electric light, even boosting the number of rest rooms, he transformed Napoleon III's Richelieu wing from a dark and dowdy cavern into a bright, logical showcase for the Louvre's unsurpassed collections.

An Apocalyptic Mess

The Venice Biennale is the world's oldest modern art festival, dating back to 1895. The 1993 edition offered its best works on the periphery: a fine homage to British painter Frances Bacon and some multimedia pieces by filmmaker Peter Greenaway and stage designer Robert Wilson. But the main exhibit,

Death in Venice: the Biennale flopped.

centered in the Italian pavilion, was an incoherent shambles. Of the other national pavilions, the best was the American one, showing sculpture by Louise Bourgeois, now 81 and at the top of her form. The chief heiress of Surrealist obsession in America, her work carries a deep strand of recollection interwoven with sexual fantasy, refracted through strange uses of material. The German pavilion, by political conceptualist Hans Haacke, featured an on-target treatment of Hitler's legacy, but Spain offered a room-size sculpture, featuring an oversize bed frame, wire mesh and chairs by Antoni Tàpies, that was vapid. The Biennale also featured a second main section, called "Aperto 93," offering apocalypic trivia, devoid of æsthetic impulse, that was generally dull, hectoring and politically simpleminded.

The glass-enclosed Marly Courtyard of the refurbished Richelieu wing of the Louvre.

With Schindler's List and Jurassic Park, the year in Hollywood was . . .

THE YEAR OF SPIELBERG

HE WAS
the most popu-
lar filmmaker of all
time. He had directed four of
the top 10 box-office smashes in history. He was the heir to Cecil B. DeMille and
David Lean, the master of sweeping scores, grand colors and grander gestures. He had revived, then ruled,
the cinema of escapism. And yet director Steven Spielberg claimed he "felt liberated for the first time in my
career" in making a gritty, realistic film in black and
white designed to confront the century's most horrible
moment, the Holocaust.

The film, *Schindler's List,* was released in December
and immediately hailed as a masterpiece. Yet, remarkably, it appeared only six months after Spielberg had
dazzled the world with the most successful of all his boy-
ish fantasy films, the science fiction thrill ride *Jurassic
Park.* Crammed with all the director's magic tricks, the
movie about dinosaurs running amuck in a futuristic
theme park was a gigantic international success, topping *E.T.* to become the highest-grossing film in history. In a single year the 46-year-old Spielberg had strung
together an unparalleled two-reeler, first crowning his
achievements as the master of pop
movies, then abandoning the throne
to find fulfillment as a serious artist.

"The movie simply needed my
clout to get made," Spielberg says of
Schindler's List, and he was not being
immodest. Since no filmmaker had a

track record like his, none had his power to encourage both a studio and the young mass audience to take a risk on a movie devoted to an inherently repellent, even terrifying, subject.

At the same time, Spielberg said, "this movie didn't need my strengths as a storyteller, because the story's already been told." Here he was being too modest. It was surely the screen storyteller in him who responded to the compelling narrative strength of Thomas Keneally's novelized life of a German Czech named Oskar Schindler, who came to Poland to make money out of the coun-

try's occupation by the Nazis and stayed to preserve 1,100 Jews, workers in the enamelware factory he established, from the death camps.

Spielberg must have understood that even though Schindler, a hypnotically ambiguous character—he was a drinker, womanizer, black marketeer and con artist— was operating in a charnel house, he was finally that classically empathetic, inspirational figure, the lone individual doing good in a desperately dangerous context. If you could get an audience to accept that context, you could involve them with a man who, though antiheroic in some of his behavior, was in his essence a movie hero of quite a familiar, beloved kind.

And Spielberg, a master of movie technique, must have sensed in this tale elements that would bring out the best in him. He had always liked to work on big, crowded canvases, but he had never challenged his skills with a subject so dense and dark as this one, nev-

er used them with more tact or to better dramatic and emotional effect. There was a kind of morality—a respect for one's tools and materials and for the intelligence of the beholder's eye—in the craftsmanship he deployed. It served the interests of the tale, not the ego of the storyteller. In the annals of Hollywood "clout," this was almost as astonishing as the movie itself.

Or, as Spielberg told the cast, "We're not making a film; we're making a document." Documents are printed in black and white, and so is *Schindler's List*. To Spielberg, these are the colors of reality. They may also be part of an effort to find the cinematic equivalent to the style of Keneally's 1982 novel, which is marvelously understated—the only way to go, really, when your subject is so overwhelming that all but the simplest words are bound to fail it.

Spielberg strove for a similar artlessness with his camera. The film was made on location in Cracow, using the actual factory Schindler operated, even the apartment he once inhabited. The scenes in which the Jews are forced into the ghetto or endure the torments of camp life are shot documentary style, with hand-held cameras. "I didn't want to direct off a Cecil B. DeMille crane," Spielberg says. "I wanted to do more CNN reporting with a camera I could hold in my hand."

To enhance this effect, he eschewed storyboards for only the third time in his 14 films. Instead, in some sequences he filled several streets with hundreds of extras after extensive rehearsal, then sent his cameras and the actors who had lines to speak into the melee, often requiring them to improvise dialogue and bits of business.

The process energized Spielberg, who was finally realizing a dream he had first entertained more than a decade earlier, only to delay while awaiting both the script he wanted (it was provided by Steven Zaillian, writer-director of *Searching for Bobby Fischer*) and the maturity in himself he felt he needed. Onlookers say

143

he never sat down, never retreated to his trailer, and one day made an astonishing 51 setups. Yet always he moved in an aura of "austere calm, a man at peace with himself," in the words of co-producer Gerald Molen. At some point, impeccable professionalism simply merged with obsession.

Ben Kingsley, who plays Itzhak Stern, the Jewish accountant who both cooked the books for Schindler's lifesaving scams and served as guide to his conscience, was astonished at Spielberg's nerve: "I didn't think he would have the courage and the panache and the command to fill an area of five blocks, a big area of action where you are receiving information from what's happening in the foreground, in the midground and also in your peripheral vision." But these are among the greatest sequences of chaos and mass terror ever filmed.

To re-create evil, especially *in situ*, and especially on this scale and at this length (3 hours, 15 minutes), is of course to confront it. And the experience was shattering. As Spielberg walked through his crowds of extras, gesturing people this way and that because he did not speak their language, it suddenly occurred to him that Josef Mengele, the notorious concentration-camp physician, "gestured people to the left or the right. One direction was death; the other was one more day of life. I felt like a Nazi."

And there was no surcease. Leaden skies poured rain and snow almost every day of the company's three-month stay in Poland. "I went in there thinking you separate work from life," says Embeth Davidtz, a member of the cast. "It's the first time that didn't happen." The goofing around that usually leavens the boredom and hardships of difficult movie locations was not available to this company. "The ghosts were on the set every day in their millions," says Kingsley. As Spielberg recalls, "There was no break in the tension. Nobody felt there was any room for levity," and people were always "breaking down or cracking up." This he had anticipated, he says, "but I didn't expect so much sadness every day."

The result of this relentless passion is not perfect. What enterprise of this scope and intensity possibly could be? In concentrating on the range of their suffering, the film loses a certain particularity among the victims. It lacks highly individual characters who would embody and dramatize their plight. Something of Schindler himself has also been lost in the transition to the screen. Keneally conceived him as a man who admired his own cleverness and may have derived the same sardonic pleasure from taking Jews away from the Nazis as he did from taking money away from them in exchange for flawed products. Added to the movie, unfortunately, is a blatantly sentimental concluding scene in which Schindler breaks down hysterically because he might have saved even more people but did not.

Spielberg claimed "no high expectations for the box-office

MAGICIAN AT WORK: For all the frightening reality of its dinosaurs, the guts and gore in Spielberg's summer hit were left mostly to the imagination of the viewer.

potential" of *Schindler's List*. But the long lines outside theaters in major cities during its first weeks in limited release augured more success than he predicted. No reporters captured Spielberg questioning the box-office potential of *Jurassic Park* before *its* release. Still, the magnitude of its worldwide success astonished even an industry that was expecting a blockbuster. The film grossed $850 million, to become the No. 1 box-office hit of all time, handily surpassing the old champ—Spielberg's *E.T.*

Jurassic Park, like every other Spielberg movie before *Schindler's List*, was couture for the masses: a cunning design, elegantly tailored. Spared no expense? Just ask the picture's sponsor, Universal, which had not had a $100 million winner at the domestic box office since 1989 (with the Spielberg-produced *Back to the Future Part II*) and urgently needed a megahit. Hence the marketing tie-in with McDonald's, the imminent *Jurassic Park* ride at Universal's theme parks and the saturation of action figures, jammies and cologne. The director did cut costs with a decent, modest cast of nonstars, and he tried shooting every dialogue scene in no more than five takes. But the expert exertions of the 483 other artists and technicians listed in the credits ensured that *Jurassic Park* would cost about $65 million, or $1 for every year since dinosaurs became extinct.

But moviegoers didn't fork over their ticket money for tie-ins. This was a monster movie, Spielberg style. So how were the monsters? Amazing. Dinosaurs live. You are there, once upon a time, before man walked or woman dreamed. You can pet a triceratops and, if you wish, examine its droppings. You can feed a vegetarian brachiosaur, whose movements are graceful, endearing. At times the beasts (animated, mostly, by the computer sorcerers from Industrial Light & Magic) move in a hazier space than the humans in the foreground, but in the intimate scenes the dinos are utterly convincing. Spielberg loves to mix wonder with horror, and he has fun creating a living Museum of Natural Fantasy.

Then he scares you witless. Here come a nosy tyrannosaur and a fan-faced, bilious dilophosaur. Nastiest of all are the velociraptors, smart, relentless punks in packs—Saurz N the Hood. They have a special appetite for kids, just like the great white shark in the movie that made Spielberg's rep. Now it has some worthy successors: primeval creatures with personality and a lot of bite. *Jurassic Park* is the true *Jaws II*.

With its next-generation effects and its age-old story line, it is a movie whose subject is its process, a movie about all the complexities of fabricating entertainment

"The worst days came when I had to have people take their clothes off and be humiliated. That tore me up the most."
—Steven Spielberg

DOUBLE VISION: After draining days filming scenes of the Holocaust in Cracow, Spielberg spent his nights editing the final cut of *Jurassic Park*.

in the microchip age. It's a movie in love with technology (as Spielberg is), yet afraid of being carried away by it (as he is). The film even has a resident conscience, chaos theoretician Ian Malcolm (Jeff Goldblum), who insists that what God has put asunder, no man should join together.

The director of such beautiful dramas as *Empire of the Sun* and *Always* knows that Malcolm is right; the director of *E.T.* and the Indiana Jones movies knows that he must be ignored. Spielberg needs the dinosaurs to run amuck, as they so handsomely, plausibly do. Yet Malcolm's words are a warning to all directors who, like Spielberg, fall under the spell of the great new toys of filmmaking. "Dennis Muren and the ILM team," Spielberg says, "have perfected the dinosaur. Now what we need are stories. Without them, technology is an orphan. Without a good yarn, it's just a bunch of convincing pictures."

Thanks to Michael Crichton's novel, Spielberg had a good yarn to work with. Thanks to his effects wizards, the pictures of monsters were convincing. Still, it was the director who put the drama into every snazzy frame of *Jurassic Park*, as he would later put the heart into every moving frame of *Schindler's List*. Thanks to his long apprenticeship in the fantasy factories, Spielberg's high craft became higher art when he trained his cameras on a story that, for once, mattered: the Holocaust death factories of a very real sort of monster. ■

Go Ahead, Make My Career

Hollywood on a saturday morning. The world's biggest box-office star is pulling his forest green GMC Typhoon out of a parking lot when four guys with clipboards dash toward him through the traffic. What would Dirty Harry do? Never mind. Clint Eastwood is not Dirty Harry. He stops, signs a few autographs and produces his patented tight-lipped smile as his supplicants bob their heads and murmur profuse thanks.

In real life, Eastwood knows how to play the self-deprecating good guy. Just listen to him explain why they wanted him to sign blank slips of paper rather than personalized greetings to Uncle Cappy in Port Clyde. "It's a business," he says. "They trade them." He pauses, grins, then adds, "You get one Steve McQueen for four of mine."

Not anymore, even though the inventory of McQueen autographs is not going to increase. 1993 was Eastwood's Year of Being Taken Seriously. The Academy of Motion Picture Arts and Sciences honored Eastwood and his dark western, *Unforgiven*, with Oscars for Best Director and Best Picture. His peers behind the camera, the Directors Guild of America, gave Eastwood their Best Director award. That was Eastwood's spring. In the summer he was in familiar territory again: lighting up screens and box offices in the tough thriller *In the Line of Fire*, a blockbuster that grossed more than $100 million. The critics' choice and the people's choice, Eastwood had crossed the divide that separates a constellation from a star and a serious filmmaker from someone who merely makes movies.

The puzzle is, How did people miss the big transition? It's not that Eastwood has been toiling in obscurity, making little jewels about the plight of the sea otter in the Gulf of Alaska. This is a man who has been the biggest draw in movie theaters for more than 20 years. How big? The 21 movies he has made for Warner Bros. since 1971 have had box-office sales of $1.2 billion worldwide.

Nevertheless, Eastwood almost fell into the trap suc-

Once he was The Man with No Name. But Hollywood forgave **Clint Eastwood** his salad days in spaghetti westerns with a pair of Oscars for *Unforgiven*

cessful actors sometimes set for themselves. For the better part of four decades, he created superficial, though memorable, characters. First there was Rowdy Yates, the carefree cowpoke in the television series *Rawhide*. Then came The Man with No Name, an avenging angel wearing spurs in Sergio Leone's spaghetti westerns. After that it was Dirty Harry, the police inspector who cleaned up the streets of San Francisco. Both his fans and his critics seemed to conspire to keep him in character: they continued to see him, for good or ill, as they first saw him, when it was easy to love him or despise him. They didn't want to grant him his complexities.

For a considerable time, Eastwood obliged them. "You have to do what is realistic for you," he said 15 years ago. "You can stretch your machinery, but the audience might not believe you." But in 1980, with the making of *Bronco Billy*, Eastwood began to reach for a richer cinematic legacy. In this Capraesque comedy about a New Jersey shoe salesman turned Wild West-show impresario, no guns are fired in anger. Instead Eastwood began to explore the limits of his often damaged characters in a quieter, more reflective way. Nor were villains dispatched bloodily three years later in *Honkytonk Man*, a melancholy movie about a drunken musician in which Eastwood starred with his son Kyle. "I'd hate to look back on my portfolio someday and think, 'Well, I did 100 *Magnum* films and one car-wreck film,'" he said after *Honkytonk Man* was released. Unfortunately, nobody out there but Eastwood was paying much attention. The film was a bomb.

Not compared with *Bird*, however. This dense but compelling biography of the saxophone player Charlie Parker disappeared without a ripple after its release in 1990. It was Eastwood's most ambitious and uncompromising effort as a director, shot in murky, natural light. If *Bird* established that Eastwood was willing to take chances behind the camera, *White Hunter, Black Heart* proved he was willing to take huge and potentially embarrassing risks as an actor. His portrayal of a film di-

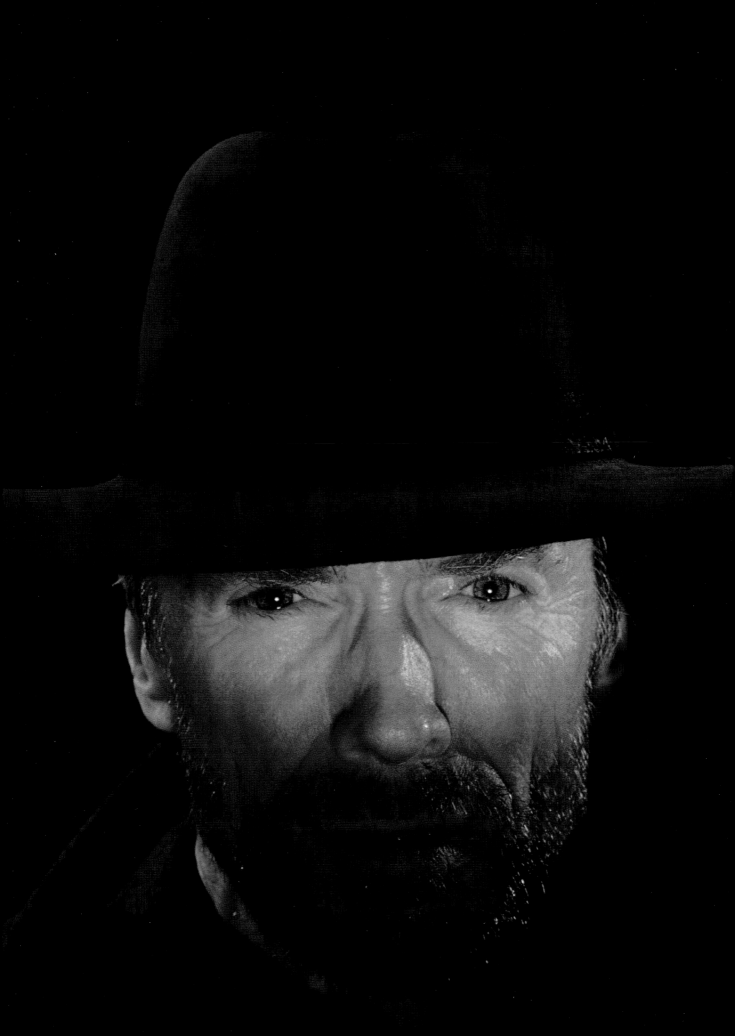

rector modeled on John Huston was as removed from the characters his public had come to expect as Orson Welles is from Donald Duck. Like *Bird*, it was a commercial failure.

Yet each experience taught him more about his craft and prepared him for *Unforgiven*, a lean and provocative anti-western in which the good guys are not so swell and the bad guys are not entirely deserving of their fate. For Eastwood it was something new, garbed in familiar cowboy clothing. Only after the final gunfight does the director allow his alter ego, the actor, to indulge in a brief valedictory to the satiric excess that characterized the Eastwood of an earlier era. "Any son of a bitch who takes a shot at me," gunman William Munny bellows into the night, "I'm not only going to kill him, I'm going to kill his wife, all his friends and burn his damn house down." As Eastwood likes to say, "Just another one of my flawed characters." Moviegoers were impressed enough to make *Unforgiven* the biggest box-office success Eastwood has ever produced.

His willingness and ability to transcend his image help answer some of the questions about the trajectory of his career, among them: How come he isn't Doug McClure, one of those TV-series hunks of the '60s who faded into anonymity? Or merely a Sylvester Stallone, one of those action heroes who have achieved nothing like the longevity Eastwood has? Neither could have, or would have, made a movie like *Unforgiven*. With the intelligent shyness that empowers many great actors, Eastwood embraced the entire craft of filmmaking, wandering the sets and picking up insights even as he was churning out B movies in his early days. "My involvement goes deeper than acting or directing," he once said. "I love every aspect of the creation of motion pictures, and I guess I'm committed to it for life."

He takes the work seriously, but not himself. During the *Unforgiven* shoot, he regaled the crew with his wicked John Wayne impersonation. When Gene Hackman kicked the hell out of him in their first saloon encounter, the script called for Hackman to stride over to the bar and pour a drink. From his position on the floor, where he was miming grievous hurt, Eastwood didn't call, "Cut!" Instead he groaned, "Pour one of those for me."

He is quick to spread the credit for his success to a loyal and veteran production crew. His wardrobe man, Glenn Wright, has been with him since *Rawhide* in the early '60s. Cameraman Jack Green has worked on 18 Eastwood films, and production designer Henry Bumstead has been on board for two decades. "Henry Bumstead likes to say that I take the bulls__ out of moviemaking. It's pros like Henry who do that for me," says Eastwood. "All I'm doing is encouraging them."

❝Hollywood pays too much attention to home runs. If all I ever did was hit one home run, the only thing I'd be now is a celebrity has-been.❞

Eastwood plans his productions like military campaigns and compares his role to that of an officer in combat. Distractions are kept to a minimum and posturing discouraged. "He says very little to you," claims Hackman, whom Eastwood lured to play the sheriff in *Unforgiven*. "I appreciate that. Most of what directors say to actors is said for the benefit of the people standing around the camera." As a result, Eastwood films are delivered under budget and ahead of schedule.

Eastwood developed his prudence as a child of the Depression. His family roamed northern California and the Northwest as his father searched for work. The determination of the father shaped the son's bedrock respect for honest labor. Eastwood attended eight grammar schools in eight years, an experience that taught him self-reliance and a suspicion of the intentions of strangers. "When you're the new kid in town, you always have to punch it out with the other kids the first day or so before they accept you," he says. If they didn't, Eastwood did not let it trouble him.

Like most natives of the San Francisco area, Eastwood grew up scorning Los Angeles. He created two lives, one based in his office on the Warner lot in Burbank, the other up the coast in Carmel. His friends there have included a schoolteacher, a former bar owner and an itinerant barber. Film is rarely a topic of conversation. Carmel residents protect his privacy, even those who disagreed with his policies when he was mayor in 1986-87.

No one in L.A. could figure out why the most powerful actor in the industry would want to be mayor of a village of 4,700 people. Unless, of course, Eastwood had larger ambitions. That made sense to them. The more Eastwood denied it, the more convinced became those who breathe the rarefied air in Bel Air and Beverly Hills that Eastwood was grooming himself to become the next Ronald Reagan. The truth was far simpler. Eastwood felt his town government wasn't working, and he was willing to sacrifice his privacy to try to fix it. Eastwood acts on his convictions.

At 63, Eastwood has finally been embraced by those who practice his craft. He reigns as one of the richest and most powerful men in an industry where the two attributes are virtually synonymous. Yet his focus is on the next task. Soon after the smash release of *In the Line of Fire*, he took a crew to Texas to start *A Perfect World*, about a Texas sheriff chasing an escaped convict who has kidnapped a child. It may not win any awards. "Hollywood pays too much attention to home runs," he says. "Singles and doubles can win the game when longevity is the goal. Besides, if all I ever did was hit one home run, the only thing I'd be now is a celebrity has-been."

That would be out of character. ∎

Toni Morrison's Gift

A sharecropper's daughter becomes the first African-American writer to win the Nobel Prize

Finding no novels that portrayed the people she knew, Morrison wrote them herself.

 NEARLY EVERYONE, including the author, was startled when in October the Swedish Academy awarded the 1993 Nobel Prize for Literature to the American novelist Toni Morrison. The last two winners also wrote in English, and Morrison's name had not appeared in speculations. Once the surprise wore off, though, the recognition that Morrison was the first African American, and only the eighth woman, to receive literature's most prestigious award, worth $825,000, provoked widespread elation. Inevitably, some people privately suspected that Morrison won *because* she was a black female. Had the prize gone to Thomas Pynchon, of course, the same skeptics would not have assumed it was because he was a white male. No one could understand, and probably laugh at, this double standard better than Morrison. She had dealt with it, triumphantly, throughout her life and through her fiction.

The two are closely akin. Although her six novels contain few autobiographical traces, they constitute intensely imaginative responses to the specific historical and social pressures she has experienced as a black woman in the U.S. The imagination is all hers; the pressures have been the inheritance of millions, including, now, those who have read her books.

Her parents were onetime Alabama sharecroppers who moved north to Lorain, Ohio, a small steel-mill town just west of Cleveland, in search of a better life. The second of four children, Chloe Anthony Wofford was born in 1931, in the teeth of the Great Depression. Her father took whatever jobs he could find and nurtured, as his daughter once recalled, an angry disbelief in "every

word and every gesture of every white man on earth." He apparently had reason. As the daughter grew older, she heard family tales about an incident that occurred when she was only two, and too young to remember. Her parents had fallen short of their $4-a-month rent, and the furious landlord had tried to torch the house, with the family inside. That someone would intentionally destroy his own property or burn people alive for a pittance seems implausible. The young girl believed it, and her writing would later be etched with the incommensurability between what hatred intends and what it achieves.

From age 12 on, she took jobs to help her struggling family's finances. She graduated with honors from high school and went off to Howard University in Washington, at that time an all-black institution. Next came Cornell, where she did graduate studies in English and, after writing a thesis on the theme of suicide in the works of William Faulkner and Virginia Woolf, earned an M.A. degree in 1955. Her degree qualified her to teach English, which she did, first in Texas and then back at Howard. Her familiarity with Faulkner's work proved invaluable when she later began to write fiction: incantatory Faulknerian cadences crop up in all her novels. While an instructor at Howard, she married a Jamaican architect named Harold Morrison and had two sons. As the marriage turned sour, Morrison began to seek

A Morrison Sampler

privacy and consolation in writing, like, as she later remarked, "someone with a dirty habit." For many years, though, her writing was confined to the off-hours when she was not being a mother or a breadwinner. After her 1964 divorce and resignation from Howard, Morrison and her children moved to Syracuse, New York, where she edited textbooks at a subsidiary of Random House. Three years later she was transferred to the publisher's Manhattan headquarters.

Morrison moved easily and successfully through the overwhelmingly white provinces of publishing and academe. At the same time, while working to improve other people's manuscripts, she had territories of her own in mind. Where in contemporary American literature were the black girls and women she had known and been? Where were the fictional counterparts of her relatives back in Lorain, portrayed in all their loving, feuding, straitened complexity?

The novels she proceeded to write constitute provisional and consummately artful answers to these questions. *Sula* (1973) examines the stormy friendship of two black women and the opposing imperatives to obey or rebel against the mores of their beleaguered community. *Song of Solomon* (1977), her only novel with a male protagonist, proved a critical and commercial breakthrough for Morrison; the phantasmagoric saga of a black man in pursuit of his past won the author rapturous praise and a greatly enlarged circle of readers.

Those who do not find *Song of Solomon* Morrison's best book almost invariably choose *Beloved* (1987), an intricate, layered, harrowing story about what an escaped slave did to save her child from bondage and the rippling effects of this act

"The black girls in New York City were crying and their men were looking neither to the right nor to the left. Not because they were heedless, or intent on what was before them, but they did not wish to see the crying, crying girls split into two parts by their tight jeans, screaming at the top of their high, high heels, straining against the pull of their braids, and the fluorescent combs holding their hair. Oh, their mouths were heavy with plum lipstick and their eyebrows were a thin gay line, but nothing could stop their crying and nothing could persuade their men to look to the right or to the left."

Tar Baby, 1981

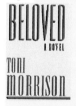

"Holding hands, bracing each other, they swirled over the ice. Beloved wore the pair; Denver wore one, step-gliding over the treacherous ice. Sethe thought her two shoes would hold and anchor her. She was wrong. Two paces into the creek, she lost her balance and landed on her behind. The girls, screaming with laughter, joined her on the ice. Sethe struggled to stand and discovered not only that she could do a split, but that it hurt. Her bones surfaced in unexpected places . . . The live oak and soughing pine on the banks enclosed them and absorbed their laughter while they fought gravity for each other's hands. Their skirts flew like wings and their skin turned pewter in the cold and dying light."

Beloved, 1987

"So by the time Joe Trace whispered to her through the crack of a closing door her life had become almost unbearable. Almost. The flesh, heavily despised by the brothers, held secret the love appetite soaring inside it. I've seen swollen fish, serenely blind, floating in the sky. Without eyes, but somehow directed, these airships swim below cloud foam and nobody can be turned away from the sight of them because it's like watching a private dream. That was what her hunger was like: mesmerizing, directed, floating like a public secret just under the cloud cover."

Jazz, 1992

through many years and lives. When it was awarded the Pulitzer Prize in 1988, after some black authors protested that Morrison had never won a major award, the honor could hardly fail to be perceived, in some quarters at least, as tainted.

No such reservations should attend Morrison's Nobel. The Swedish Academy cannot be lobbied. It made an honorable, correct choice in awarding her the Nobel, but probably for at least one wrong reason. Explaining Morrison's selection, the academy wrote, in part, "She delves into the language itself, a language she wants to liberate from the fetters of race." This was wrong, as were the many critics over the years who praised Morrison for "transcending" the blackness of her characters and bestowing on them a universality that everyone can understand.

In practice—and this is the great lesson that her fiction has to teach—Morrison does just the reverse. White authors are seldom praised for transcending the whiteness of their characters, and Morrison has demanded, through the undeniable power of her works, to be judged by the same standards. She has insisted upon the particular racial identities of her fictional people—black women and men under stresses peculiar to them and their station in the U.S.—because she knows a truth about literature that seems in danger of passing from civilized memory. The best imaginative writing is composed of specifics rather than platitudes or generalities; it seeks not to transcend its own innate characteristics but to break through the limitations and prejudices of those lucky or wise enough to read it. Madame Bovary is not Everywoman; she is a living complex of new knowledge and experience in the lives of all who have met her. Sethe, the tormented former slave in *Beloved*, is not Everywoman either; she is Toni Morrison's gift to those who desperately need to know her. ∎

The Mushmeister Rings Twice

Novelist Robert James Waller clones a lachrymose best seller

AS ROBERT JAMES WALLER, THE MOST POPULAR writer of 1993, put it in his runaway best seller *The Bridges of Madison County:* "Where great passion leaves off and mawkishness begins, I'm not sure." Maybe so, but Waller did a good deal of exploring along that border during the year, leading a wagon train of believers. *Bridges*, which offered a weepy tale of 52-year-old photographer Robert Kincaid and fortyish Iowa farm wife Francesca Johnson meeting and spending four days in forbidden aerobics, sold more than 4.5 million copies and spent all 52 weeks of 1993 among the top five slots on the New York *Times* best-seller list, more than half of them as No. 1. That's a lot of hankies.

In November *Bridges* finally yielded first place to Waller's equally teary new novel, *Slow Waltz in Cedar Bend*. Like *Bridges*, it featured a sensitive, middle-aged leading man. Waller, 54, who held down a day job as professor of management at the University of Northern Iowa, liked to point out the similarities between himself and his fictional heroes.

Slow waltz; fast sales. The second novel sold more than 2 million copies within two months of its release. But Waller wasn't finished. He just happened to tell somebody at Warner Books that he had been a semipro, Saturday-night-at-the-Holiday-Inn sort of guitarist and singer since college. And, yes, he had written a song called *The Madison County Waltz*. Next thing you know, Atlantic Records was releasing a CD, *The Ballads of Madison County*, and Waller had another first: a bodice-ripper album. Waller's novels not only satisfied millions of sobbing readers; they gladdened the hearts of cynical reviewers, who delighted in denouncing them. The writer, of course, cried all the way to the bank. By year's end Steven Spielberg had bought the movie rights to *Bridges*, and Robert Redford and Clint Eastwood were reported to be angling for the leading role of Robert Waller/Kincaid. ■

BRIDGES OF CEDAR BEND

Robert Waller's novels, *The Bridges of Madison County* and *Slow Waltz in Cedar Bend*, both topped the New York *Times* best-seller list in 1993. That's not all they had in common.

The Bridges of Madison County	Slow Waltz in Cedar Bend
STORY	
A passionate middle-aged woman, stuck in a lifeless marriage, is reborn because of a lusty yet sensitive middle-aged man.	A passionate middle-aged woman, stuck in a lifeless marriage, is reborn because of a lusty yet sensitive middle-aged man.
HERO	
Robert Kincaid, photographer. Wears sandals from India, faded blue jeans, khakis. Smokes; Zippo lighter.	Michael Tilman, professor. Wears sandals from India, faded blue jeans, khakis. Smokes; Zippo lighter.
HERO'S WHEELS	
A truck he calls "Harry."	A motorcycle he calls "The Shadow."
HEROINE	
Francesca Johnson, farmwife. Black hair, face showing first lines. Wears silver hoop earrings and tight-fitting jeans.	Jellie Braden, graduate student. Black hair, face showing first lines. Wears silver hoop earrings and tight-fitting jeans.
EXOTIC SETTING FOR HEROINE'S RECKLESS AFFAIR	
Naples.	India.
HEROINE'S HUSBAND COMPARED WITH HERO	
"She knew ... Richard was ... no match intellectually or physically for Robert Kincaid."	"'He's ... reminded of his limitations just by being around people like you, Michael.'"
OLD WAYS	
"Stop in Bangkok ... and look up the silk merchant's daughter who knows every ecstatic secret the old ways can teach."	"And then came the Trivandrum Mail running southward into traditional India, where the old ways endured."
SUNSET IN LAST LINE	
" ... about twilight ... "	" ... last sunlight ... "

ALL THE RAGE

A vibrant alternative scene turned rock on its ear, while the hottest stars hid from the hype

SMASHING PUMPKINS Singer Billy Corgan says the dogmatism of rock's indie scene repelled him.

SOUL ASYLUM After 10 years, the times caught up with this band's blend of punk energy and folk melodies.

O nce upon a time a gas-station attendant and high school dropout grossed more than $50 million for a record company. But because his success was based on scorning success, he lived unhappily ever after. In 1990 Eddie Vedder was working the night shift at a service station in San Diego, sometimes telling people he was a security guard to impress them. Three years later, the 28-year-old singer and lyricist for the alternative-metal band Pearl Jam had become rock's newest demigod. His group's debut album, *Ten*, had sold nearly 6 million copies and still ranked in the Top 30 of the *Billboard* album chart more than 90 weeks after its release. In October 1993 the Seattle-based quintet released its second album, called simply *Vs.*, which roared to the top of the charts, selling more copies in its first week of release than any other album in history.

Eddie Vedder had all the rock-idol moves down. A painful, shadowy past? Check. An air of danger and sensuality reminiscent of Jim Morrison? You bet. Refusal to adopt the trappings of a rock star, thus demonstrating that he was such a genuine article he didn't need stardom? Absolutely. Was he happy to be featured on the cover of TIME? No way.

Vedder was a product of the thriving world of alternative rock, a musical genre that rejected the commercial values of mainstream pop. Alternative had no strict definition, but it had a feel. Its musicians rejected showbiz glitz. They supported progressive social causes. Many of them avoided dating groupies and models. Their music was usually guitar-driven, with experimental touches. While pop songs are often about love, alternative lyrics were usually about tougher feelings: despair, lust, confusion. Alternative rock was a reaction, especially among the twentysomething generation, to all the years of being subjected to Madonna's changing hair color and MTV close-ups of George Michael's butt.

Alternative rock had been simmering for years, ready for this moment of boiling over. The Georgia-based band R.E.M. was an alternative pioneer in the mid-'80s that went mainstream years before Pearl Jam was even formed. What was new in 1993 was that the record charts were crowded with alternative bands

PEARL JAM Says vocalist and front man Eddie Vedder: "Sometimes when I see my face [in] a magazine, I hate that guy."

ranging from the arty-rock quartet Smashing Pumpkins to the folk-tinged Soul Asylum.

And therein lay the controversy: alternative music had become one of the most potent forces in the mainstream, triggering an identity crisis and rancorous debate among musicians and fans. If these rockers are stars now, fans asked, haven't they become everything we're against? Nothing better symbolized the struggle for this musical genre's soul than the success of Pearl Jam, a band adored by followers but reviled by some fellow musicians as sellouts, poseurs or opportunists riding on the fame of their fellow Seattleites, Nirvana.

Pearl Jam came together as a serendipitous offshoot of a Seattle band called Green River, whose bassist Jeff Ament and guitarist Stone Gossard split off to form Mother Love Bone, a group that combined a heavy-metal sound with bouncy tunes. Just as the group seemed

ready to break through in 1990, its lead singer died of a heroin overdose. Enter Eddie Vedder. He was born in Chicago, the oldest of four children. He never knew his real father. He was raised by a man who he thought was his father and with whom he often clashed. By the time his mother told him the truth, Vedder had migrated to San Diego, and his biological father had died of multiple sclerosis. Vedder was living in San Diego when a musician friend gave him a cassette marked simply STONE GOSSARD DEMOS '91 and told him the guitarists on the tape were looking for a singer. Vedder listened to the tape, then wrote three lyrics and recorded himself singing them over the melodies. Vedder sent the demo tape back to Seattle, where bassist Ament listened to the deep, intense growl of the California stranger. He played the tape three times, then picked up the phone. "Stone," he told his pal, "you better get over here."

Vedder followed the tape to Seattle, where guitarist Mike McCready and, a bit later, drummer Dave Abbruzzese rounded out the new band's lineup; their first album came out in 1991.

What really put the band over the top was its live performances, dominated by Vedder's vocal power and mesmerizing stage presence. Especially in the first year or so, he hurled himself into crowds, surfing on upraised hands. He climbed the scaffolds around a stage, dangling from dangerous heights. Pearl Jam cemented its reputation in August 1993 at the MTV Music Video Awards, where the band won four awards, including best video of the year for *Jeremy*, and joined Neil Young for a stirring version of his song *Rockin' in the Free World*.

Despite Vedder's flamboyance, most alternative musicians were a far cry from the strutting, white-male rockers of decades gone by. They tended to be anti-sexist, pro-tolerance and pro-underdog. The same went for female rockers. Members of the independent music community were wary, almost paranoid, about the movement's being copied or co-opted by the mainstream. Yet any scene that paid so much homage to purity and anticommercialism was bound to be divided by charges of hypocrisy, especially when the lure of big bucks was at hand. In 1993 the alternative crowd found itself drifting from the ideals that gave it birth: to express anti-Establishment ideas and make music for misfits. When 5 million people buy an album, they can't all be outcasts. Some of them are going to be Rush Limbaugh fans who just like the beat. ∎

DAVE (AND AL)
An ashtray-smashing
Veep helps Letterman
to the top of the heap.

LATE NIGHT WITH...

Television's sleepiest hours wake up with new faces, old Chases— and old faces in new places

TOM BROKAW, THE NBC ANCHORMAN, COULDN'T escape the subject even during a vacation in Africa following a reporting stint in Somalia. After a day of "birding and fishing and dodging hippos" in a remote area of Botswana, Brokaw said, a guide noticed his cap from NBC's *Late Night with David Letterman* show and asked, "Do you think Letterman is going to CBS?"

Only in the floodlit world of network television could a simple career move cause such shock waves. As the networks continued to react to the yawning gap in the late-night slot left by the 1992 departure of NBC's 30-year-man, Johnny Carson, the battle to attract the night-owl audience generated TV's most interesting fare of 1993. Carson's designated heir, Jay Leno, struggled to maintain the supremacy of NBC's *The Tonight Show*, while David Letterman switched to CBS at a time slot directly opposite Leno. Fox brought in Chevy Chase to begin a new show, NBC chose the unknown Conan O'Brien to fill Letterman's old time slot, and Arsenio Hall stayed put in syndication, hanging on for dear life.

Letterman announced early in January that he would leave NBC when his contract expired in late June and resurface on CBS in late August with a show airing opposite Leno, at 11:30 p.m. Eastern time. CBS reportedly paid $42 million over a period of three years for the ironymonger's services. His manager gave NBC a one-month period to match the CBS bid, but NBC's only chance of keeping Letterman was to dump Leno as *Tonight* host and give Letterman the job—something its programming executives had publicly ruled out. After a siege of executive indecision, the network decided to stick with Leno, who had taken over from Carson in May 1992. The result: NBC lost both Carson and Letterman in little more than a year.

With Letterman's future now determined, the buzz in the TV world turned to *his* replacement. In late April the network surprised everyone by picking comedy writer Conan O'Brien to fill Letterman's shoes. O'Brien was not simply unknown; he was inexperienced. He had been recommended by *Saturday Night Live* producer Lorne Michaels, whom NBC had tapped to run the post-Letterman *Late Night*. O'Brien's new show would go on the air September 14, capping a two-week stretch that was emerging as D-day for the entire time period: Letterman's show was set to debut on August 30, and the new Chevy Chase show a week later on Fox.

JAY

A funny thing happened on the way to premier week: NBC declared it owned the rights to some of Letterman's most famous routines from his days at *Late Night*. "There are certain intellectual-property issues that do not travel with Dave," warned Robert C. Wright, president of NBC, referring to such Letterman shtick as Stupid Pet Tricks, the hapless Larry "Bud" Melman character portrayed by Calvert De Forest and the famous Top 10 list. NBC never brought the suit; even Leno had been milking the story for sharp laughs. Meanwhile, when Letterman's new show premiered in the renovated Ed Sullivan Theater on Broadway, the host seemed reborn. Attracting guests like Vice President Al Gore and dispatching his cameras into the New York streets around his new playhouse, he managed to retain his trademark oddball humor, yet seemed less prickly than in the past. His command of the late-night format was more evident than ever when contrasted with the unfortunate spectacle of Chevy Chase flopping

ARSENIO

One week after Chase's disastrous debut, it was Conan O'Brien's turn. His first show was the occasion mainly for a big sigh of relief. The little-known former writer for *The Simpsons* defused the hype over his arrival with aplomb and good humor. In a taped opening bit, he was seen jauntily walking to work on D-day, as everyone from his apartment doorman to NBC anchorman Tom Brokaw warned, "You'd better be good." As O'Brien settled into the job, however, his neophyte weaknesses began to show. He leaned into his guests like a high school kid on a job interview. His sidekick, Andy Richter, was a superfluous appendage. The prepared comedy bits were occasionally funny but more often tacky. O'Brien decorated his rec-room set with pictures of TV personalities like Ernie Kovacs and Jack Paar. Unfortunately, he came across more as a preppie Mr. Rogers.

By December the dust was settling on the field of battle, and the ratings told the tale. With each point representing 942,000 homes, Letterman

just about everyone

heavily in his debut on Fox a week later.

Chase was always the longest shot in the late-night horse race. As a prospective talk-show host, he offered too little experience and too much ego. His competition was too entrenched, his audience too ill-defined, his comic sensibility too dated. Nothing short of a miracle, it seemed, could make him a hit.

The only miracle about *The Chevy Chase Show* was that the star managed to show his face on the air for as long as six weeks. His debut hour was the sort of disaster TV fans might someday recall for their grandchildren. Nervous and totally at sea, Chase tried everything, succeeded at nothing. He shot basketballs from the stage, fawned embarrassingly over guests (Goldie Hawn and Whoopi Goldberg), took pratfalls that fell flat and, in one desperate moment, boogalooed in the middle of the stage, pleading with the apathetic crowd, "Everybody, shake it." Few were surprised when Fox pulled the plug on October 17.

CONAN

was averaging a 5.2 rating, translating into 4.8 million households. Leno was averaging a 4.1 rating, Arsenio Hall was getting a 2.2, Conan O'Brien was drawing a 1.8, and Chevy Chase was licking his wounds.

Once all the ballyoo died down, however, viewers had a right to feel disappointed. A year that promised to bring a new sense of vitality to television had produced a batch of clones. Each new show fit comfortably into the Letterman-fashioned late-night mold: another tall, Waspy male with a facetious, wise-guy attitude, drawing writers from the same pool of ex–*Harvard Lampoon* staff members to help deliver a nightly mix of topical jokes and goofy comedy bits. In their search for someone to take over in late night, the networks seemed paralyzed, unwilling to try something different. NBC appeared to have broken the mold by choosing O'Brien, the late-night host nobody knew. But once he arrived, the audience seemed to know him all too well. ∎

CHEVY

Dave's Prime Time

What, me happy? After 11 years, David Letterman tops TV's late-night race. And he even admits he's enjoying it

THE REIGNING MASTER OF THE late-night television world strides into his new office in his workday outfit of T shirt, shorts and sneakers. "Look at this," he says. "It's brand-new. Clean walls. New carpet. Office furniture. I used to have a paper route, and now I have three floors of a theater building on Broadway in New York City. I'm the luckiest man alive."

After a decade of the fabled David Letterman irony, one can be excused a skeptical pause. Is he serious? Or is this another Letterman put-on, one of those statements meant to convey its precise opposite—the way "those fine, fine people at General Electric" on his old show usually meant Dave had had another dustup with his bonehead corporate bosses. Letterman's new headquarters—located a few stories above New York City's Ed Sullivan Theater, where in late August of 1993 he unveiled his new late-night talk show on CBS—are clean, all right, but not without intrusion. The smell of roasting chicken wafts up every afternoon from the fast-food place downstairs and causes most of the staff to make faces. "I don't mind it," Dave says cheerily. "You build the place over a chicken restaurant, what's it gonna smell like—catfish?"

No getting around it; David Letterman sounds, well, *happy* for a change. Or, at least as happy as an insecure, driven, angst-ridden performer with a pathological fear of failure can be. Certainly no one has more of a right to enjoy himself for a spell. For two years, Letterman had been the most wrangled-over, gossiped-about, sought-after star in television. When Jay Leno was chosen to succeed Johnny Carson as host of the *Tonight Show*, it was Letterman, the disappointed office seeker, who drew the sympathy vote. In the fall of 1992, when his contract with NBC was coming due after 11 years as custodian of the post-Carson time period, he was besieged with offers. In January, when he announced he was jumping to CBS for a reported $14 million a year, Letterman reached the superstar pantheon. By the fall of 1993, following the most frenzied battle for viewers in late-night TV history, Letterman was the clear winner. He was handily topping pretender-to-the-throne Leno in

the ratings, and Chevy Chase's new show on the Fox network had died a mercifully quick death.

Letterman's new TV incarnation represents more than just a change of networks and an earlier bedtime; it marks the ascendance of a new generation. When *Late Night with David Letterman* made its debut on NBC in 1982, it was the prankish outsider, a subversive send-up of talk shows, television, the entertainment world in general. Letterman refused to fawn over guests; with the help of Vegas-obsessed bandleader Paul Shaffer, he took deadpan aim at show-biz phoniness. He griped about his NBC bosses, turned stagehands into stars, conducted elevator races in the hallway. His medium-twisting inventiveness was influenced by Ernie Kovacs, his man-on-the-street playfulness by Steve Allen. But Letterman seasoned them with his own sardonic, cranky, cooler-than-cool personality.

Like its star, Letterman's new lair is steeped in TV history. It's the old Ed Sullivan Theater—where Elvis and the Beatles were once presented by the Great Stone Face—following a complete overhaul. In his new setup Letterman has a more cavernous auditorium, a bigger audience (about 400 seats, nearly double the capacity of his old NBC studio) and a whole new neighborhood for his snoopy cameras to roam around in. "You can leave the stage, go down three or four steps, open the door, and you're right on 53rd Street," says Letterman. "I can scream every night at *Miss Saigon*. I can literally holler at her. I can make enough noise on our sidewalk to disrupt their show every night."

His crankiness may be exaggerated for effect, yet Letterman, 46, remains an aloof, almost opaque celebrity. In conversation he is articulate, disarmingly modest and genuinely, effortlessly funny. Having shed 30 pounds since leaving NBC, he seems more relaxed and upbeat than ever before. Yet he guards his emotions tightly and talks only reluctantly about his private life.

Colleagues say one reason is that there isn't much of it. Letterman, by most accounts, is consumed by his work, has few close friends and spends little time socializing outside the office. Girlfriend Regina Lasko used to

work on his show (she became production manager for *Saturday Night Live*), but most staff members were unaware of their relationship until after the two had been dating for months. Letterman has mentioned her name publicly only once and regrets it. "People started following her family around," he says.

Others attribute Letterman's reclusiveness to his Midwestern reticence and a sincere discomfort with playing the celebrity game. "It's good taste," says Steve O'Donnell, who spent eight years as the show's head writer. "He doesn't want to lay that stuff on you."

Despite his kids-in-the-hall casualness around the office, Letterman is a fiercely driven perfectionist who controls virtually every detail of his show. "There's more tension than any place I've ever worked," says an ex–staff member. Letterman rejects reams of material submitted by his team of a dozen writers, and he crosses off potential guests by the score. "We'd hand in a list of 50 guests, and he'd say no to 48," says a frustrated former booker. He is also notoriously moody and has last-minute pangs of self-doubt. "In the makeup room five minutes before the show," says head writer Rob Burnett, "Dave will suddenly say, 'This bit is not going to work.' Sometimes he needs to be almost pushed in front of the camera." After the show, he typically replays the videotape and broods about mistakes or bits that misfired. "He's incredibly insecure and very self-torturing," says Merrill Markoe, his former girlfriend, who helped create *Late Night,* devised such popular bits as Stupid Pet Tricks and wrote for the show until 1986. "He doesn't ever reward himself for a job well done. He always feels that he screwed up. In fact, in all the years I knew him, I never once heard him say he thought something went pretty well. The most he ever gives himself is remarks like, 'Well, I guess that stuck to the tape.'"

Yet off-camera Letterman can also seem much like the on-camera, prank-playing fraternity boy. Staff members recall the chaos that ensued during an office celebration several years ago, when he set off a flare in a colleague's office and triggered the building's smoke alarms. Letterman's outside interests mostly involve sports. He jogs and swims (more of the latter since he injured his neck in a car accident two years ago), plays basketball and went to the All-Star baseball game in July 1993. His No. 1 passion is auto racing, which has a nostalgic appeal for Letterman, who grew up in Indianapolis and fondly recalls visiting the speedway as a boy. He keeps a collection of foreign sports cars in an airplane hangar in Santa Monica, pores over British racing magazines and takes a different friend each year to the Indianapolis 500, part of his campaign to show that the sport is "more than cowboys in cars going as fast as they can."

" I can scream every night at *Miss Saigon.* I can make enough noise on our sidewalk to disrupt their show every night. "

Letterman treats his Midwestern roots with a mixture of ironic detachment and affection. He visits his mother a couple of times a year; one visit was after the 1993 Indy 500. Letterman says he was tickled by the experience. He called the house at 7 p.m. and came by after dinner. "I got there at 8:30, and Mom says to me [affecting her quiet, church-lady voice], 'David, would you like some strawberry pie?' I go into the kitchen, and there's a brand-new, fresh-baked strawberry pie. I said, 'When did you make this?' She said, 'I started right after I got off the phone with you.' It was just the cutest. I was so touched. Isn't that motherhood? She gets off the phone, drops what she's doing and *bakes a pie.*"

Letterman's father, a florist who died when David was 27, was a "polar opposite. When he would walk through a room, lamps would rattle. He was funny and energetic and a goofball, screaming and hollering, making corny jokes. Then when he died, the focus shifted obviously to my mother, and none of us realized how quiet and undemonstrative she was. It took some re-getting used to. My first 27 years, I'm living in a fraternity house. It was all thunder and lightning. And with my mom now, it's kind of a gentle spring rain."

Letterman married his college sweetheart and moved with her to California, where they divorced after nine years. Friends say he was rarely without a steady girlfriend thereafter, though Letterman gets a troubled look whenever the subject of female relationships comes up. "Every relationship that's failed in my life has been my fault," he says.

In his Midwestern modesty and reserve, Letterman recalls no one so much as the man he publicly idolizes, Johnny Carson. Like Carson's, much of Letterman's appeal comes from the counterpoint between his heartland Wasp looks and his edgy irreverence. The two have become closer since Carson retired, Letterman says. "I'm more at ease around him now." Letterman had dinner at Carson's house in the spring of 1993 along with former *Tonight* producer (and now Letterman executive producer) Peter Lassally. Carson served meat loaf and mashed potatoes and talked about his recent African safari. "He had learned Swahili," says Letterman. "I'm thinking, 'Is this a dream?' I'm here in Johnny Carson's dining room, and he's speaking Swahili."

But in one area the pupil does not plan to emulate the master: "I'm not going to be around as long as Carson," Letterman vows. "After a period of time with this, I will leave and go on. I'll probably never be on television again, on any kind of regular basis. This will be my new and final project."

A pause for the old self-doubt to surface. "You can hear America breathing a sigh of relief." ∎

■ THEATER

The Gay White Way

Angels in America and other new works
bring homosexual themes to Broadway

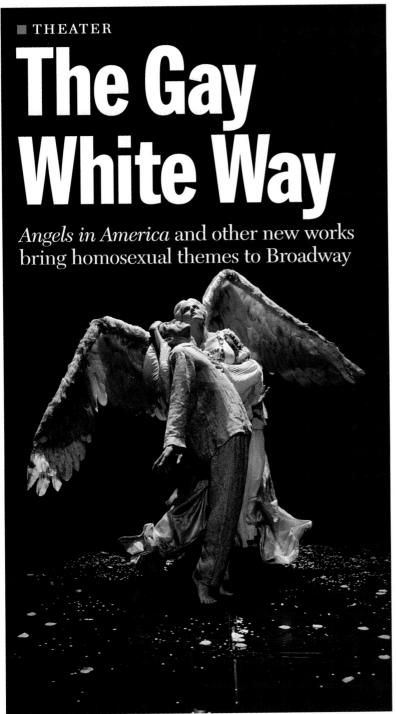

ANGELS: Tony Kushner's imaginative, two-part exploration of gay identity and social mores won the Pulitzer Prize for Drama.

movies viewed from a campy gay perspective. The year's ablest comedy, *The Sisters Rosensweig*, sympathetically portrayed a bisexual man who romances one of the title siblings, then leaves her because he prefers men. The season's foremost drama, *Angels in America* [whose first part, *Millenium Approaches*, opened in May and was followed by the second part, *Perestroika*, in November] positioned the gay experience at the center of America's political and spiritual identity.

Angels, the seven-hour epic subtitled *A Gay Fantasia on National Themes*, was the first gay-centered play to win the Pulitzer Prize in drama. The runner-up was the best show of the off-Broadway season, the equally gay and angry memoir of AIDS activist Larry Kramer, *The Destiny of Me*. A decade ago, the theater establishment collectively winced when its vital self-advertisement to Middle America, the telecast of the Tony Awards, opened with a best-play prize to the flamboyant Harvey Fierstein for *Torch Song Trilogy*. In 1993 virtually every Tony category featured shows with gay elements. Among the other contenders: Lynn Redgrave's one-woman *Shakespeare for My Father*, which alluded to the bisexuality of Sir Michael Redgrave, and the rock opera *Tommy* with its homosexual, pedophile uncle.

Broadway had welcomed gay material before. But a breakthrough in unabashed candor and commercial viability came with 1992's best musical, *Falsettos*, which centered on a father who leaves his wife and son to take up with a male lover who dies of AIDS. While it sounds grim, the show was in large part a cheerfully neurotic comedy; its mordant wit in the face of death is yet another index of a gay aesthetic. The producers shrewdly emphasized the show's celebration of families of all kinds in testimonial ads touting it as fit for rabbis and priests, Midwestern tourists and suburban firemen. Having long since turned a profit on Broadway, *Falsettos* launched a once unimaginable national tour.

What accounted for the surge? The gay civil rights movement, for one thing. The theater has always been home to a disproportionate share of gay artists because the environment was tolerant and, perhaps, because their lives already involved illusion, role playing and disguise. Many artists have come out of the closet in life and insist on doing so in their work. In addition, AIDS has given gay male playwrights a clarity and tenacity of vi-

THE THEATER HAS LONG BEEN A HAVEN FOR GAY artists—provided they addressed straight topics. But in 1993, gay characters and stories abruptly took center stage. After decades on the fringe, gay-themed works enjoyed lavish Broadway productions that were embraced by mainstream heterosexuals. "The trend really peaked this year," said John Harris, editor of *TheaterWeek*. "All the hot properties seem to be gay."

Broadway's best musical, *Kiss of the Spider Woman*, merged a homoerotic love story with homage to bygone

159

KISS OF THE SPIDER WOMAN: Chita Rivera triumphed in the title role as the embodiment of a gay prisoner's dreams of bygone Hollywood glamour.

sion that comes from facing mortality. "Gay writers have life and death to write about," said Kramer, who chronicled his early activism in *The Normal Heart* and confronted having the AIDS virus in *Destiny*.

Above all, as Congress and the states debated gay civil rights and President Clinton struggled to certify the role of gays in the military, many gay writers saw their *milieu* as inherently dramatic. Like Jews, blacks and women in prior decades, gays promoted their struggle for equality into the spotlight.

KISS OF THE SPIDER WOMAN CERTAINLY ELECTRIfied audiences with its squalid story of two Argentine cellmates, shot through with a dazzling dollop of Latin American magic realism. Though the show featured torture and threats of anal rape, for most audience members the artistry of the production overcame its harshness. Many particularly enjoyed the ending, which managed to be at once cynical, unhappy, exultant and uplifting. The show was

graced with a strong performance by Canada's Brent Carver as a fey, movie-obsessed interior decorator imprisoned for his homosexuality. But the star turn was the comeback of veteran Broadway diva Chita Rivera as the embodiment of the decorator's Hollywood fantasies. Rivera's presence afforded mainstream audiences a comfortable entry into a violent and homoerotic world. Still, director Harold Prince confessed, "We couldn't have gotten this project financed a decade ago."

The same could be said for *Angels in America*, which galvanized audiences with its radical political perspective and literary style, even though its New York production was visually ugly, less magical and less convincing than an earlier staging in Los Angeles. *Angels* disproved truisms about the unmarketability of political drama with its aggressive scorn for Ronald Reagan and Republicanism, for Mormons and moralizing, and its demonic view of lawyer-dealmaker Roy Cohn, a gay-bashing closet gay and a top-level G.O.P. influence peddler for more than three decades. Instead, the play compellingly reasserted the theater's place in the public debate. Hearteningly to theater partisans, *Angels* generated excitement about a drama comparable to the biggest buzz about musicals. Above all, Kushner's work demonstrated that plays can matter in a pop culture dominated by electronically recorded performances rather than live ones.

Angels operated on two levels: as a soap opera about three intertwined households inhabited by homosexuals and as a preachment about religion, social politics and the meaning of America. Playwright Kushner impressively sustained the soap-opera interest through both 3½-hour sections of the complete work, but fumbled his sermon. Part Two, *Perestroika*, was full of absorbing incident: sometimes campy and funny, sometimes unnervingly bold. Whenever Kushner waxed philosophical, however, the second half rendered his epic smaller, shrinking steadily through its final act as it reduced the mystical and allegorical to banal leftist slogans.

But the lengthy work passed its most difficult test. Like the highly successful *Kiss of the Spider Woman*, it attracted mainstream playgoers far beyond its guaranteed audience of homosexuals, sympathetic straights and theater mavens. Defying some predictions that it was too gay-oriented to flourish on Broadway, *Angels* played to 98% of capacity. Said a triumphant Kushner: "There's a healthy curiosity among straight audiences. People are braver now because they don't feel that they're going to be tainted." ∎

CONCERT CHAMPÊTRE, CIRCA 1509

■ ART

Brush with Genius

The toast of Paris: a show of Titian and his sublime, influential artistry

THE BIG DRAW OF PARIS IN THE SPRING OF 1993 WAS the show titled "The Century of Titian," which filled the Grand Palais with the most comprehensive exhibition devoted to the work and influence of a single Renaissance painter in living memory—a feast for the eyes and a landmark in modern museum history.

Few artists have ever dominated a period, and a cultural frame, the way Titian did. His public career as an artist began with the new century, around 1505; it lasted until 1576, when he was carried off by the plague, still painting, at the age of about 90. Titian's work, so masterly in its effects, so profoundly inventive, so grand in scope and yet relieved by such suppleness and intimacy of feeling, continued to set the tone of aspiration for Rubens in the 17th century and, through Rubens, for painters like Delacroix well into the 19th.

Titian was the son of a provincial notary, born in Pieve di Cadore in north Italy in 1478 or 1479. Apprenticed to a Venetian artist before his 10th birthday (no child labor, no Renaissance), he learned from the two painters whose work incarnated the "modern style," Giovanni Bellini and Giorgio da Castelfranco, alias Giorgione. Bellini supplied the prototypes for one side of early Titian: his suave construction of pictorial space and pragmatic realism. The imagery of Giorgione, Titian's exact coeval, was more mysterious and poetic.

The most enduring product of the relation between Titian and Giorgione was the pastoral, the landscape of pleasure, the earthly paradise derived from Latin literature, with its shepherds, gallants and nymphs. The picture that starts this long train is Titian's *Concert Champêtre,* circa 1509, which is one of the most hermetic and disputed images in all Western art. No theory will ever quite account for the magic of the scene, with the two naked women in the mature and fruitful landscape and the two clothed men, one standing for Culture—as his city dress, his lute and the rhyme between his elegant hat and sharp profile and the architecture on the hill behind him proclaim—while the other, rustic and mop-headed like the tree behind him, signifies Nature. This originally pagan, arcadian image would come to permeate Venetian culture, even affecting religious art.

Learned but never pedantic, steeped in the classics, Titian could mediate fluently between the world of Ovid and what to him was modern life. His integration of idea, observation and pictorial gesture was seamless. He consolidated a style of portraiture that would radiate throughout Europe: the official mask in the grand manner, suffused with mobile thought and subtle indications of personality. Titian's nudes may not conform to modern erotic taste. They are too plump and "womanly." But when his unbounded sensual curiosity played upon the idealized territory of the classical nude, he changed the whole sexual balance of the naked body in art, creating an inexhaustible domain of feeling for others as well as himself. In his late years Titian sought only to release his deepest feelings in whatever roughhewn language they required. Old Titian is like old Michelangelo, the master of apparent incompletion. Old Titian is the astonishing predecessor of Expressionism: smooth modeling in continuous, rational space gives way to the agitated sea of paint, the broken emphatic touch, the gleam of marshlight or fire on darkness laid into yet more darkness. ■

THE HUNTER (CATALAN LANDSCAPE), 1923-24

The Purest Dreamer in Paris

A lavish show of Joan Miró exults in his precise, poetic vision

MIRÓ, IN SPANISH, MEANS "HE LOOKED"—AN absurdly good name for a painter. Joan Miró died in 1983, and 1993 marked the centenary of his birth. It was celebrated by a major retrospective at the Museum of Modern Art in New York City: 291 paintings, drawings, sculptures and ceramics. Miró got his first retrospective, at MOMA, more than half a century ago, and now he received the treatment reserved for the heaviest guns of 20th century art: Picasso in 1980, Matisse in 1992.

Miró was a marvelous artist—some of the time. Late Miró is dull fodder, but this takes nothing away from the brilliance of his earlier work, especially that of the '20s and '30s, when he was in Paris and making the finest paintings associated with the Surrealist movement.

Miró used to be referred to as "the great Spanish artist," which is technically true but culturally wrong. He was a *Catalan* artist, and the difference mattered greatly to him. Catalans think of their culture as both older than most of Spain's (Barcelona was a great medieval city when Madrid was mud huts) and newer as well: the roof on which the rain of north European avant-gardes fell before its patter reached the rest of Spain.

Miró was born and raised in Barcelona. But his parents had a farm near Tarragona, at Montroig, and the countryside would always exercise a peculiar fascination for him. The farm was the symbol of what Catalans call *enyoranca*, a sort of global, unappeasable nostalgia, a longing for the past and for one's roots.

Miró was set on going to Paris, knowing that the French avant-garde set the standard. Once he was there, it was his power of recall that caused the Surrealists to adopt him. His art seemed to open a direct line to the repossession of childhood through unedited memory. His own habits contrasted oddly with the Surrealists': he was shy and abstemious. But he was the purest dreamer in Paris, and they needed him.

His sinuous and elastic line took part of its character from Art Nouveau calligraphy, the pervasive civic style of Barcelona in his boyhood. His bestiary of images, wild and swarming and drawn with a line as exact as a knife's cut, comes from multiple sources. One, obviously, was Hieronymus Bosch. Another was the decorative art of Islamic Spain, with its precise yet often hallucinatory stylization of animal and vegetable shapes. And then there were the mosaic inventions of the Catalan artist Josep Maria Jujol, whose wandering line and isolated words set in tile clearly stayed in Miró's mind when he was doing his poem-pictures.

Miró's work would stay populated with images of specifically Catalan identity. "Hard at work and full of enthusiasm," he reported to a friend from Montroig in 1923. "Monstrous animals and angelic animals. We must explore all the golden sparks of our souls." *The Hunter (Catalan Landscape)*, 1923-24, is full of such sparks, starting with the figure of the hunter himself, with his floppy cap and his heart, burning with neat little flames of patriotic ardor, somewhat resembling an anarchist's grenade about to go off.

Miró's work was to have an immense influence on abstract painting, and yet it never lost its sense of wonder at the world or ceased to anchor itself in sharp little signs denoting the specific. At one point his work narrowed to focus on the nail of the big toe, which then got conflated with the crescent moon: a small step for mankind, but a big one for a foot. ∎

162

FAMILY ROMANCE, 1992-93

A Fiesta of Whining

Preachy and political, the Whitney Biennial celebrated cant and cliché

IT IS AN AXIOM THAT, NEXT TO RUNNING THE NA-tional Endowment for the Arts, curating the Whit-ney Biennial is the worst job in American culture. Every two years, the dread summons to represent the most vital currents in American art looms before the museum. During the 1980s, the Whitney Biennials tended passively to reflect the fashions of the art market without showing more than an occasional glimmer of independent judgment. The 1993 version was scaled to a chastened art world. The sour taste of the collapsed '80s star system galvanized the "new" Whitney into a veritable transport of social concern. This Biennial was not a survey but a theme show, a saturnalia of political correctness, a long-winded immersion course in margin-ality. The aesthetic quality (that repressive, icky word!) was for the most part feeble. The level of grievance and moral rhetoric, however, was stridently high.

Instead of the Artist as Star, we had the Artist as Vic-tim, or as Victim's Representative. The key to the show, the skeptic might say, was its inclusion of the tape of the Los Angeles police bashing of Rodney King taken by George Holliday, a plumbing-parts salesman not known for his artistic aspirations before or since. The '93 Bien-nial was anxious to present all its artists as witnesses, just like Holliday. Witnesses to what? To their own feelings of exclusion and marginalization. To a world made bad for blacks, Latinos, gays, lesbians and women in general. It was one big fiesta of whining agitprop, in the midst of which a few genuine works of art and some sharp utter-ances (mainly in video) managed to survive.

The bulk of the show was video, photography, instal-lations, a few sculptures and words on the wall. There were only eight painters out of 81 artists. But that was because it was more or less given that painting is a form of white male domination, implying "mastery." As an al-ternative, the unprepared visitor met with the wretched pictorial ineptitude of such artists as Sue Williams, who couldn't draw at all, but whose installation featured a dandy splash of plastic vomit.

No sodden cant, no cliché of therapeutic culture went unused. Much of the art on view conformed to the recipe for postmodernist political utterance set out, with lapidary accuracy, by art critic Adam Gopnik. That is, you take an obvious proposition that few would disagree with—"Racism is wrong" or "One should not persecute gays"—and encode it so obliquely that by the time the viewer has figured it out, he or she feels, as the saying goes, included in the discourse.

Some work got above this level. Charles Ray spe-cializes in weird dislocations of scale; his 45-ft.-long red toy fire truck parked outside the museum was an arresting street presence, while his naked nuclear fam-ily inside (father, mother, daughter and son, all exactly the same size) was distinctly spooky in a way that derives from Magritte. The found-object assemblages by the Cherokee artist Jimmie Durham—parodic weapons made out of rusty gun parts, salvaged wood, plastic pipe—dealt with race and cultural resistance, but did so by imaginative, not merely rhetorical, means.

Of course this show wasn't the end of civilization as we know it, but it was glum, preachy, sophomoric and aesthetically aimless. Indifferent to pleasure, it became college-level art for college-level thinking about civic virtue. It contributed nothing fresh, and little of intel-ligence, to America's quarrels and complaints about gender, race and marginality. ■

The Best

1 The Age of Innocence

Martin Scorsese's impeccable yet daring adaptation of an Edith Wharton novel brings together a gentle man (Daniel-Day Lewis) and a worldly woman (Michelle Pfeiffer). But the true subject is reticence, its charms and perils—the mannerly, orderly life that most of us try to live. Tiptoeing through the plush parlors of old Manhattan, the film finds passion in the kissing of a lady's wrist, and heartbreak in a sigh. Scorsese has composed a tragic opera, sung in whispers.

2 Schindler's List

An unlikely, enigmatic hero rescues 1,100 Polish Jews from the Holocaust. Epic cinema, tragic drama, Steven Spielberg's austere but monumental film is an act of remembrance that transcends the ordinary critical categories.

3 Léolo

Little boy lost: French-Canadian writer-director Jean-Claude Lauzon takes this old theme and replaces its sentimentality with surrealism. No family could be more horrifying than little Leo's, no movie bolder in fashioning domestic tragedy into art.

4 In the Name of the Father

Daniel Day-Lewis is brilliant as Gerry Conlon, the Belfast lad falsely accused of I.R.A. terrorism and imprisoned with his long-suffering dad. Jim Sheridan's movie is informed by an angry passion for justice.

5 Farewell My Concubine

To make this show-biz epic, director Chen Kaige may have risked his professional life. This half-century panorama of the Peking Opera is at heart a swirling entertainment—outsize passions drawn on a vast, colorful canvas.

6 The Snapper

A fractious Dublin family faces an awkward fact: the eldest daughter is soon to give birth to an illegitimate baby. This crowded, wayward, funny film, written by Roddy Doyle and directed by Stephen Frears, is a hymn to family values without the usual piety.

7 Tim Burton's The Nightmare Before Christmas

Every Burton film is Halloween scary and candy-cane sweet. So it's apt that he dreamed up this stop-motion fable about a Halloween ghoul who wants to play Santa Claus. *Nightmare* is Disney's weirdest cartoon ever: chilly, rollicking, endlessly inventive. And it's animated by Danny Elfman's magical-spookical score. Is this the first Hollywood musical to set every one of its 10 songs in a minor key?

CONCUBINE: Maoist exposé.

8 King of the Hill

In Depression-era St. Louis, a 12-year-old (played with wary, wily reserve by Jesse Bradford) mobilizes both imagination and practicality to survive on his own after his family breaks up. Director Steven Soderbergh takes a strongminded look at a hard-luck life.

9 Like Water for Chocolate

Home cooking is the sorcery of the oppressed. In this sprawling banquet of a romantic Mexican melodrama, forbidden love finds the recipe for fulfillment—even if it takes a lifetime and beyond. Screenwriter-novelist Laura Esquivel and her husband, director Alfonso Arau, capture a savory passion that comes straight from the hearth.

10 Shadowlands

The oddest of couples. An emotionally choked Oxford don, literary critic, fairy-tale writer and Christian apologist meets a high-spirited American poet, and they find a transforming moment of happiness in confronting her imminent demise. Richard Attenborough's film gains strength from the performances of Anthony Hopkins and Debra Winger as the live-and-learn lovers.

LEOLO: Luscious surrealism meets domestic tragedy in a Canadian gem.

Of 1993

1 Toni, Tony, Tone

Sons of Soul (Polygram). This trio may hail from Southern California, but they left their hearts in Motown. The Tonys evoke past greats such as the Jackson Five with vibrant vocals and melodies, but they never settle for mere imitation. No computer beats, no fakery: the Tonys are a real band, with real instruments, who have brought the art of R&B songwriting back to the future.

2 Billy Joel

River of Dreams (Columbia). The Piano Man time-travels through a song cycle that begins on the emotional edge and ends baptized in hope and harmony. *River of Dreams* revives a pop era when hooks were called melodies and a strong man could show a sweet side.

3 Ella Fitzgerald

The Complete Ella Fitzgerald Song Books (Verve). Porter, Ellington, Berlin, the Gershwins: Fitzgerald honored them all, and while she was at it set herself up not only as a great jazz vocalist but as a trusted custodian of some of American pop's richest treasure.

4 Handel: The Water Music

John Eliot Gardiner conducting the English Baroque Soloists (Philips). Gardiner's original-instruments essay of Handel's ebullient instrumental suite excels for the crisp precision and unerring intonation of the playing, and for its irresistible rhythmic energy.

5 Digable Planets

Reachin' (A New Refutation of Time and Space) (Pendulum). Combining upscale jazz and proletarian hip-hop, Digable Planets has brought two sides of the black experience together, uniting buppies and b-boys from Howard University to Howard Beach.

6 Gavin Bryars

Jesus Blood Never Failed Me Yet (Point Music). An old derelict sings a religious anthem in a raspy voice, accompanied by a loop of the song with Bryars' kaleidoscopic underpinning of strings, winds and horns, with Tom Waites concluding with a 10-minute duet of almost mystic poignancy. The new-music album of the year.

7 Emmylou Harris

Cowgirl's Prayer (Asylum). In her 22nd album, country music's hippest traditionalist turns to God as the best part of life: wise parent, firm friend, ultimate beau. This sheaf of fine songs and intimate readings makes divine love sound like a kiss in the back of a

HARRIS: Powerful, delicate melodies.

pickup. If there's a honky-tonk in heaven, Harris will be the star act on stage.

8 Smashing Pumpkins

Siamese Dream (Virgin). This co-ed group stood out because it dared to criticize the sometimes pretentious nature of the alternative rock scene. Cool albums date as quickly as milk in a convenience store; *Siamese* remains compelling after repeated listening.

9 Dvorak: Complete Piano Trios

The Lanier Trio (Gasparo). The Dvorak piano trios are glories of the chamber-music literature; the sorrow and the pity is that they are little known. The Lanier Trio—William Preucil, violin; Dorothy Lewis, cello; and Cary Lewis, piano—lavish impeccable ensemble and golden tone on each piece.

10 Ice Cube

Lethal Injection (Priority). Ice Cube's raps about police brutality and white immorality enter the ear and expand in the brain like a Black Talon bullet. His lyrics are sometimes inexcusable, but his logic is often inescapable, disgusted with a system that offers only drive-by compassion. Ignore his high-caliber insights at your peril.

FITZGERALD: Treasures.

1 The Positively True Adventures of the Alleged Texas Cheerleader-Murdering Mom

(HBO). Holly Hunter's hilarious, high-strung, compulsively chattering turn as Wanda Holloway, the homemaker accused of plotting to eliminate her daughter's cheerleading competition, was just part of the fun of this delicious send-up of TV's ripped-from-the-headlines docudramas. Michael Ritchie's deadpan direction, Jane Anderson's script and Lucy Simon's infectious, country-flavored score also sparkled.

2 The Great Depression

(PBS) In the tradition of *The Civil War* and *Eyes on the Prize*, this documentary series (from *Eyes* creator Henry Hampton) brought another patch of American history to life with an artist's eye and an educator's passion. Everything from the breadlines to the political battles was made fresh, dramatic, relevant.

3 Laurel Avenue

(HBO) A working-class black family in Minnesota battles against drugs, crime and assorted family crises. This two-part drama, directed by Carl Franklin (*One False Move*), was startling in its frankness yet leavened by a stubborn optimism, a far cry from the usual easy sentimentality dished up by network programmers.

4 Bakersfield P.D.

(Fox) The little series that couldn't. This loopy comedy about a provincial police department provided more laughs than any new show of the season, yet ratings never budged from the Nielsen basement. After much praise and more patience than usual, Fox programmers finally pulled it off the air. And so goes the saddest story of '93.

5 NYPD Blue

(ABC) Here's the happiest: Steven Bochco returned to form with a fierce, unfashionably hard-edged police drama—and scored a surprise hit. Stars David Caruso and Dennis Franz provide solid character groundwork that has eclipsed the well-publicized (and very occasional) glimpses of nudity.

6 Perot vs. Gore

(CNN) Perhaps not since the Army-McCarthy hearings in 1954 has a public figure been so thoroughly undone by a TV performance. Gore exposed the meanspirited bluster of the little man from Texas. The second big loser of the evening: the strangely passive moderator, Larry King.

7 Wild Palms

(ABC) O.K., Oliver Stone's and Bruce Wagner's futuristic miniseries eventually ran out of gas. Still, the ride was bracing—full of unnerving images, a richly imagined vision of the technofuture, and a paranoid atmosphere more convincing than anything Stone managed in *JFK*.

8 The Larry Sanders Show

(HBO) A sitcom about a talk show, starring a real-life talk-show host, who last starred in a sitcom as himself, a comedian with a sitcom. This wicked exposé of show-business narcissism is TV's shrewdest satire of itself since *Tanner '88*.

THE GREAT DEPRESSION: Moving.

9 60 Minutes . . . 25 Years

(CBS) The anniversaries keep piling up, but this time Mike, Morley, Ed, Andy and the rest of the gang did more than the obligatory clip job. They gave us a piquant peek at the show's foibles as well as its triumphs. And they reminded us that, for all their recent imitators, the Old Guard still does it best.

10 Hard Copy

(Syndicated) But the new kids are changing the rules. Less tacky than *A Current Affair*, more fun than *Inside Edition*, this compulsively watchable tabloid show strikes the right balance between sensationalism and enterprising journalism. Sometimes everyone else seems a day behind.

WILD PALMS: The best network mini-series of the year.

NON FICTION

1 President Kennedy

by Richard Reeves. **We knew he was no saint. Now we have 800 carefully researched pages to tell us that J.F.K. was more Hollywood than Harvard, a gifted politician who relied on his personal charm rather than deep understanding and conviction. He was often "careless and dangerously disorganized." The image of vigor was also an illusion: hormone shots and amphetamines kept him pumping.**

2 Lenin's Tomb: The Last Days of the Soviet Empire

by David Remnick. What do good journalists do when they find themselves in the middle of the story of a lifetime? If the reporter is David Remnick and the story is the fall of the U.S.S.R., you dig till you drop and type like hell. Remnick covered thousands of miles for hundreds of interviews to explain who did what to whom when the Kremlin came tumbling down. The result is history still hot from the crucible.

3 W.E.B. Du Bois: Biography of a Race

by David Levering Lewis. The first of a planned two parts, this volume tracks the controversial black intellectual—"The Old Man" to generations of black leaders—from his middle-class roots in Massachusetts to Paris for the 1918 Pan-African Congress. Lewis reveals the crusading editor and author of *The Souls of Black Folk* to be an aloof thinker struggling with contradictory ideas about racial inclusion and separatism.

4 Leni Riefenstahl: A Memoir

by Leni Riefenstahl. At 91, the German dancer turned actress and filmmaker has a lot to remember. Her Late Romantic style won raves from Hitler and invitations to his mountain lair. Her documentaries about the 1934 Nazi Party Congress and the 1936 Olympic Games glorified the New Order with innovative and striking techniques. Whether one thinks of her as indomitable or abominable, Riefenstahl is an energetic writer with a vivid memory of intimacies in an amoral time.

5 A History of Warfare

by John Keegan. Casting a cold eye over 4,000 years of mortal combat convinces this British historian that making war is basically a bad habit. Alive with sudden, unexpected delights of knowledge, the book ranges across time and distance to brilliant effect. Unromantic but admiring, Keegan provides the grim details about the profession of arms with a stoic clarity that blurs all flags and levels all battlefields.

FICTION

1 Smilla's Sense of Snow

by Peter Hoeg. **The exploitation of Greenland's mineral resources by Denmark seems unlikely background for a detective thriller about the mysterious death of a six-year-old Inuit boy. Unlikely too is the investigator, one Smilla Quaavigaaq Jaspersen, a woman caught between the native Greenland culture of her hunter-tracker mother and the well-appointed world of her Danish father, a physician and scientist. Like Ross Macdonald, Hoeg creates an unfamiliar but palpable world that steadily envelops the reader.**

2 Operation Shylock

by Philip Roth. The uncontested master of comic irony comes up with another ticklish situation: a writer named Philip Roth journeys to Israel to confront a Philip Roth imposter who is trying to persuade Jews to go back to Europe and re-establish Yiddish culture. Seriously funny about Middle East madness, Roth riffs with an abandon not seen since *Portnoy's Complaint.*

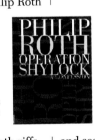

3 Remembering Babylon

by David Malouf. A celebrated Australian novelist re-imagines his country's pioneer past with a haunting tale of a white man raised by Aborigines. It is the mid-19th century, and the struggling Queensland settlers are homesick for the British Isles and afraid of the natives. Malouf works the themes of culture clash and racial fears into a seamless lyric narrative.

4 The Shipping News

by E. Annie Proulx. Winner of this year's National Book Award, Proulx's rambunctious second novel zeroes in on a coastal Newfoundland community coming apart economically and socially when the fishing and seal hunting industries fail. Proulx's sharp ear for regional speech and barbed style can be both startling and humorous.

5 The Pugilist at Rest

by Thom Jones. A collection of short stories about damaged men that poses important questions: Is courage a virtue, or is it simply testosterone poisoning? Is God just a neurochemical event, part of the tantalizing aura that precedes an epileptic fit? Jones is an ex-Marine and former amateur prizefighter who puts a wallop in his prose.

1 Kiss of the Spider Woman
Better than the movie, bolder than the book, this brassy musical is centered on a homosexual flirtation in an Argentine prison. Scenes of torture cross-cut to remembered flights of film fantasy, with lots of hunks and feathers. Comebacks all around—for title star Chita Rivera, director Harold Prince and especially composer John Kander and lyricist Fred Ebb—plus the debut of the year by Brent Carver as the brave window dresser. The show's point: there can be no freedom without sexual freedom.

2 Sunset Boulevard
A disappointment in London, where it played as a tragedy, Andrew Lloyd Webber's latest megamusical was reborn in Los Angeles as a gothic comedy. Glenn Close dispelled her chilly persona in a moving portrait of a bygone movie queen who remains a legend in her own mind.

3 Two Rooms
Lee Blessing's meditation on a Beirut hostage and his grieving spouse was the play of the year, its poetic pain matched only by Laura Esterman's gutsy portrait of the wife

and the imaginative staging—with the couple separated in reality yet entwined in fantasy.

4 Keely & Du
No play was more topical than pseudonymous Jane Martin's what-if about right-to-life extremists kidnapping a pregnant woman and holding her until it is too late for her to abort. Martin subtly traced the evolving bond between the streetwise captive (Julie Boyd) and her principal captor (a superb Ann Pitoniak).

5 Three Hotels
No longer just promising, Jon Robin Baitz is now a major playwright. Off-Broadway, three searing monologues by a husband and wife unveiled a sardonic saga of international corporate greed and the resulting wreckage of one executive's career, family and beliefs.

6 Antigone in New York
Polish emigre Janusz Glowacki is the U.S. stage's foremost writer on the Eastern European immigrant experience and an incisive satirist. This odd lark, derived from Greek myth, about two derelicts' attempt to give a fallen

TOMMY: Surprise! Now he's a Playbill wizard.

comrade a decent burial, was interspersed with caustic remarks about the KGB and trendy Manhattan.

7 The Song of Jacob Zulu
Tug Yourgrau's script about the making of a black South African terrorist was uneven but unforgettably performed in Eric Simonson's epic staging. Zakes Mokae excelled as several elders, and Ladysmith Black Mambazo, the a capella singing group, served gloriously as a modern Greek chorus.

8 Tommy
There wasn't much emotional depth or even adolescent rebellion left in the granddaddy of rock operas, but there was the most arresting light show ever to reach Broadway, superb storytelling by director-adapter Des McAnuff, and that great Pete Townshend score.

SUNSET BOULEVARD: Star turn.

9 A Perfect Ganesh
Two aging matrons take a vacation in India that turns into a much-needed spiritual quest. Terrence MacNally's off-Broadway tragicomedy costarred the Indian god of the title, who appears in many guises and takes the audience on a similar journey of the soul.

10 Fool Moon
However you labeled this wordless exercise by two inspired clowns (Bill Irwin and David Shiner), its visual imagery delighted children while enchanting the most cerebral elders.

1 Notre Dame vs. Florida State

Two unbeaten powerhouses, No. 1 and No. 2, met with the innocent hype only the college game can provide. And then an upset, as the Irish sedated the favored Seminoles for three quarters and hung on a for 31-24 palpitator. Why, it was the Game of the Century—for one week, until Notre Dame lost to Boston College on that game's last play. FSU was restored to the top of the polls—by writers and coaches—when it overcame undefeated Nebraska in the Orange Bowl. Attention, NCAA: Give those scholar-athletes some exercise in December by holding an eight- or 16-team tournament.

CHINESE FOOD: Diet of worms.

2 Evander Holyfield vs. Riddick Bowe

The former champ was supposed to be too small, too old, too darned nice to regain his heavyweight title against Bowe's imposing bulk. In their furious November bout, the only advantage Evander had was a huge heart. His victory was a comeback of class.

3 The N.F.L. vs. Sominex

Pro football has become the 60-yard game, as conservative teams trudge (one-two-three, kick) between the red zones. Teams settle for wussy little field goals (up 47% this year) instead of going for the big manly touchdown (up only 12%). And once again the behemoth National Conference seemed headed for lopsided victory in the Stupor Bowl. So why would the Fox network want to pay $1.58 billion for four years of this No-Fun League?

4 Mitch Williams vs. the Strike Zone

The Wild Thing's eccentric fast ball had helped the Philadelphia Phillies beat the superior Atlanta Braves in the play-offs, but in the World Series against Toronto, he lost all sense of navigation and blew two crucial games. The closer has closed in Philly: he was abruptly traded to Houston.

5 Steffi Graf vs. the Ghost of Monica Seles

With Wimbledon, French and U.S. Open victories, Fräulein Forehand had her best year. Yet still hovering like the shade of Banquo was this question: What if Seles had not been stabbed on the court by a man who said he did it to help Steffi be No. 1? (He was later convicted but sentenced to only two years' probation.)

6 Chinese Women Runners vs. Vegetarians

Wang Junxia and her teammates shattered world records in the 10,000 meters, 3,000 meters and 1,500 meters during one memorable weekend at the Chinese National Games in Beijing. Their coach credited their success in part to a diet spiced with gourmet dried worms.

7 Michael Jordan vs. Himself

The wonder warrior led his Chicago Bulls to a three-peat N.B.A. title. He conquered Madison Avenue with his thousand-megawatt smile. He battled the press over inquiries into his high-stakes gambling. But after his father's murder this summer, Jordan decided he'd had enough of fighting. His retirement stunned the hoop world and left the top spot in sport stardom vacant.

8 England vs. France

When the World Cup comes to the U.S. in 1994, this is the vaunted matchup that *won't* take place; both teams were eliminated in the trials. Americans will still be treated to a summer clinic in the world's most popular sport—and without the antics of Britain's soccer hooligans.

9 Leon Lett vs. His Brain

From showboat to goat: in the Super Bowl, this defensive star's premature TD celebration cost his Dallas Cowboys a touchdown. On Thanksgiving the Cowboys lost to Miami because Lett couldn't keep his hands off a loose ball. This hotdog keeps ending up a wiener.

10 The Fans vs. Miss Manners

The Fan Man parachutes onto the ropes during the Bowe-Holyfield brawl. Wisconsin fans run amuck after their football team beats Michigan. Saints' QB Wade Wilson collapses, and hometown boors cheer. Now behave, people, or we'll send Vince Coleman after you.

WILD THING: He made hearts sting.

Michael Jordan: Goodbye to All That

His basketball talent was so singular that **MICHAEL JORDAN**, 30, often seemed to be competing only against himself, against the memory of his last impossible dunk, his last acrobatic steal, his last whizzing cross-court assist. But he was the captive of his own megacelebrity, rarely even leaving his hotel room when on the road. Close to his parents, he was heartbroken when his father was senselessly murdered in August. Finally, Jordan quit basketball, stunning fans and fellow players in October by retiring from the Chicago Bulls, the team he had led to three consecutive N.B.A. championships. The Jordan Era was over.

Wedded Bliss? Try to Trump This

Married. **DONALD TRUMP**, 47, publicity-addicted casino operator; and **MARLA MAPLES**, 30, occasional actress; two months after Maples gave birth to their daughter Tiffany. More than a thousand guests attended the 15-minute ceremony in the Grand Ballroom of The Donald's Plaza Hotel, causing limolock in surrounding streets. Among the invited: soap-opera villain Susan Lucci, fight czar Don King, raider Carl Icahn, ex-jock O.J. Simpson, shock-jock Howard Stern. In their wake trailed 17 TV-camera crews, 90 paparazzi, many bodyguards.

Frank's Ranks

The pantheon of **FRANK SINATRA** devotees opened its gates to some new and unlikely faces. First, Zonic Shockum, Jawbox and 30 other obscure punk bands did it their way, recording a two-CD set of Sinatra standards, *The Chairman of the Bored.* Then Old Blue Eyes himself released an album of *Duets* recorded with such surprising partners as U2's Bono and Gloria Estefan. The album was a smash, even though new technology allowed the duets to take place over special telephone lines, and the harmonies were phoned in.

BACK TO BASICS

Earlier in the year she sang for Bill Clinton, dined with Janet Reno, buddied up to Colin Powell. Then **BARBRA STREISAND** shifted gears from Political Animal to Very-Well-Paid Vegas Casino Act. After a long absence from the stage, she thrilled her fans by returning to live performing with two glittering New Year's appearances at MGM's Grand Hotel. Her take: a reported $20 million.

A TRIBUTE TO BAD TASTE

WHOOPI GOLDBERG and boyfriend **TED DANSON** achieved the impossible—lowering the moral tone of a Friars' roast—when the *Cheers* star improbably showed up in blackface to pay an epochally crude tribute, liberally sprinkled with racist jokes, to his then girlfriend. New York City Mayor David Dinkins claimed Danson was "way over the line," and talk-show host Montel Williams resigned from the Friars Club in protest. But Goldberg stood by her man, claiming she had helped write the material herself. Perhaps to prove her point, she later vexed the Anti-Defamation League by publishing a recipe for "Jewish American Princess Fried Chicken." Unhappily for lovers of romance, the two soon split up.

The Spirit of Bipartisanship

They were America's most celebrated avatars of the old theory that opposites attract: one managed Bill Clinton's presidential campaign, the other was a key strategist for George Bush, yet they had been an item for more than three years. On Thanksgiving Day, to the delight of 150 guests—who included the likes of Rush Limbaugh, George Stephanopoulos and Timothy Hutton—**JAMES CARVILLE** and **MARY MATALIN** laid down their ideological differences and married on Carville's home turf, New Orleans. Following a 20-minute civil ceremony, the couple, accompanied by a brass band, led their wedding party through the streets to a Creole turkey dinner at the city's landmark restaurant, Arnaud's. Sensitive to the potential for fractiousness among their diverse group of guests, Mr. and Mrs. Carville wisely designated one bar for Republicans and a second for Democrats. Both poured liberally.

Di Turns Shy

Early December marked the first anniversary of the separation of the Prince and Princess of Wales, and **PRINCESS DIANA,** 32, celebrated the occasion by developing a sudden allergy to the cameras that had followed her everywhere—even on her vacation in St. Kitts. In early November the *Sunday Mirror* published a series of photos, ostensibly taken through a hidden camera, of the svelte princess in tight gear working out at London's LA Fitness Club. Though Diana lividly decried this invasion of her privacy, some thought the pictures were planted in an attempt to steal the limelight from Charles, who was making a high-profile trip through Arab states the same week. Later in the month Diana left a royal charity gala in tears: "a migraine" was the official explanation.

A few days later, a chin-up Diana appeared at a London benefit and told the crowd, "If it is all right with you, I thought I would postpone my nervous breakdown." Then she announced she would reduce the extent of her public appearances in 1994.

Man in the Mire: The Travails of Michael

The year began well for **MICHAEL JACKSON**, with an appearance at Bill Clinton's Inaugural, a Super Bowl half-time spectacle and a TV chat with Oprah Winfrey on which he allowed he was just a regular guy with a skin problem who was dating Brooke Shields. But then came the summer of disaster. Charged with child molestation, targeted by ensuing criminal inquiries and lawsuits, he admitted to drug addiction, disappeared for "treatment" after abandoning a world tour, then mysteriously returned to his secluded Neverland Ranch in California. In late December he declared his innocence of the sexual-abuse allegations.

UNWED. How did the magic unravel? After five years of marriage, **Burt Reynolds** sued **Loni Anderson** for divorce

in an extremely snarly conflict. The high point—spectacle-wise—came when Reynolds, on TV, challenged his ex to truth-serum and lie-detector tests to prove that she cheated on him before he cheated on her. **WON'T WED.** They had certainly overstayed their welcome, but **Amy Fisher**

and **Joey Buttafuoco** just wouldn't disappear from the public eye. In the spring all three major networks featured docudramas recounting the infamous story of adultery and attempted murder on Long Island. In the fall Fisher's story—if not her shooting of Mrs. Buttafuoco—was apparently vindicated when Joey pleaded guilty to a charge of statutory rape.

DIDN'T WED. For months gossip columnists speculated about when **John F. Kennedy Jr.,** America's Prince Charming, would marry **Daryl Hannah**, moviedom's bohemian blond. The couple's choice was unexpected: a breakup, for now.

Call Me Madam—or Just Call Me

She was a new kind of madam, neither a rouged and overweight 60-year-old nor even a pedigreed East Coast socialite. Young, skinny and hip, **HEIDI FLEISS, 27,** was charged with running a ring of high-priced L.A. prostitutes. Basking in the publicity, Fleiss threatened to name names from her oversize appointment book, throwing Hollywood moguls into late-summer turmoil. Rocker and alleged customer Billy Idol maintained, "Fortunately, I've never had to pay for sex." One movie exec tickled Hollywood by issuing a statement denying contact with Ms. Fleiss, before anyone got around to accusing him of any.

BONING UP ON KATE

Throwing fear into the hearts of those women who found the consumption of food essential to good health, a new wave of skinnier-than-thou models created the "waif look." In the vanguard: **KATE MOSS,** 19, a breezy 98-pounder who became one of the world's most photographed models and Calvin Klein's latest skivvie hawker. The fanfare for the famished reflected the most dramatic change in tastes since the arrival of Moss's British forebear Twiggy, and Moss was blamed for prompting anorexia among admiring girls.

THE 10 MOST

REQUESTED CELEBRITY LOOK-ALIKES IN LOS ANGELES

1. Michael Jackson
2. Bill and Hillary Clinton
3. Sharon Stone
4. Heidi Fleiss
5. Cindy Crawford
6. Madonna
7. Sylvester Stallone
8. Elizabeth Taylor
9. Beverly Hills 90210 cast
10. Robert de Niro

Banned Man Meets Band Man

1993 was another year on the lam for **SALMAN RUSHDIE,** 46, still the victim of a Muslim fatwa, the sentence of death decreed by clerics for *The Satanic Verses.* But Rushdie got around, appearing at Massachusetts Institute of Technology to receive an honorary post, chatting briefly with President Clinton in Washington, and surprising a pop crowd at London's Wembley Stadium by showing up onstage in the middle of a U2 concert to poke fun at the group's bemused lead singer and anti-Danson, **BONO.**

GANGSTA RAPPERS FACE THE CLAPPER

They called their music "gangsta rap," and its stars earned the title. **SNOOP DOGGY DOGG,** 22, was charged as an accomplice to murder three months before his record *Doggystyle* debuted at No 1 on the charts. Dr. Dre, 28, whose album *The Chronic* sold 2 million copies, pleaded no contest to battery for breaking a man's jaw. Tupac Shakur, 22, a rapper with Digital Underground, was arrested in the shooting of two off-duty police officers in Atlanta; later he was arrested in New York and charged with sexual assault on a young woman.

Brat Packing

Poor **SHANNEN DOHERTY.** Old boyfriends called her rage prone; coworkers called her snotty. Even marrying Ashley Hamilton, the 19-year-old son of George Hamilton, didn't help her keep her job at *Beverly Hills 90210.* She reportedly won't be back.

A Terrible Swift Sword

Before their little spat made headlines, **JOHN** and **LORENA BOBBITT** were just another unglamorous couple with a lot to work out; the tough ex-Marine and the Ecuadorian-born hairdresser apparently had a tempestuous union. Then, on a June night—after, Lorena later claimed, John had raped her—she cut off his penis with a carving knife, drove off with it and threw it from her car some miles from the couple's home. A medical team retrieved the organ and surgically reattached it in a 9½-hour operation. John, who was tried and acquitted of marital sexual assault, appeared as a jovial guest on the *Howard Stern Show,* while Lorena, who became something of a feminist folk hero, was expected to plead temporary insanity at her trial for malicious wounding in January 1994.

My Very Own Eraserhead

Following a rumor-filled hiatus from movies, Pretty Woman **JULIA ROBERTS** surprised just about everyone when she wed country-western star **LYLE LOVETT,** music's quirkiest, most talented un-hunk. Both stars had appeared in Robert Altman's send-up of Hollywood, *The Player,* but not together. Their courtship was brief, their wedding plans almost whimsical. The marriage was held in Marion, Indiana, where Lovett was touring; the bride was barefoot. At that night's concert, Roberts entered in her wedding gown to introduce her new husband.

Academy Awards

Best Picture
Unforgiven

Best Actor
Al Pacino, *Scent of a Woman*

Best Actress
Emma Thompson, *Howards End*

Best Director
Clint Eastwood, *Unforgiven*

Best Suppporting Actor
Gene Hackman, *Unforgiven*

Best Supporting Actress
Marisa Tomei, *My Cousin Vinny*

Lifetime Achievement
Federico Fellini

Top Films at Box Office

(WORLDWIDE)
1. *Jurassic Park*
2. *The Fugitive*
3. *Aladdin*
4. *The Bodyguard*
5. *Indecent Proposal*
6. *The Firm*
7. *Cliffhanger*
8. *Sleepless in Seattle*
9. *In the Line of Fire*
10. *A Few Good Men*

Top 10 TV Programs

FALL SEASON, 1993
1. *Home Improvement*
2. *60 Minutes*
3. *Roseanne*
4. *Seinfeld*
5. *Coach*
6. *Frasier*
7. *Grace Under Fire*

8. *N.F.L. Monday Night Football*
9. *Murder, She Wrote*
10. *CBS Sunday Movie*

Best-Selling Books

FICTION:
1. *The Bridges of Madison County*
   Robert James Waller
2. *The Client*
   John Grisham
3. *Like Water for Chocolate*
   Laura Esquivel
4. *Griffin & Sabine*
   Nick Bantock
5. *Without Remorse*
   Tom Clancy
6. *Einstein's Dreams*
   Alan Lightman
7. *Pigs in Heaven*
   Barbara Kingsolver
8. *Pleading Guilty*
   Scott Turow
9. *The Golden Mean*
   Nick Bantock
10. *Vanished*
    Danielle Steel

NONFICTION:
1. *Women Who Run with the Wolves*
   Clarissa Pinkola Estes
2. *Care of the Soul*
   Thomas Moore
3. *The Way Things Ought to Be*
   Rush Limbaugh
4. *Embraced by the Light*
   Betty J. Eadie
5. *Healing and the Mind*
   Bill Moyers
6. *Bankruptcy 1995*
   Harry E. Figgie &
   Gerald J. Swanson
7. *The Te of Piglet*
   Benjamin Hoff
8. *Reengineering the Corporation*
   Michael Hammer and
   James Champy
9. *Listening to Prozac*
   Peter Kramer
10. *The Hidden Life of Dogs*
    Elisabeth Marshall Thomas

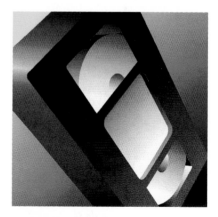

Top 10 Videos

SALES:
1. *Aladdin*
2. *Pinocchio*
3. *Home Alone 2*
4. *Sing Along Songs: Friend Like Me*
5. *Once Upon a Forest*
6. *Beauty and the Beast*
7. *Terminator II*
8. *Homeward Bound: The Incredible Journey*
9. *101 Dalmatians*
10. *Richard Simmons: Sweatin'*

RENTALS:

1. *Unforgiven*
2. *Scent of a Woman*
3. *The Bodyguard*
4. *A League of Their Own*
5. *Sneakers*
6. *Under Siege*
7. *A Few Good Men*
8. *Bram Stoker's Dracula*
9. *The Last of the Mohicans*
10. *Single White Female*

Tony Awards

Best Play
Angels in America: Millennium Approaches

Best Musical
Kiss of the Spider Woman

Best Revival
Anna Christie

Best Actress, Play
Madeline Kahn,
The Sisters Rosensweig

Best Actor, Play
Ron Leibman, *Angels in America: Millennium Approaches*

Best Actress, Musical
Chita Rivera,
Kiss of the Spider Woman

Best Actor, Musical
Brent Carver,
Kiss of the Spider Woman

Nobel Prizes

PEACE:
Nelson Mandela, President of the African National Congress, and **F.W. de Klerk**, President of the Republic of South Africa

LITERATURE:
Toni Morrison, the first black American to receive the honor

MEDICINE:
American **Philip Sharp** and Briton **Richard Roberts** for their independent discoveries in 1977 of "split genes"

ECONOMICS:
U.S. economic historians **Robert Fogel** of the University of Chicago and **Douglass North** of Washington University in St. Louis

PHYSICS:
American astronomers **Joseph Taylor** and **Russell Hulse** for their 1974 discovery of the first binary pulsar

CHEMISTRY:
American **Kary Mullis** and British-born Canadian **Michael Smith** for their individual accomplishments in genetic research

Sports

BASEBALL
World Series: The Toronto Blue Jays over the Philadelphia Phillies, four games to two, the second consecutive Series win for the Blue Jays

BASKETBALL
N.B.A. Championship: The Chicago Bulls over the Phoenix Suns, four games to two, the third straight title for Chicago
NCAA Men's Championship: North Carolina over Michigan, 77-71
NCAA Women's Championship: Texas Tech over Ohio State, 84-82

FOOTBALL
Super Bowl XXVII: The Dallas Cowboys over the Buffalo Bills, 52-17, Buffalo's third straight Super loss

HOCKEY
N.H.L. Stanley Cup: The Montreal Canadiens over the Los Angeles Kings, four games to one, the 24th Cup for the Canadiens

BOXING
Heavyweight: Evander Holyfield over Riddick Bowe in Las Vegas to regain the title from Bowe

HORSE RACING
Kentucky Derby: Sea Hero
Preakness: Prairie Bayou
Belmont Stakes: Colonial Affair
Breeders' Cup Classic: Arcangue

GOLF
Masters: Bernhard Langer
U.S. Men's Open: Lee Janzen
PGA Championship: Paul Azinger
Mazda LPGA: Patty Sheehan
British Open: Greg Norman
U.S. Women's Open: Lauri Merten

TENNIS
Australian Open:
Monica Seles, Jim Courier
French Open:
Steffi Graf, Sergi Bruguera
Wimbledon:
Steffi Graf, Pete Sampras
U.S. Open:
Steffi Graf, Pete Sampras

MOTOR SPORTS
Daytona 500: Dale Jarrett
Indy 500: Emerson Fittipaldi
Le Mans: Geoff Brabham, Christophe Bouchut, Eric Helary

Films: *Variety.* Television: Nielsen Media Research. Books: Simba/Communications Trends. Videos: *Video Business.*

Marian Anderson, 96, singer. Shut out by Jim Crow laws from performing on the American operatic stage, Anderson began touring Europe in the 1920s, drawing vast acclaim. After Anderson was barred in 1939 from singing in Washington's segregated Constitution Hall, Eleanor Roosevelt intervened and arranged for her to perform at the Lincoln Memorial. When 75,000 blacks and whites assembled on Easter 1939, they came not just to hear the glorious register of Anderson's voice but also to witness a force that was quietly conquering color boundaries. Her grace under stress conveyed to all Americans a message that blacks had a profound contribution to make to the country's cultural life.

Anderson first began singing at age six, learning spirituals at the Union Baptist Church in her hometown of Philadelphia. Her personal fortitude grew out of her faith. Whether singing in the White House (1939), or as the first black to sing in New York City's Metropolitan Opera (1955), she never raised her voice except in song. And when she sang, the walls came tumbling down.

Dave Beck, 99, labor leader. Beck was a laundry-truck driver when he joined the International Brotherhood of Teamsters in 1914. By 1952, he had become the organization's president, and in the five years he held that office he forged the 1.6 million Teamsters into the nation's most powerful union. Beck's tenure was marked by accusations of Mob ties and corruption, charges that eventually led to his ouster and 30 months in prison for tax evasion and embezzlement.

Anthony Burgess, 76, writer and composer. Burgess was the author of more than 50 novels, radio and television scripts and innumerable articles and essays, and a composer of operas, symphonies and concertos. Yet his fame, much to his chagrin, rested largely on Stanley Kubrick's violent 1971 film adaptation of *A Clockwork Orange*, the dystopian, futuristic novel Burgess published in 1962. A lifelong linguist, he wrote *A Clockwork Orange* in an invented slang of English, Russian and even a dash of Gypsy.

Raymond Burr, 76, actor. As television's Perry Mason, Burr had a towering bulk and thundering baritone that terrified malefactors, who routinely confessed all in the face of his withering accusations. Burr returned to series TV as the crotchety, wheelchair-bound crime solver Ironside.

Sammy Cahn, 79, lyricist. Cahn's hundreds of pop-culture epiphanies include the words to *Love and Marriage* and *I Fall in Love Too Easily*, as well as Oscar-winning ditties *Call Me Irresponsible, All the Way, High Hopes* and *Three Coins in a Fountain* and the lyrics for Broadway shows, including *High Button Shoes*.

Roy Campanella, 71, baseball catcher. Born of an Italian father and a black mother in Philadelphia, the phenomenally gifted Campanella joined the Brooklyn Dodgers in 1948, one year after Jackie Robinson had broken baseball's color barrier as a player for the team. Over the extraordinary decade that followed, he was named Most Valuable Player in three seasons, and he set a single-season home-run record for a catcher—41 homers in 1953. But his career ended in January 1958, when a car accident left him with no movement below his shoulders. He faced paralysis with admirable courage, and in 1969 he entered the Hall of Fame.

A Spirit of Fire and Grace

THERE WERE SO MANY long odds and so many graceful triumphs in the lifetime of tennis star **ARTHUR ASHE**. More than seemed plausible for a black kid from segregated Richmond, Virginia, playing in a white man's game. More than seemed reasonable for a man who suffered the first of several heart attacks at age 36. More than seemed attainable to stunned observers who wept with him in April 1992 when he announced that he had AIDS— probably the result of a blood transfusion after a second bypass operation in 1983.

The tears did not last. Ashe, the pragmatist, set up an AIDS foundation, became active in AIDS research, spoke to scores of gatherings on the nature of his disease, on race relations, on the lessons of life lived in the shadow of mortality. The dignified discourse ended prematurely in February 1993 as Ashe, 49, succumbed to the disease.

Of the protean figures responsible for the integration of sports in America, Ashe stood in the first rank, with Jesse Owens, Jackie Robinson and Muhammed Ali.

With a serve that sprayed aces and a ground stroke of laser-like precision, Ashe never displayed his unorthodox brilliance better than on Centre Court at Wimbledon in 1975, when he faced the enfant terrible of tennis, Jimmy Connors. Connors swaggered onto the court as the bookmakers' darling. Ashe turned him into an unexpected runner-up with a four-set lesson in pinpoint placement. Tantrums took over tennis after that, but Ashe would have none of it. The game, like life, had to be conducted with passion, but dignity had to be maintained.

Cesar Chavez, 66, famed labor organizer. Chavez grew up in a migrant family and became a national figure as president of the United Farm Workers in the late 1960s, when he began unionizing poorly paid Mexican migrant workers to raise them out of squalid working and living conditions. His successful boycotts against various grape growers and the producers of iceberg lettuce were widely accepted by Americans during the 1970s.

John Connally, 76, politician. Connally's greatest influence and patron was Lyndon Baines Johnson; he played a key role in Johnson's brutal 1948 Senate race. As governor of Texas, Connally was riding through Dallas with John Kennedy when the President was shot; Connally was seriously wounded. He served as a popular Governor until 1969, and in 1971 Richard Nixon appointed him Secretary of the Treasury. After Connally became a Republican, in 1973, his political career ended with the 1980 G.O.P. presidential primaries, during which he won only a single delegate. After initial business successes, Connally found himself overleveraged and declared personal bankruptcy in 1988.

Agnes de Mille, 88, dancer and choreographer. In the 1943 musical *Oklahoma!*, De Mille transformed Broadway dance from mere ornament to an essential, expressive element of theatrical storytelling. Her triumphant collaboration with composer Aaron Copland in the 1942 ballet *Rodeo* brought De Mille to the attention of Rodgers and Hammerstein. Her other Broadway successes included choreography for Kurt Weill's *One Touch of Venus* and Lerner and Loewe's *Brigadoon*. A stroke in 1975 barely slowed down De Mille; she published an account of her recovery in *Reprieve: A Memoir*, the 11th of her 12 books, in 1981.

James H. Doolittle, 96, aviator. In April 1942, America was still dumbstruck by the attack on Pearl Harbor when word came of an impossibly bold daylight air raid on Japan. Leading the attack was its architect, Lieut. Colonel Doolittle, who had in a few months secretly trained volunteer pilots to fly normally land-based B-25 bombers from the deck of the aircraft carrier *Hornet*. Doolittle, already a legend for such aviation feats as making the first flight guided entirely by instruments, now became the war's first hero—he received an instant promotion and the Medal of Honor. Doolittle went on to a series of posts in the European theater, and his Eighth Air Force devastated Germany's military factories while shooting down 10,000 enemy planes.

Don Drysdale, 56, Hall of Fame baseball pitcher. During his 14 major league seasons with the Dodgers, "Big D" and his fastball terrorized opponents for more than strictly competitive reasons: he set a 20th century National League record by hitting 154 batters. Drysdale played in five World Series, and in 1968 pitched 58 scoreless innings, a record that stood for two decades.

Doris Duke, 80, American Tobacco Company heiress, socialite and philanthropist. Called the "richest girl in the world" after she inherited most of her father's millions at the age of 12, Duke kept gossip columnists busy for decades with her luxurious life and unhappy romances. Among her many philanthropic interests were Duke University, AIDS research, the environment, animal rights and historic preservation. Childless, she left an estate of at least $750 million.

William Clarence (Billy) Eckstine, 78, singer. At the peak of "Mr. B's" postwar popularity, no one could duplicate the honeyed, baritone vibrato that turned *Everything I Have Is Yours*, *Fools Rush In* and *I Apologize* into romantic standards. Eckstine became pop music's first black male sex symbol. Earlier, as guiding spirit of the Billy Eckstine Band, he brought together such patriarchs of bebop as Charlie Parker and Dizzy Gillespie.

Federico Fellini, 73, film director. Most directors are content to Xerox the world. Not Fellini; he created his own world on film. In *La Dolce Vita* (1960), *8½* (1963), *Amarcord* (1974); and 20 other films, overripe images spilled out of his cornucopia: clowns and courtesans, prelates and zealots, creatures from a fantasist's bestiary. His work and his world were bigger than life, from the days when he came from Rimini to Rome, sketching caricatures on tablecloths. Fellini films were often showcases for the talents of Giulietta Masina, who for 50 years was Signora Fellini. She often played the average, put-upon feminine spirit, just as Marcello Mastroianni was the gallantly anguished soul of modern man.

Vincent Foster Jr., 48, President Clinton's deputy legal counsel. Foster, whose friendship with the President began four decades earlier in Hope, Arkansas, was a brilliant litigator and Hillary Rodham Clinton's colleague at the Rose law firm in Little Rock. A target of early critics of the Administration over the insufficient vetting of nominees and the abrupt firings in the White House Travel Office, Foster became depressed and took his own life with a gun in a Virginia national park. The removal of files from his office after his death fueled suspicions that he was perhaps holding damaging secrets in the Clintons' Whitewater real estate case.

John Birks ("Dizzy") Gillespie, 75, jazz trumpeter and a founding father of bebop. On the wings of two unlikely angels, Gillespie and Charlie Parker, bebop jumped off swing into the high ozone. Gillespie played the role of the good-timing, glad-handed buddy, but in matters of chops and talent he played a supporting role to no one. Born in South Carolina in 1917, he taught himself trombone and trumpet; before he left his teens he was playing in a band and had got himself his nickname. With his cheeks expanding far past normal size when he played his upward-tilting horn, his music flowed from a kind of high spirit, a purposeful passion that the horn symbolized and the silliness deflected.

Lillian Gish, 99, silent movie star. Before cinema had sound, it had something every bit as expressive: the face of Lillian Gish, who debuted on stage at five and went on to become the pre-eminent actress of pretalkie Hollywood, best remembered for her work in such D.W. Griffith classics as

Intolerance and *Way Down East.* Gish also triumphed in theater and talking motion pictures as recently as 1987's *The Whales of August.*

William Golding, 81, author. Golding's first published novel, *Lord of the Flies,* won critical acclaim for its disturbing depiction of the descent of marooned schoolboys into barbarism. Golding, who published nine other novels, won the Nobel Prize for Literature in 1983 and was knighted in 1988.

Stewart Granger, 80, swashbuckling star of more than 60 films. Born in Britain, Granger played opposite many of Hollywood's most glamorous actresses, including Vivien Leigh, Ava Gardner, Grace Kelly and Elizabeth Taylor. Among his films are *King Solomon's Mines* (1950), *The Prisoner of Zenda* (1952) and *Beau Brummell* (1954).

Fred Gwynne, 66, actor. Television comedies made Gwynne's rumbling bass and skyscraper frame familiar to millions during the 1960s, first as the amiable officer Francis Muldoon in *Car 54, Where Are You?* and then as a suburban Frankenstein's monster in *The Munsters.* But the Harvard-educated Gwynne also left a legacy of major work for the stage: he won raves, for example, as Big Daddy in the 1974 Broadway revival of *Cat on a Hot Tin Roof.*

Harry Robbins (Bob) Haldeman, 67, Nixon White House chief of staff. Of all the President's men, H.R. Haldeman was the most ferocious in his protection of his boss's interests. Haldeman joined Nixon's vice presidential re-election campaign in 1956, and in Nixon's 1960 campaign for President was his chief advance man.

Although he counseled Nixon not to run, Haldeman managed Nixon's failed 1962 campaign for Governor of California. As Nixon's chief of staff, Haldeman played an essential role in the cover-up of the Watergate break-in. He also oversaw a secret $350,000 slush fund for the Watergate burglars. He was convicted of obstruction of justice and lying to the FBI and a federal grand jury and was imprisoned for a year and a half.

Helen Hayes, 92, actress. Hayes distinguished herself over eight decades in a succession of roles, most memorably in her on-stage portrayals of royalty (*Victoria Regina, Mary of Scotland*). Along the way, Hayes achieved a certain royalty in her own right and was ultimately dubbed "the First Lady of the American theater," a tribute to both her craft and her commitment to the stage.

John Hersey, 78, novelist and war correspondent. Hersey was born in China to traveling American missionaries. Early in his writing career he covered the Far East as a TIME correspondent. Hersey's 1945 novel, *A Bell for Adano,* which won him a Pulitzer Prize, and his 1946 *Hiroshima,* a searing report of the world's first atom-bombing, are considered classics of war literature.

Ruby Keeler, 83, 1930s movie-musical star. As actor and singer, she was forgettable; as a dancer, rarely better than proficient. But as the summation of America's most legendary decade, Keeler was matched by few. Her spunky innocence sparkled in *Gold Diggers of 1933, Footlight Parade* and *42nd Street,* in which Warner Baxter warned, "You've got to come back a star!" She did.

Polly Klaas, 12, dimpled youngster from Petaluma, California, whose abduction from a slumber party in her own house by a knife-wielding intruder on October 1 led hundreds of distressed volunteers to conduct a weeks-long search for her. Richard Allen Davis, an ex-convict arrested for a parole violation, confessed to the kidnap-murder and directed authorities to a wooded thicket where he hid the girl's body after strangling her.

Film's Fairest Lady

HER FIRST MAJOR FILM ROLE, the one that introduced her to the world and made her a star, was as the young princess in *Roman Holiday.* It also defined her—as star-making parts will—in film and in life. When **AUDREY HEPBURN** died, at 63, it was as if we had to surrender the marvelous princess of our dreams.

Born in Belgium in 1929, she spent her adolescence in World War II Holland. She lost family to the Nazis, often went desperately hungry, and occasionally carried messages for the Resistance in her shoes. After the brutal war, the world found a grace in her that it yearned for. She seemed serene, but she was quick to laugh. She was ethereal, but she could be sensual and knowing, whether in the mock innocence of her Holly Golightly in *Breakfast at Tiffany's,* or, later, in the painful cunning of the beleaguered wife in *Two for the Road.* Surely she must have been thoroughly sick of hearing all about her gamin quality, her elfin smile, her graciousness and class, even though she was too gracious and too classy to say so. She played the star as if by natural right.

She was married and divorced twice (her first husband was Mel Ferrer, who acted opposite her in *War and Peace* and directed her in *Green Mansions*). In recent years she

lived in Switzerland and threw her energies into arduous charity work for UNICEF; she traveled to Somalia and appeared on television with early pleas to help the starving.

Her last film appearance was in the Steven Spielberg romantic fantasy *Always.* She played an angel, and she was radiant, doing what she always did: working with a great director, bringing to her part an unforced sovereignty of spirit, fulfilling our need to believe in the dream.

Ferruccio Lamborghini, 76, founder of the company that produced the sleek Italian sports cars bearing his name. Finding a faulty clutch in his Ferrari in 1961, Lamborghini decided to branch out and make his own cars. After shedding his majority interest in the automaker in the 1970s, he turned his attention to cultivating wine grapes.

Irving ("Swifty") Lazar, 86, talent agent. For decades the Hollywood cliché was "Every good writer has two agents: his own and Swifty Lazar," and frequently the person making the observation was Lazar himself. He represented just about every well-known literary figure who worked in the movies—Tennessee Williams, Truman Capote, Noël Coward and Ernest Hemingway—as well as actors like Humphrey Bogart, who gave Lazar his nickname after the agent locked up five screen properties for Bogart on a single day in 1955. Lazar's annual Oscar-night party was scarcely less notable than the awards ceremony itself.

Erich Leinsdorf, 81, orchestra conductor. Born in Vienna, Leinsdorf was a rising young conductor when his career in Austria was thwarted by Nazi-fueled anti-Semitism in the 1930s—but not before Arturo Toscanini discovered his talents and recommended him to New York's Metropolitan Opera. The brutally demanding conductor went on to lead and record with some of the world's great ensembles, including his legendary leadership of the Boston Symphony Orchestra in the 1960s.

Ling-Ling, 23, tourist attraction. A crowd pleaser for two decades at the National Zoo, at the time of her death Ling-Ling was the oldest giant panda outside China. She is survived by mate Hsing-Hsing, the initially reluctant father of her five cubs—all of which died within days of their birth.

Myrna Loy, 88, movie star. Loy's wry blend of intellect and sensuality made her the "Queen of the Movies" in the late '30s. Her breakthrough role was Nora Charles, wife and soul mate of William Powell's tippling, crime-solving Nick Charles in 1934's *The Thin Man*, a B movie that became an unexpected hit. Loy and Powell made

Fanfare for an Uncommon Man

AFTER HIS DEATH IN JANUARY at 84, retired Supreme Court Justice **THURGOOD MARSHALL** lay in state in the Court's Great Hall as a steady flow of people filed past his casket, which was supported by the same bier on which Lincoln's coffin had rested.

The Justice would have been surprised by the outpouring. A strong and consistent liberal, he was no sentimentalist. He possessed a rather dim view of human nature, nurtured by his constant battling against the oppressive days of Jim Crow in the South. It was in good part thanks to the efforts of the great civil rights leader, lawyer, and Supreme Court Justice that those days of racial segregation were long past.

Born in Baltimore, Marshall graduated first in his class at Howard Law School and sued successfully to integrate the University of Maryland law school, which had rejected him because he was black. After years of traveling through the South to argue civil rights cases, Marshall became chief lawyer for the N.A.A.C.P. He won 29 of 32 cases he argued before the Supreme Court, including *Brown v. Board of Education*, the landmark case in which Marshall argued that the Constitution prohibits racial segregation in public schooling. In 1967 he was appointed by President Lyndon B. Johnson to become the Supreme Court's first black justice.

Once at the Court, Marshall became known for his passionate sympathy for all downtrodden people, his delightfully unfashionable dress, and the sharp questions he directed at attorneys in oral argument.

six *Thin Man* films, to establish Loy's image as "the perfect wife": witty, beautiful and a good sport.

Salvatore Anthony Maglie, 75, pitcher. In the '40s and '50s, the sometime Yankee, Giant and Brooklyn Dodger boasted one of the deadliest arsenals in baseball: an intimidating glower, a perfectly sculpted curve ball, and a fast ball that sliced within a whisker's breadth of embattled batters, earning Sal the nickname "the Barber."

Joseph L. Mankiewicz, 83, film director, writer and producer. Mankiewicz loved words; he filmed words; he realized that *talking* pictures were just that. He won an Oscar for best director and best screenplay for *A Letter to Three Wives* (1949) and won both those awards again for *All About Eve* (1950). He also directed one of the

biggest film flops of all time: *Cleopatra* (1963, starring Elizabeth Taylor). But his cinematic successes like *The Philadelphia Story* and *Woman of the Year* were legion, and legendary.

George ("Spanky") McFarland, 64, child movie star. With pudgy authority, McFarland played the leader in Hal Roach's *Our Gang* shorts between 1931 and 1945. Imperious and often hapless, Spanky became beloved by subsequent generations when the *Our Gang* series was rerun endlessly on TV under the name *The Little Rascals*.

Carlos Garcia Montoya, 89, Madrid-born guitarist and composer whose passionate improvisations made him one of the world's finest flamenco guitarists. In the late 1940s he began giving solo recitals, establishing a global following for the Spanish folk form.

Garry Moore, 78, television personality whose soothing manner made him an early star of the new medium of television as the host of a variety show. Moore also helped create the game-show form, hosting *I've Got a Secret* and *To Tell the Truth* with genial authority.

Willie Mosconi, 80, pocket billiards master. The Philadelphia native won the world championship 13 times between 1941 and 1956. His most amazing record: running 526 straight balls in a 1954 exhibition.

Pat Nixon, 81, First Lady to Richard Nixon. In 28 turbulent years in the political vortex, Pat Ryan Nixon got scant credit for her lasting contributions as First Lady, or even for being a real person behind the tautly composed image. She was a child of the frontier, born in scruffy Ely, Nevada; a daughter of the Depression, helping to coax a living out of four acres of South California soil; a wife of the '50s, on the ladder to success. She met young lawyer Richard Nixon at an amateur-theatrical tryout; he proposed on the first date. They were married in 1940; daughters Tricia and Julie followed. She never wanted a life in politics, and never quite captured the fancy of the American public, but excelled at keeping the White House a national treasure and expanded the role of First Lady as foreign emissary. Bitter after Watergate, she became virtually a recluse, first at San Clemente and then in New York and New Jersey, where she died surrounded by her family.

Norman Vincent Peale, 95, author and preacher. Peale's 1952 blend of pop theology and self-help nostrums, *The Power of Positive Thinking*, remains one of the most popular books in history, despite—or perhaps because of—the simplicity of its message, summed up in such chapter titles as "Expect the Best and Get It" and "I Don't Believe in Defeat." Peale spread his philosophy in 46 books that achieved sales of 21 million in 41 languages. His negative side emerged when he led the anti-Catholic opposition to John F. Kennedy's run for the presidency.

Herbert Philbrick, 78, infiltrator of the U.S. Communist Party for the FBI during the 1940s. Philbrick's best-selling 1952 autobiography, *I Led 3 Lives*, promptly adapted into a television series, chronicled his life as an advertising executive, a communist and an anticommunist snitch.

River Phoenix, 23, actor. The oldest of five children of a hippie couple who served in Latin America as missionaries for the Children of God, Phoenix made his first impact at 16 in *Stand By Me* and was an Oscar nominee for his role as the son of fugitive radicals in *Running On Empty*. Audiences saw a vulnerable decency in the young actor, who could play a devoted son, a loyal pal, a gentle first love or a lost boy. Early on Halloween morning, he staggered out of the Viper Room, a Hollywood hot spot, and collapsed writhing on the sidewalk; later, tests showed he had overdosed on a combination of drugs.

Vincent Price, 82, tall, erudite, suavely menacing character actor who delighted audiences in countless gothic horror films with his masterly tongue-in-cheek portrayals of assorted rogues, villains and madmen. Educated at Yale, Price began his acting career on the London stage in the mid-1930s and quickly moved to Broadway. In 1953 he first established himself as the Olivier of ghoulery by playing a crazed sculptor in the 3-D thriller *House of Wax*. A succession of classic horror films followed, among them *The Fly* (1958) and, in the 1960s, a series of Edgar Allan Poe adaptations including *The House of Usher, The Pit and the Pendulum* and *The Masque of the Red Death*. Price was also a noted art collector and a popular writer of art and cooking books.

A Young Lion Leaping

H E WENT DOWN DEFI-antly, all guns firing. Until the very end of his long struggle with AIDS, **RUDOLF NUREYEV** continued to live ravenously, leading an active life, conducting when he could no longer dance, traveling. When he died at 54, he was mourned as not only a great dancer, but also as a rare source of energy in the arts.

The first of the postwar ballet superstars, he burst upon the West, defecting in Paris at age 23. His partnership with Margot Fonteyn, prima ballerina of London's Royal Ballet, was the most famous of the century: her ineffable femininity, his feral grace. She called him "a young lion leaping," and wild he was.

He was born hungry. His parents were Tartar peasants from Bashkir, near the Ural Mountains. From age six, when he saw his first dance performance, he was obsessed by movement. Against the odds, he clawed his way to Leningrad and the Kirov school at age 17—very late to start serious classical training. His sheer will and magnetism won the day. Once in

the West, he danced everywhere in a huge variety of roles, from the full-length classics to modern works. In 1983, as aging robbed his powers, he became artistic director of the Paris Opéra Ballet, where he served for six colorful years. Taking his last bow there in October 1992, he was gaunt and emaciated, but swathed in a huge gold-and-scarlet cape. The style—and the heroism— were intact.

General Matthew B. Ridgway, 98, former Army Chief of Staff. During the Second World War, he developed the paratrooper attack and converted the 82nd Infantry Division into an airborne unit that landed in Sicily in 1943 and on the Normandy beaches on D-day. In the latter assault, Ridgway skydived into action with his troops. In 1951 he replaced the dismissed Douglas MacArthur in Korea. He won that war, overseeing the counteroffensive that drove North Korean and Chinese troops out of the South. Ridgway kept a grenade taped to his uniform, a habit that became legendary among his men. In 1953 he was named Army Chief of Staff by President Eisenhower.

Albert Sabin, 86, medical researcher. Sabin devised the oral version of polio vaccine, which did the most to conquer the disease. During World War II, Sabin's vaccines protected thousands of U.S. troops against such diseases as dengue fever and Japanese encephalitis.

Harrison Salisbury, 84, journalist and author. Salisbury wrote elegant historical accounts of epic 20th century struggles, such as *The 900 Days: The Siege of Leningrad* and *The Long March: The Untold Story*. At the same time, Salisbury made his mark as an editor and reporter at the New York *Times*, winning a Pulitzer Prize in 1955 for a pioneering series on Stalinist atrocities and serving as the first editor of the Op-Ed page, which became an influential national forum.

Dr. George Sheehan, 74, physician, author, running enthusiast. Perhaps more than anyone else, Sheehan was the inspiration for the vast increase in popularity running experienced in the 1970s and still enjoys today. An accomplished middle-distance runner in college, he abandoned the sport when he took up medicine, only to resume it in middle age with renewed enthusiasm. In 1969 he became the first man older than 50 to run the Boston Marathon in less than five hours.

William Shirer, 89, author and journalist. In the 1930s Shirer covered Europe for the Chicago *Tribune* and befriended Edward R. Murrow, who hired him as a correspondent for CBS. His diaries smuggled out of Nazi Germany became the basis of his worldwide best seller, *Berlin Diary*. A columnist for the New York *Herald Tribune* and a CBS commentator after the war, Shirer had difficulty finding a job in the '50s, when his political opinions put him on the wrong side of the McCarthy era. The involuntary sabbatical gave Shirer the time to produce his masterpiece, *The Rise and Fall of the Third Reich*.

Donald ("Deke") Kent Slayton, 69, one of the original Mercury 7 astronauts. The Wisconsin native and Korean War-era test pilot was grounded by a heart murmur in 1962 just before a Mercury flight that would have made him the second American in orbit. But by July 1975 his ailment had disappeared, and at age 51, Slayton participated in the famous Apollo-Soyuz mission, in which an American spacecraft docked with a Soviet counterpart.

Wallace Stegner, 84, author. Stegner won a 1972 Pulitzer Prize for his novel *Angle of Repose* and a 1977 National Book Award for *The Spectator Bird*. He first received acclaim in the 1940s and enjoyed a late success with his 1987 novel *Crossing to Safety*. Long preoccupied with the American West, Stegner was admired for his subtle, lucid style and his persuasive skepticism toward the frontier myth.

Lewis Thomas, 80, scientist and author. A skilled biomedical researcher who served on the faculties of Johns Hopkins, Yale and New York University, Thomas enjoyed a second career as explicator of the mysteries of life. His best-selling 1974 book, *The Lives of a Cell: Notes of a Biology Watcher*, won a National Book Award, and its equally popular 1979 sequel, *The Medusa and the Snail: More Notes of a Biology Watcher*, won the American Book Award for paperbacks in 1981.

Conway Twitty, 59, country music singer. His given name was Harold Jenkins, and he started off as a rock 'n' roller. He wasn't the handsomest guy in the world, and he didn't have the greatest voice, but he became one of the most popular country stars ever and a canny manager of his career.

His lyrics said the things women want to hear and men wish they could say. "It's 99% the song, not what I do," Twitty once said. He played the percentages and came out a winner.

Major General Edwin A. Walker, 83, retired army officer. A career military man, Walker rose through the ranks as an artillery officer, a combat commander in World War II and Korea, finally becoming a major general in 1957. A member of the far right-wing John Birch Society, Walker in 1961 was relieved of his command in West Germany when it was learned that he was using his position to indoctrinate the troops with his extreme views. Admonished by the Army Secretary, Walker resigned. In the years that followed, he ran a losing campaign for Texas Governor and for a while was the darling of ultraconservatives. But his obsession with mysterious forces supposedly plotting his persecution eroded his following. In April 1963 Walker was fired upon by an unknown gunman. Months later, the Warren Commission concluded the assailant had been Lee Harvey Oswald.

Thomas Watson, 79, computer executive. The World War II pilot put aside his dream of a career in commercial aviation to join IBM, the company his father had founded. After young Watson became chief executive in 1956, he transformed the manufacturer of typewriters into the Big Blue behemoth of computing.

Frank Zappa, 52, musician. The noted rock iconoclast, best known for his work with the seminal 1960s band the Mothers of Invention, was in many ways the prisoner of his own image: hirsute hippie freak; opinionated crank; First-Amendment scourge of Tipper Gore. Yet Zappa was the most protean and adventurous composer of his generation. In addition to his numerous rock recordings, he collaborated with the likes of composer Pierre Boulez and conductor Zubin Mehta. Born in Baltimore and a self-taught musician, he could be amateurish and juvenile, but his best music was a dazzling merger of Stravinsky and Varèse with rock, rhythm and blues. ∎

When two photographs appear on one page, credits run from top to bottom or left to right; if more than two appear, credits run clockwise from top left of page.

The Year in Review: iv Fritz Hoffman—JB Pictures **1, 3** Mark Pemberthy (art) **4** Bill Nation—Sygma **6** Cynthia Johnson for TIME **7** Paul Watson—Toronto Star—Sygma **8** Mike Goldwater—Network—Matrix **9** Andrey Salaviov—Sipa **10** Antoine Gyori—Sygma **12** Imperial Household Agency **13** NASA **14** Klaus Bergman—Conti Press—Sipa **15** Joel Richardson—Washington *Post* **16** John Mantel—Sipa, no credit **17** Steve Helber, AP pool, James Keyser for TIME

In the Spotlight: (left to right, from top left) Bill Nelson, Gary Kelley, Paul Davis, Bill Nelson, Mark Pemberthy, Josh Gosfield, Hanoch Piven, Mark Frederickson, David Sandlin, Chris Payne, Smith Georges, Robert Grossman, Christian Clayton, Bill Nelson, Paul Davis, Josh Gosfield, Chris Payne

Nation: **20** Diana Walker for TIME, Don Ryan, Rick Rickman—Matrix (fire) **21** Barry Iverson for TIME, Los Angeles *Daily News*—Sygma **22** Diana Walker for TIME **23** Cynthia Johnson for TIME **24** Cynthia Johnson for TIME **25** Alex Quesada—Matrix for TIME **26** Brooks Kraft—Sygma **27** Sam Kittner—CNN **28** Gary Knight—Saba for TIME **29** CNN/ABC **30** Bob Pearson—Agence France Press **31/32** Phillip Saltonstall (art) **33** Ron Edmonds—AP **34** Alex Quesada—Matrix **36** John Duricka—AP, Diana Walker for TIME, Dirck Halstead for TIME **37** Alex Quesada—Matrix for TIME (2), Rick Friedman—Black Star for TIME **39** no credit, White House, W. Geoffrey Hartmann for TIME, Cynthia Johnson for TIME, no credit, Jeff Mitchell, Mike Stewart—Sygma **40** Diana Walker for TIME **41** Chick Harrity *US News & World Report* pool **42** Jerry Hoefer—Fort Worth Star Telegram—Sipa **44** Rod Aydelotte—Waco *Tribune Herald*—Sygma **45** Network Nine—Australia **46** Rodger Mallison—Fort Worth *Star Telegram*—Sipa **47** Cynthia Johnson for TIME, Brad Markel—Gamma Liaison **49/50** Terry Ashe for TIME **51** U.S. Army—National Archives **52** Christopher Morris for TIME **53** Joe Tabacca—AP **55** Porter Gifford—Gamma Liaison **56** ABC News **57** Steve Berman—Gamma Liaison for TIME **58** Bill Gillette—Gamma Liaison **60** Fritz Hoffman—JB Pictures for TIME **61** Ron Haviv—Saba for TIME **62** Alex Quesada—Matrix for TIME, Najlah Feanny—Saba for TIME, Ron Haviv—Saba for TIME **63** TIME map by Joe Lertola **64** Jeff Topping—Gamma Liaison, Ron Haviv—Saba for TIME **65** Andrew Holbrooke—Gamma Liaison

World: **66** Pacemaker, Steve Liss for TIME, Julian Simmonds—Select (oil tanker) **68** Anthony Suau for TIME **70** Ron Haviv—Saba for TIME, Stanley Greene—Agence Vu **71** Anthony Suau for TIME **72** Sergei Guneyev for TIME (2) **73** Coskun Aral—Sipa, Malcolm Linton—Black Star for TIME, Mike Persson—Gamma Liaison **74** Jeffrey Aaronson—Network **75** Robin Moyer for TIME **76** Forrest Anderson for TIME **77** Paul Davis (art) **78** Jon Jones—Sygma **80** Luc Delahaye—Sipa **81** Alexandra Boulat—Sipa for TIME **82** Chris Rainier—JB Pictures for TIME, Tom Haley—Sipa for TIME **83** Louise Gubb—JB Pictures for TIME **84** Ricki Rosen—Saba for TIME **86** Esais Baitel—Gamma Liaison **87** Gregory Heisler for TIME (4) **88** Don McCullin—Magnum, Ricki Rosen—Saba for TIME **89** Ian Berry—Magnum, Louise Gubb—JB Pictures **90** Gregory Heisler for TIME **91** Gregory Heisler for TIME **92** Dirck Halstead for TIME **93** Gilles Caron—Gamma Liaison **94** Gregory Heisler for TIME **95** Gregory Heisler for TIME **96** no credit **97** Ernest Shirley

Business: **98** *Dateline NBC*, Yves Forestier—Sygma (Euro Disney) **99** James Keyser for TIME, Bill Swersey—Gamma Liaison **100** Chip Simons for TIME **102** no credit, Coca Cola **103** no credit, James Keyser for TIME **104** Joe Lertola (art) **105** no credit **106** Frank Ockenfels 3—Outline **107** Michael Tighe—Outline for TIME, Brian Smith—Outline **108-111** Gregory Heisler for TIME

Society: **112** Lennox McLendon—AP, Kim Kulish—Los Angeles *Daily News*—Sygma (domes) **113** Anthony Verde, MTV **115** Stephen Shames—Matrix **116** Kenneth Jarecke—Contact for TIME **117** Kenneth Jarecke—Contact for TIME **118** Chuck Nacke **119** Red Morgan for TIME **120** Limor Inbar **121** Eugene Burton—Gamma Liaison **122** Sears **123** Sears, Culver Pictures (TV) **125** Anthony Brusso—Outline for ENTERTAINMENT WEEKLY (Stern), Max Aguillera Hellweg—Onyx for TIME (Limbaugh), Photo manipulation by Ron Plyman **126** Kimberly Butler—LGI, Anthony Brusso—Outline for ENTERTAINMENT WEEKLY **127** Theo Rudnak (art)

Science: **128** Chemical Design Ltd.—Photoresearchers, SSC, Jay Colton (pyramid) **129** Prof. Peter Goddard—Photoresearchers, Ken Balcomb **130-133** Gregory Heisler for TIME **134** NASA **135** Robert Giusti (art) **137-138** Louis Psihoyos—Matrix **139** Theo Rudnak (art)

The Arts & Media: **140** Henry Groskinsky, Barnes Collection, Michel Setboun—Sygma (Louvre) **141** Douglas Kirkland—Sygma, Daniel Geeraerts—Gamma Liaison **142/143** David James—Universal (*Schindler*), Murray Close—Amblin—Universal (*Jurassic*) **144** Murray Close—Amblin—Universal **145** David James—Universal **147/148** Eddie Adams—Sygma **149** James Keyser for TIME **151** Marty Reichenthal—AP **152** David Titlow—Retna, Mark Sullivan—LGI **153** Steve Gullick—Retna **154** Alan Singer—CBS **156** Gwendolyn Cates—Outline, Timothy White—Onyx, Timothy White—Onyx, Gwendolyn Cates—Outline **157/158** Gregory Heisler—Outline for ENTERTAINMENT WEEKLY **159** Joan Marcus **160** Michael Cooper **161** Louvre **162** MOMA **163** Ted Thai for TIME

The Best of 1993: **164** Columbia Pictures, Miramax, Fine Line **165** Chris Cuffaro—Outline, R. Corkery—LGI, H. Farmeyer—LGI **166** Ken Sax, Library of Congress, ABC Photos **167** Sandra Johnson for TIME, Rigmor Mydtskov **168** Martha Swope, Joan Marcus (2) **169** B. Masck—Allsport, M. Ponzini—Focus on Sports, G. Mortimore—Allsport

People/For the Record/Milestones: **170** David Liam Kyle for SPORTS ILLUSTRATED, Ron Gallela, Firooz Zahedi—Boitash Group **171** Diane Cohen—Hotshots, Sipa, Storm/Flint—Norfoto—Gamma Liaison **172** Robert Rocco—Sygma (Fleiss), Terry O'Neill—Sygma, Stowers Kemp—Sygma, no credit (2), John Mantel—Sipa **173** Schafer—Onyx, Jonathan Green—Globe, Wilfredo Lee—AP pool, Larry Morris—AP pool, A. Murray—Sygma, **174-175** Daniel Pelavin (art) **176** Claudio Edinger **177** Motion Picture and Television Archives **179** Brian Lanker **180** Cecil Beaton

DATE DUE